Dinsmore's
Complete Map
OF THE
RAILROADS & CANALS
IN THE
UNITED STATES & CANADA
Carefully Compiled from Authentic Sources
BY
RICHARD S. FISHER,
EDITOR OF THE
American Rail Road & Steam Navigation Guide.
NEW-YORK.
PUBLISHED BY DINSMORE & COMPANY.
Nº 9 SPRUCE ST.
ENGRAVED IN RELIEF FOR POWER PRESS PRINTING
HY. SCHÖNBERG & Cº. ACROGRAPHERS.
75 Nassau Street New York.
1850

Entered according to Act of Congress in the year 1850 by Dinsmore & Co in the Clerks Office
of the District Court of the U.S. for the Southern District of New York.

REFERENCES.
Rail Roads in Operation
Rail Roads in Progress
Rail Roads Projected
Canals

RAILROAD

Timetables
Travel Brochures
& Posters

New York, New Haven and
Hartford public timetable,
1939. Rare.

RAILROAD
Timetables
Travel Brochures
& Posters

A History
and Guide
for Collectors

Brad S. Lomazzi

Golden Hill Press

First Edition, October 30, 1995
Text Copyright © 1995 by Brad S. Lomazzi

Cover Design © 1995 Golden Hill Press

Library of Congress Catalogue Card Number 94-076651
ISBN 0961487682

Published in the United States of America by Golden Hill Press, Inc., Spencertown, NY.

Jacket and book design by Rich Kraham of SmithKraham Design, Chatham, NY.

Photographed by Michael Fredericks, Ghent, NY.

Text is typeset in Sabon Antiqua 11 on 13. Headlines are set in Gill Light, 36 point.

Printed in China by Twin Age, Ltd., Hong Kong

Front Jacket, left to right: Southern Pacific public timetable, 1897, Rare; Northern Pacific travel brochure, 1925, Rare; Union Switch & Signal Company Traffic Centralized Control brochure, 1935, Very Rare.

Back Jacket, left to right: Rock Island public timetable, 1939, Rare; California Expositions travel brochure, 1914, Rare; White Pass and Yukon travel brochure, ca. 1920, Very Rare.

Left Flap: Baltimore & Ohio public timetable,

FOR MARY, JAMIE, & LAURA

*Erie Railway public
timetable, 1888, Very Rare.*

FOREWORD

As a railroad paper collector I have, in over thirty years, accumulated an impressive amount of paper, both in volume and weight. Some might say I am obsessed with the hobby. I say I am *fascinated by history*.

No one taught me about collecting railroad paper. I had my notion of what was interesting and what was not, and went from there. After meeting many other railroad paper collectors at various times in my life, I have come to the wry realization that there are no limits to the excesses some humans will go to, no matter what their endeavor.

My particular affinity is for railroad timetables, and as Brad Lomazzi depicts in this tome, they come in many sizes, colors, and served different purposes. My particular interest is employee timetables, issued only to employees of the railroad and offering quite detailed information about how it is to be operated.

Having developed a long perspective on railroad paper, I can attest to the fact that doing a book about railroad paper collectibles is not for the faint of heart because of the incredible amount of information that can be included or, worse, overlooked. Brad Lomazzi has admirably met this challenge. In this book, he offers the reader a fine overview of the history of railroading through the many publications produced over a century and more.

By working with Brad to include many items from my collection for use in the book, I had the enjoyment of seeing many things quite new to me. It confirmed my feeling that time travel is happily possible just by opening any old timetable and following a train across the railroad.

America was brought together by steel rails and flanged wheels. Railroad timetables brought order to seeming chaos. Take time to savor from the railroad paper collectibles herein, the delights of train travel in the past.

WILLIAM J. NEILL
MARCH, 1995

PEAKE, TOO, PREPARES TO
Sleep like a Kitten

CHESSIE'S SECRET

. . . of how to Sleep like a Kitten:
Have you ever observed how cats prepare for sleep? Loosely they curl up . . . give a little snuggle . . . go limp in every muscle . . . and away into dreamless sleep. Refreshing slumber comes so easily on a Chesapeake and Ohio train! For here every condition is perfect . . . your berth a miracle of downy comfort . . . your car insulated against noise. Genuine air-conditioning cleans, warms and humidifies your rolling bedroom—maintains sea-level pressure on even the highest mountain. You glide along super-smooth roadbed, lulled by cradlewise motion, soothed by a feeling of security. Try Chessie's formula for restful sleep on THE GEORGE WASHINGTON — THE SPORTSMAN — THE F.F.V.! The ticket agent of any railroad can route you via Chesapeake and Ohio.

CHESAPEAKE AND OHIO LINES

Advertisement from a Chesapeake and Ohio Railroad public timetable, January 21, 1940. Rare.

PREFACE

"YOU COLLECT WHAT?" people would ask about my hobby. "I collect railroad timetables and travel brochures," was my reply.

Since many people did not know what this meant, I would try to explain. After years of explaining, I finally realized that the best answer to this question was "I collect railroad history."

And that is what the many railroad travel publications of the past are, the history of America through the eyes and ideas of the people who created them. For anyone interested in learning not just history, but with a little imagination, experiencing it, this is the way to go!

Without some type of logical organization it would be difficult to fully describe the many different railroad travel publications that were produced. This turned out to be one of the greatest challenges in writing this book. Some categories were, of course, obvious, such as public and employee timetables. In others, there were many similarities and significant overlap not only in the publication's content, but also in the time periods during which they were produced. At first, these ambiguities created a somewhat distorted and confusing picture. After completing a thorough study of examples produced over the entire expanse of time in which they were published, their roles and thus a practical way of organizing them, became clear. I hope the categories and descriptions in this book will help anyone who is interested in collecting railroad paper ephemera to more fully appreciate the history they contain.

The effort to produce a comprehensive work on the subject of railroad travel publications mandated a thorough review and study of as many originals as possible. Given the volume of fine examples that have survived in collections today, the endeavor, at times, seemed overwhelming. But for this work to have any real value to collectors and historians, I felt this was what had to be done.

I have presented and described here the best examples I found in each category. For an illustrative example to qualify as "best," it had to have interesting content that may not have necessarily been extraordinary, but was worthy of note and significant in telling the complete story. Considering the mass of railroad travel publications that were produced, I have absolutely no doubt that there are many more "best" examples out there that I have not seen. It is my sincere hope that those readers who have additional examples, information, or opinions to expand this knowledge base or, heaven forbid, who spot errors, will please contact me through Golden Hill Press.

Over the years and during the countless hours it took to produce these chapters, I was part of a travel adventure like no other I had experienced. The review process revealed much more about these publications, their content, and American history than I had ever known. They truly tell their own story. Their history lies within them and nowhere else. It is this unique historical perspective and advantage they enjoy that I have tried to convey in my writing. Let them, in their pure form, be the story tellers.

Enjoy your journeys into the past.

BRAD S. LOMAZZI
AUGUST, 1994
ROSEVILLE, CALIFORNIA

ACKNOWLEDGMENTS

THIS HISTORY of railroad paper collectibles would not be what it is save for the help of many fine people. All who contributed share the same enthusiasm that I do in wanting to show to all the fascinating history these collectibles contain.

I would like to extend special thanks to my friend and fellow collector Mr. William J. Neill, who generously shared many items from his large collection. Bill also provided technical input on railroad operating practices which included clarification of the concepts and history behind many of the rules.

No less a debt is owed to Ms. Jacqueline J. Pryor, archivist for the Railway and Locomotive Historical Society, whose extensive ephemera collection is housed in the California State Railroad Museum Library. Jackie is a dedicated researcher who was kind enough to provide not only expert assistance, but a comprehensive review of this book's concept and draft manuscripts as well.

My special thanks also go to Ellen Halteman and Kevin Bunker of the California State Railroad Museum Library for their help in locating additional material used in this book. Let no one ever underestimate the recall abilities of these two archivists, or their dedication to railroad history. They work very hard and know their collections!

Others whom I would like to thank for their support and contributions to this project are: Mr. Stephen Drew, Curator of the California State Railroad Museum Library, Dr. Blayne P. Lamb of the California State Archives, Bill Kratville and Don Snoddy of the Union Pacific Railroad Museum, and Richard A. Cooley of the Colorado Railroad Museum.

The many artists, illustrators, and writers who created the original folders were true American pioneers. Their positive words and images helped invoke the nation into realizing its great, vast natural beauty, and the potential in all of us to make it as good a place as we wanted it to be. Their creative talents no doubt helped thousands harness dreams that led them to full and happy lives.

Words are not enough to express my thanks to Mary Zander, my editor and publisher, for the tremendous opportunity to do this project. Her desire to put forward only the best, a philosophy that I share, made the publishing process more challenging, but the results much finer. Also our thanks go to Mary and her partner Lorraine Zagarola for their gracious hospitality on our trip to New York City, a travel adventure we will never forget, even though we took a plane!

My writing is only half the book. My sincere thanks also go to the designer, Rich Kraham, who being a railfan and historian himself, was perfect for this project, and to Michael Fredericks for his photographic skills in copying some very difficult originals. Also, thanks to Stuart Murray for his fine work as copy editor and Maria Iglesias Baxter for her word processing.

BRAD S. LOMAZZI
FEBRUARY, 1995

CONTENTS

connecting
2 great cities

"Follow the Flag"

WABASH

NO BETTER TRAINS—ANYWHERE!

"Banner Limited"		"Midnight Limited"	
Leave Chicago	10:05 a. m.	Leave Chicago	11:45 p. m.
Arrive St. Louis	6:00 p. m.	Arrive St. Louis	7:41 a. m.
Leave St. Louis	12:20 noon	Leave St. Louis	11:52 p. m.
Arrive Chicago	7:59 p. m.	Arrive Chicago	7:50 a. m.
Splendid Dining Car Service under supervision of competent stewards.		Midnight Luncheon and Breakfast in Club Cars.	

New
ALL-STEEL
Equipment

Chicago

WABASH

St. Louis

*Advertisement from a
Wabash Railroad public
timetable, 1924. Rare.*

INTRODUCTION

IN EARLY 19th century America, railroads were considered little more than engineering novelties. Soon, however, they came to be recognized as a very practical concept, and within a relatively short time, as an indispensable network joining together parts of this vast country.

In the 1830s, travel and freight hauling needs were barely met by the existing system of canals and wagon roads. Canal boat routes were limited. Poor road conditions were common. Both methods of transportation were very slow. These limitations seriously hampered commerce and growth in the new nation. It was the efficient all-weather steel "roads" that gave railroads a unique advantage over other forms of transportation. This advantage accelerated their growth at a phenomenal rate, allowing railroads to remain relatively unchallenged as the most efficient mode of transportation until the mid-20th century, over a hundred years after their beginnings.

The profoundly practical concept of the railroad itself was only half the story. Once railroad services became available, they had to be effectively publicized, or such rapid growth would not have been possible.

Communication and Growth

Communication in the 19th century was very different than it is today. The world was presented to all with printed illustrations and words. People depended entirely on printed matter not only for factual information, but for entertainment as well. With that, it is reasonable to foresee the inevitable beginnings and looming significance of railroad travel publications.

With the great tide of emigrants coming from all over the world and a continent full of unknowns, communication through railroad travel publica-

tions would also become a necessary component responsible for the rapid growth of railroads and of the United States. Pioneer Americans were eager to create images in their minds of where they could go and what they would find there. Railroad travel publications made this possible. Often, these publications were all the information that early settlers had to lead them into the new lands. Dreams were inspired and hopes were realized by them.

By the mid-19th century, Americans in the midst of industrial revolution were beginning the move away from a primarily rural, agrarian society. They were more than ever drawn to the beauty of the vast, often still unexplored, continent. Railroads could now easily take them to these places. Amidst growing wealth and leisure, a flourishing tourist industry promoted mountain resorts and forest retreats. Our system of National Parks grew out of the lobbying efforts by the railroads. Railroads promoted vacationing in America well into the automobile age, and AMTRAK still does.

The Publications

Railroad paper ephemera show us—in text and pictures—how the railroads presented their many functions to those who would use them. These many publications—timetables, posters and broadsides, brochures, tourist and travel guides—were designed to motivate and facilitate individuals and businesses using the railroads. Fast freight services, excursion trains for settlers, and still later, for tourism, the areas they served, and the trains themselves all were subjects to be presented to the public. Timetables, whose initial function was as a tool to efficiently run trains, were soon distributed to the public and advertised railroad services, including land availability and travel information, within their pages. Eventually tourist and travel guides took over these latter functions. The extensive use of these publications accelerated the growth of an already burgeoning railroad industry.

Reviewing these publications now, one sees the history of 19th and early 20th century America reflected in their advertisements, illustrations, and texts. The evolution of a nation is reflected in the changing subjects and pictures. Clothes, technologies, architecture, scenery, national interests and events, as they evolved over more than a century, are here to be seen and stimulate the imagination. Beautiful etchings, stunning graphics, some in black and white and many in color, grace their pages, along with nostalgic or, sometimes, amusing advertisements for those products deemed useful by our forebears.

This book allows the reader to look at some of the very rare railroad paper ephemera still extant. As well, it gives many examples of rare and common materials. Little very common material is presented here because it exists in such abundance. Also not presented here are categories of railroad paper that are less popular material or very specialized. The major categories of interest: public, employee, suburban and freight timetables, tourist and travel guides, travel brochures, passenger train brochures, timetable and travel posters, and tickets and other small paper ephemera, are the subject of this book.

Because it was paper, and therefore fragile, much material from early railroading has been lost. Fortunately, there is still much of it to be seen, and to collect, because it was saved—sometimes by people who did not ever intend to start collections.

Collecting

Nineteenth-century travelers were themselves the first collectors of railroad paper ephemera. Timetables, tourist guides, travel brochures and tickets were used for purposes of travel, and then as souvenirs of the journey. Also, travelers enjoyed sharing their travel experiences with friends and family, and travel memorabilia provided reading entertainment and topics for conversation.

Travel brochures and public timetables were tucked away in shoe boxes. Tickets were pasted in photo albums. Tourist and travel guides survived in collections of books or were buried in trunks of personal possessions. Employee timetables and rule books from years on the job were saved in a box on a shelf in the garage. They could be retrieved at any time to relive one's travel adventures. By saving these mementos, early travelers were also preserving history, and unknowingly creating the beginnings of a popular hobby.

Travelers were not the only ones to sense the value of railroad paper ephemera. Railroads routinely saved copies of all their publications in company archives for reference. Museums and historical societies preserved material from countless donors in their communities, building respectable collections. Most of the very earliest material still in existence today was preserved in these ways. Knowing it would be saved, travelers and retired railroad employees who had accumulated paper ephemera often gave it to such historical organizations and institutions.

Old timetables and travel brochures may not have had much intrinsic value, but they were too precious to be thrown out. They represented too much history. It was this simple appreciation that caused them to be saved in the first place, put away for all those years, and finally passed on in the hopes that someone else would enjoy them.

Younger members of families and other interested individuals became the caretakers for collections of railroad paper passed on to them. Appreciating their aesthetic worth, and having an interest in railroad history, many collectors started down the paper road not sure of where they were headed, but knowing for certain that this "stuff" was very interesting to look at.

Collecting railroad paper emerged as a serious hobby in the 1940s, when dealers who traded exclusively in it began to appear. Until that time, railroad material was generally included in the broader offerings of dealers selling all types of historical paper. This was so because of the relatively few different railroad paper collectibles printed in the 19th century, the few surviving pieces, and the small number of collectors. After the turn of the century, large-volume printings of many different travel brochures greatly increased the number of collectible publications available. The artistic and informational content of these publications also made them more desirable aesthetically. With so much more available to collect, and with its intrinsic historical value firmly rooted in popular American history, collecting railroad paper ephemera came into its own.

The railroad paper ephemera hobby accelerated in the late 1960s as the era of great American passenger trains drew to a close. The near-extinction of private-passenger train service focused the attention of historians and collectors on the far-reaching, enormous impact that American passenger trains once had on our culture. Collecting railroad paper ephemera became an even more popular way to relive the history and excitement of travel by train.

The interest and demand for railroad paper collectibles has never been greater. A renaissance of interest in railroad history in recent years has led to the establishment of railroad museums and railroad historical groups in communities throughout the country. Railroad collectibles and model train shows are held in increasing numbers everywhere. Communities steeped in railroad history hold annual heritage celebrations. Steam and diesel locomotives have been restored, to operate in their former glory. As ever, railroad history is adventure. No collectible artifacts bring the travel experience of our past closer to the sense of actually being there than do railroad paper collectibles. The demand for the adventures they provide will always be great.

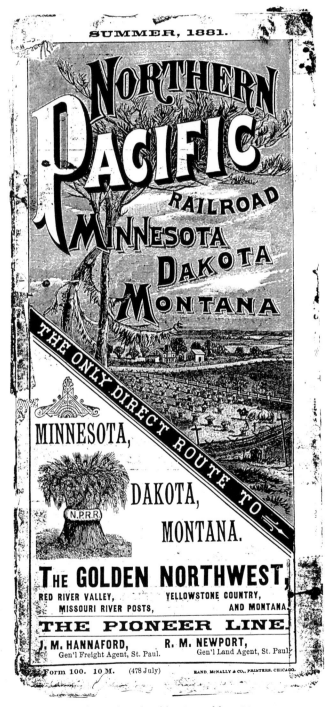

Northern Pacific Railroad public timetable, 1881.
Very Rare.

BOSTON AND MAINE RAILROAD.

UPPER ROUTE.

BOSTON TO PORTLAND,

Via Charlestown, Somerville, Malden, Stoneham, South Reading, Reading, Wilmington, Ballardvale, Andover, North Andover, Bradford, Haverhill, Atkinson, Plaistow, Newton, Kingston, East Kingston, Exeter, South Newmarket, Newmarket, Durham, Madbury, Dover, Somersworth, South Berwick, North Berwick, Wells, Kennebunk, Saco, and Scarborough.

SPRING ARRANGEMENT.....1847.

On and after **MONDAY, MARCH 1, 1847,** Passenger Trains will run Daily, (Sundays excepted,) as follows, viz :

Leave BOSTON for PORTLAND at $7\frac{1}{4}$ A. M., and $2\frac{1}{2}$ P. M.
Leave BOSTON for GREAT FALLS at $7\frac{1}{4}$ A. M., $2\frac{1}{2}$ and $4\frac{1}{2}$ P. M.
Leave BOSTON for HAVERHILL at $7\frac{1}{4}$ and $11\frac{1}{4}$ A. M., $2\frac{1}{2}$, $4\frac{1}{2}$ and 5.50 P. M.
Leave BOSTON for READING, at $7\frac{1}{4}$, 9, and $11\frac{1}{4}$ A. M., $2\frac{1}{2}$, $4\frac{1}{2}$, 5.50 and 8 P. M.
Leave PORTLAND for BOSTON at $7\frac{1}{2}$ A. M., and 3 P. M.
Leave GREAT FALLS for BOSTON at $6\frac{3}{4}$ and $9\frac{1}{4}$ A. M., and $4\frac{1}{2}$ P. M.
Leave HAVERHILL for BOSTON at $6\frac{3}{4}$, $8\frac{1}{2}$ and 11 A. M., 4 and $6\frac{1}{2}$ P. M.
Leave READING for BOSTON at $6\frac{1}{4}$, $7\frac{3}{4}$, $9\frac{1}{2}$, and $11\frac{3}{4}$ A. M., $1\frac{1}{2}$, 5 and $7\frac{1}{4}$ P. M.

MEDFORD BRANCH, { Leave Medford, at 6.30 and 8 A. M., 1.45 and 5.15 P. M.
{ Leave Boston, at 7.15 and 9 A. M. 2'30 and 5.50 P. M.

Every **THURSDAY,** an Extra Train will leave Reading for Boston at 10.30 P. M., and Boston for Reading at 11.30 P. M.
Every **SATURDAY,** an Extra Train will leave Reading for Boston at 9 P. M., and Boston for Reading at 10 P. M.

Passengers are not allowed to carry Baggage, above $50 in value, and that PERSONAL, unless notice is given and an extra amount paid, at the rate of the price of a Ticket for every $500 additional value.

FEB. 27, 1847.   S. N. DICKINSON & CO., Printers, Boston.   CHAS. MINOT, SUP'T.

Boston and Maine Railroad broadside, February 27, 1847.
Its finely detailed engravings accompanying the complete
schedules for the railroad are typical of broadsides from
this era. Very Rare.

CHAPTER ONE
PUBLIC TIMETABLES

TRANSPORTATION choices are simple in the 1830s. You can ride a horse, hitch one to a buggy or wagon, ride a stagecoach, or venture on the waterways and canals, where freight barges and packet boats are available. Since all of these travel options are relatively expensive, you walk almost everywhere. This and the other transportation modes have two limitations: poor road conditions and how much the traveller can carry or send.

Then, one day in 1834, you see a broadside (poster) advertising a "Packet Boat and Rail-Road Arrangement" to Buffalo. It shows a packet boat being pulled by horses, walking on a canal bank, and a steam locomotive with several "wagons" of freight and passengers hitched behind. The poster reads: "A Packet BOAT will leave Schenectady Daily, for Utica, Rochester and Buffalo, at Half past 10 o'clock A.M." A bold footnote adds: "These are the only Cars that run to the Packets." You are reading one of the first railroad public announcements or "notices."

Mohawk & Hudson Railroad, 1834. Very Rare.

In 1834, the concept of the railroad is only a few years old but has met with considerable success in Great Britain, where the idea originated, and in early experiments throughout many of the United States. As shown in the poster, some railroads are being built to connect canal systems. This new form of transportation draws your attention as well as that of thousands of others.

There is controversy regarding the safety of riding behind the fire-breathing steam locomotive, an invention not yet entirely proven and often prone to blowing up! Ladies are concerned about ash and cinders dirtying their hair and dresses. Gentlemen are skeptical that any machine could out-perform the reliable horse. And there is inevitable resistance from the established means of travel: Owners of toll roads, canals and stage lines are attempting to discredit the new railroad industry and its capabilities.

You and most others are very impressed, however, for it doesn't take long to realize the many advantages railroad systems have to offer: Carrying many "wagons" full of people and freight behind one mechanical "horse." "Roads" that are less at the mercy of the weather, usually easier to build and less expensive to maintain than wagon roads. Speed! You can now travel greater distances in less time and take more with you!

The fact that overland travel is easier than ever is tremendously appealing. In this new nation, huge beyond your wildest imagination, the new railroads can take you and your belongings to many different destinations for a relatively small price.

SOUTH-CAROLINA RAIL-ROAD,

Between Charleston and Hamburg, S. C. opposite Augusta. (Geo.)

Distance 136 miles, performed in daylight, from 6 A. M. to 6 P. M.
President, John Ravenel. *Directors*—Wm Aiken, A. Black, Wm. Bell, J. J. Bulow, Dr. S. H. Dickson, John Dixon, H. F. Faber, John Haslett, B. J. Howland, Dr. Joseph Johnson, T. Tupper. *Auditor,* Henry Ravenel. *Secretary,* J T Robertson. *Principal Engineer,* H. Allen.

RATES OF PASSAGE.

From Charleston to		Miles	$ Cts.	From Hamburg to			Miles	$ Cts.
Woodstock,	- -	15	50	Aiken,	-	- -	16	75
Summerville,	- -	21	75	Blackville,	-	- -	46	2 25
Inabnet's,	- -	32½	1 62½	Midway,	-	- -	64	3 25
Branchville,	- -	62	3 00	Branchville,	-	- -	74	3 75
Midway,	- -	72	3 50	Inabnet's,	-	- -	103½	5 12½
Blackville,	- -	90	4 50	Summerville,	-	- -	115	6 00
Aiken,	- -	120	6 00	Woodstock,	-	- -	121	6 25
Hamburg,	- -	136	6 75	Charleston,	-	- -	136	6 75

And from one intermediate Station to *another*, FIVE CENTS per MILE. *Children under 12 years and Coloured Persons, half price*

Regulations for the Passenger Carriage.

1st. All baggage at owner's risk—75 lbs. allowed. 2d. servants the not admitted, unless having the care of children, without the consent of all the Passengers. 3d. Passengers not allowed to stand on the outside platform. 4th. smoking prohibited. 5th. No Gun or Fowling Piece shall be permitted to enter the Car unless examined by the Conductor. 6th. The feet not to be put on the Cushions, nor the Cars soiled, defaced or injured in any way. 7th. Dogs not admitted into the Passenger Cars. 8th. At the ringing of the Bell, Passengers will be allowed one minute to take their places. 9th. Seats must be engaged and paid for fifteen minutes previous to the hour of departure. As a general direction, the conductors of the Carriages are instructed not to permit any conduct that is inconsistent with good order, or the comfort and safety of the Passengers : for which especial end these Rules have been established, and are required to be enforced with civility but strictly.

HOURS OF DEPARTURE AND ARRIVAL.

UPWARD PASSAGE.

LEAVE CHARLESTON, at 6 A. M.
To Woodstock, running time and stoppages 1h. 5m.
Not to arrive before 5m. past 7 A. M.—Breakfast 20 minutes.

Some timetables in periodical ads included other helpful information for travelers of the day, as shown by this very early (1835) example of the timetable-maker's art for the South-Carolina Railroad. This is believed to be the first regularly scheduled steam-powered freight and passenger railroad service in the United States: December, 1830. Another periodical advertisement from this early era for the Central Railroad (right) offered seats in the passenger car or baggage car. Both Very Rare.

Early Timetables

Simple in appearance, the first public railroad "timetables" were *broadsides* posted conspicuously about town, and small handbills (flyers) distributed freely to the public. Timetables also were printed as *advertisements* in newspapers and periodicals. Almost all featured engravings of steam locomotives pulling horse-drawn-type or carriage-like cars filled with passengers or piled high with barrels and bales. Such images were new and exciting.

Information given in very early timetables included only a departure and destination point, along with arrival and departure times. These times were much less precise than those of today. For instance, an 1837 broadside for the "PIONEER Fast Line" from Philadelphia to Pittsburgh stated simply that it "starts every morning."

Handbills were widely distributed because they were practical and relatively inexpensive to print. They could be found on hotel counters, at newspapers offices, in road houses and taverns, at livestock and commodity exchanges, and of course, at railroad depots. Handbills were also given out freely by young boys who were employed to carry baskets of food and tobacco to sell on trains. (There were no dining cars.) Distributing handbills became an increasingly popular advertising method. Many originals from the same large printings survive in collections today.

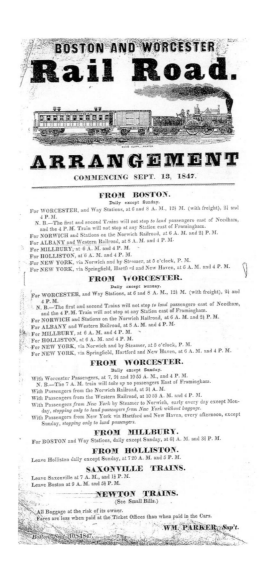

This early 1847 broadside advertised the "Arrangement" schedule for the Boston and Worcester Rail Road. The "See Small Bills" refers to the small handbills giving schedules for the Newton trains. Very Rare.

BOSTON AND MAINE
RAIL ROAD!

Spring Arrangement, 1846. Change of Hours, &c.

On and after March 2d, 1846, Passenger

Trains will leave as follows, viz :

Boston for Portland at 7 1-4 A. M. and 2 1-2 P. M.
Boston for Great Falls at 7 1-4 A. M., 2 1-2 and 3 1-2 P. M.
Boston for Haverhill at 7 1-4 and 11 1-2 A. M. 2 1-2, 3 1-2 and 6 P. M.
Portland for Boston at 7 1-2 A. M. and 3 P. M.
Great Falls for Boston at 6 3-4 and 9 1-4 A. M. and 4 3-4 P. M.
Haverhill for Boston at 6 3-4, 8 1-2 and 11 A. M. 3 and 6 3-8 P. M.

CHA'S MINOT, Sup't.

Boston, Feb. 21st, 1846.

Timetable handbills gave complete schedules or "arrangements." The Boston and Maine Rail Road's (above) entire timetable in 1846 was printed on a one-page handbill. Times are shown in quarter hour increments, a unit of time then deemed adequate for the operation of trains. Special announcement handbills, such as for this July 4, 1845 trip from Great Falls to Boston (right), advertised schedules for special trains for holidays, or for church or social events. Both Very Rare.

JULY 4, 1845.

An extra train of second class cars will leave Great Falls for Boston at 5 A. M. Returning it will leave Boston one half hour after the close of the exhibition of Fireworks on he Common. Should the weather be such hat the exhibition does not take place, the rain will leave Boston at 7 P. M.

Tickets for both ways, and for this train only, will be sold for one half the usual rates of fare.

June 30, 1845. CHARLES MINOT,
Superintendent B. & M. R. R.

Announcements for new railroad companies and their lines were common during the 1840s and the early 1850s as such enterprises proliferated throughout the Northeast and South. The same engraving by Devereux & Brown was used on an 1846 Fall River Railroad handbill (below, Very Rare), an announcement from the Greenfield and Boston "R. Roads" between Greenfield and Boston (not illustrated), and on a May, 1848, announcement for the Cape Cod Branch Railroad between Boston and Sandwich (left, Very Rare). The use of the same engraving by several railroads in this early era reflects the amount of work necessary to produce an engraving on brass—a time-consuming and expensive process. It also suggests that the printing firm with the latest and most attractive illustration was in demand by competing new railroads.

An 1849 Naugatuck Rail Road timetable (not illustrated) provided information on freight services in addition to passenger schedules. The value of both was considered on par in the early railroad years. Overnight freight service was offered from stations on the line to New York or New Haven, an advertising tactic that is still used today to attract parcel business. A note "FARE REDUCED" reflects a number of things that were happening to railroads during the late 1840s: increased ridership; competition from other railroads; more efficient equipment and increases in capital expenditures.

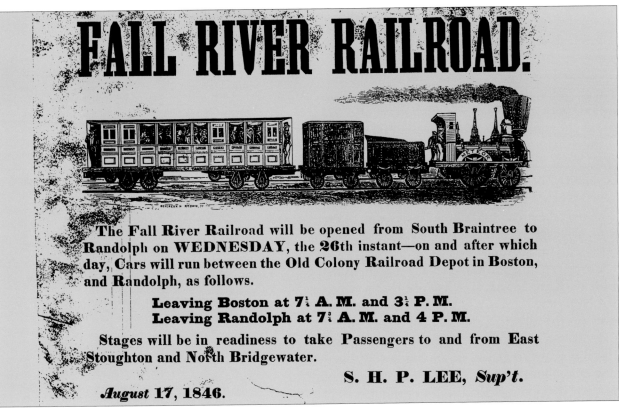

Expansion of Railroads

Figures available from the Association of American Railroads show railroads expanded rapidly from the 1830s through the 1850s. In 1834, there were 633 miles of railroad in the United States. By 1859, this number had increased to 9,021. This expansion created pressure to make printed advertising work harder to attract freight and passenger business, because there were now so many routes and schedules between eastern and midwestern cities.

Changes in Timetable
Format and Distribution

Rapid growth meant the format of various types of early railroad timetable advertising had to change. More trains running required printing longer and more complicated schedules, making periodical ads very expensive. Ads were also impractical, since periodicals reached only limited or local markets. Broadside timetables required larger and larger spaces on walls and fences. Also, they became lost in the sheer volume of postings for other products and services. Further, the amount of information broadsides could contain was limited by their size.

To better reach larger numbers of potential customers, railroads began to focus more on what had always been their cheapest and most effective means of advertising—the handbill. Handbills, however, with only two sides of information on a small page, had somewhat the same limitation. Expanding the amount of information these contained required modifying their format and increasing their free distribution. In this way, many more passengers could easily be solicited and provided with the schedules needed for travel.

Greater distribution was partially accomplished using publicity houses, such as Peck-Judah, which had been established by this time. Their sole purpose was the collection and distribution of railroad and other transportation timetables nationwide. Travel bureaus (agencies) in the business of planning railroad travel were also an important part of the early distribution network for timetables.

Through the 1850s and into the early 1860s, most of these early single-sheet public timetables

used a *list format* in which city names were followed by as many departure and arrival times as there were trains serving them. As railroads grew larger and the number of trains increased, the many entries in this list method made the format less readable, compelling railroads to seek an improved schedule format.

As a solution, railroads borrowed, from the scientific community, the concept of arranging information in "tables." There, rows and columns were commonly used for recording statistical data. Large railroads with many lines were quick to adopt this flexible style, producing the first true timetables. Even though this *double-column* format was easier to read, many smaller roads—as in this very rare Old Colony & Fall River (1859) timetable below—still found it practical to use the old list format, which continued to appear through the 1880s.

Oct. 1, 1859.

OLD COLONY & FALL RIVER R. R.

TRAINS LEAVE BOSTON FOR

Savin Hill, 8.50, 11.30 A.M.; 1, 2.15, 3, 4, 6, 6.30, 9.15* P.M.; RETURN 6.42, 7.57, 8.07, 8.36, 10.27 A.M.; 1.51, 2.17, 5.21 P.M.
Harrison Square, 7.20, 8.30, 8.50, 11.30 A.M.; 1, 2.15, 3, 4, 5.10, 6, 6.30, 9.15* P.M. RETURN 6.39, 7.55, 8.04, 8.31, 9.28, 10.24, 11.05 A.M.; 1.49, 2.14, 5.19, 4.53 P.M.
Neponset, 7.20, 8.30, 8.50, 11.30 A.M.; 1, 2.15, 2.30, 3, 4, 5.10, 6, 6.30, 9.15* P.M. RETURN 6.35, 7.51, 8, 8.30, 9.23, 10.20 11 A.M.; 1.45, 2.10, 4.49, 5.15 P.M.
Atlantic, 7.20, 11.30 A.M.; 2.30, 6.30, 9.15* P.M. RETURN 6.32, 8.25 A.M; 1.42, 4.46 P.M.
Wollaston, 8.30, 11.30 A.M.; 2.15, 4, 6.30, 9.15* P.M. RETURN 6.29, 8.07, 8.23 A.M.; 1.39, 4.13 P.M.
Quincy, 7.20, 8.30, 11.30 A.M.; 2.15, 2.30, 4, 5.10, 5.40, 6.30, 9.15 P.M. RETURN 6.25, 7.42, 8.03, 8.20, 9.15, 10.51 A.M.; 1.35, 4.41, 5.38 P.M.
S. Quincy, 8.30, 11.30 A.M.; 4, 5.10, 6.30, 9.15* P.M. RETURN 6.23, 8, 8.17 A.M; 1.32, 4.38 P.M.
Braintree, 7.20, 8.30, 11.30 A.M.; 2.15, 2.30, 4, 5.10, 5.40, 6.30, 9 15* P.M. RETURN 6.19, 7.35, 7.56, 8.14, 9.10, 10.45 A.M.; 1.29, 4.35, 5.33 P.M.
S. Braintree, 7.20, 8.30, 11.30 A.M.; 2.15, 2.30, 4, 5.10, 5 40, 6.30, 9.15* P.M. RETURN 6.15, 7.27, 7.52, 8.10, 9.06, 10.35, A.M.; 12 09, 1.25, 4.28, 5.23 P.M.
N. Bridgewater, 7.20, 11.30 A.M.; 2 15, 4, 5.40 P.M. RETURN 7, 8.44, 11.52 A.M.; 1, 5.05 P.M.
Bridgewater, 7.20, 8.30 A.M.; 2.15, 2.30, 4, 4.45, 5.10, 5.30 P.M. RETURN 6.55, 8.21, 9.10, 11.33 A.M.; 3, 4.42 P.M.
Fall River, 7.20 A.M.; 2.15, 4.45, 5.30 P.M. RETURN 7.15, 10.30 A.M; 3 40 P.M., & 5.30 P.M. for Myrick's.
Plymouth, 8.30 A.M.; 2.30, 5.10 P.M. RETURN 6.45, 9.20 A.M.; 3.15 P.M.
New Bedford & Fairhaven, 7.20 A.M.; 2.15, 4.45 P.M.
Cape Cod Railroad, 7.20 A.M.; 4.45 P.M.
Granite Bridge, Milton L. Mills and Mattapan, 8.50 A.M.; 1, 3, 6 P.M. RETURN from Mattapan, 7.50, 10.10 A.M.; 2 5.05 P.M.

* Saturdays at 10 P.M. Tuesdays at 11.15 P.M.

☞ Trains leave Myrick's for Fall River, at 7.45 and 9.15 A M., or on the arrival of the Train from New Bedford and Taunton. Leaves Fall River at 5.30 P.M., connecting with the N. Bedford Train at Myrick's.
The 7.15 A.M. Train from Fall River will not stop after leaving Middleboro', and the 4.45 P.M Train from Boston will not stop at stations North of Bridgewater.

A. HOLMES, Pres't.

PHILAD'A & READING R. R

1855.   Spring Arrangements.   1855.

The Great Northern and Western U. S. Mail Routes.

SPEED INCREASED AND FARE REDUCED

Little
Schuylkill,
Catawissa,
Sunbury & Erie

Williamsport
and
Elmira R. R.

Through to Buffalo	in 16 hours	Through to Detroit	in 24 hours
" Niagara Falls	16 "	" Chicago	34 "

Through to St. Louis in 48 hours.

TICKET OFFICE, N. W. Corner Sixth and Chesnut Sts. and Reading R. R. Depot, Corner Broad and Vine Streets.

On and after Monday, May 7th, THREE PASSENGER TRAINS will leave the Philadelphia & Reading R. R. Depot, Corner Broad and Vine Streets, DAILY, (Sundays excepted,) as follows:

DAY EXPRESS—6, A. M.

Stopping at Phœnixville and Reading only—connecting with Catawissa, Williamsport and Erie, and Williamsport and Elmira Railroad, arriving at Elmira at 4, P. M. Connecting with New York and Erie and Buffalo and New York City Railroads for Dunkirk and Buffalo, and from thence, via Steamers on Lake Erie or Lake Shore Railroad to Cleveland, Toledo, Monroe, Sandusky and Detroit; also with New York and Erie, and Buffalo, Corning and New York City Railroad for Bath, Danville, Avon Springs and Rochester; also with Elmira, Canandaigua and Niagara Falls Railroad, connecting at Canandaigua with New York Central R. R. East and West, and at Suspension Bridge with Great Western and Michigan Central R. R. for Detroit, Chicago, St. Louis, and all points in Canada and Western States.

MAIL TRAIN—7.30, A. M.

Stopping at all Stations and running to Pottsville only.

NIGHT EXPRESS—3.30, P. M.

(Running Every Day,) stopping at all Stations, and running to Pottsville—connecting at Port Clinton with Catawissa, Williamsport and Erie, and Williamsport and Elmira Railroads, arriving at Elmira at 4 A. M. Connecting with New York and Erie, Buffalo and New York City and Lake Shore Railroads for Buffalo, Dunkirk, Erie, Cleveland, Cincinnati, Toledo, Chicago, and all points West; also, with Elmira, Canandaigua and Niagara Falls Railroads, arriving at Niagara Falls at 10.30 A. M., connecting with Day Express or Great Western Railroad for Detroit, Chicago, &c.

This Route, with its connections, forms the Shortest and Most Direct Route to Canada and the Lakes.

☞ Only one change of Baggage between Philadelphia and Canada or the Lakes.

Passengers purchasing Tickets by this Line, have the privilege of stopping at any of the above points, and resuming their seats at pleasure.

FARES FROM PHILADELPHIA TO

Tamaqua,	$2.95	Batavia	$9 00
Catawissa	4.35	Rochester, via N. Y. & Erie, Buffalo, Corning and	
Rupert	4.40	New York City,	8.00
Danville	4.80	Buffalo, via N.Y. & E. & Buffalo & N.Y. City R.	10.00
Milton	5.15	" Tonawanda,	10.00
Williamsport	5.90	Niagara Falls, via Elmira & Canan. & N. Fall R.	10.00
Elmira	7.00	" " Buffalo,	10.00
Jefferson	7.65	Suspension Bridge	10.00
Starkey	7.95	Cleveland	11.70
Penn Yan	8.00	Toledo	14.75
Gorham	8.00	Cincinnati	16.00
Geneva, via Gorham	8.00	Detroit, via Rail	16.00
" Steamer Jno. Arnot	8.00	" Buffalo and Lake	13.00
Canandaigua	8.00	Chicago, via G't West & Mich. Central R.	20.00
Honeoye Falls	8.50	" Buff. & Lake Shore & Mich. South R.	20.00
Caledonia	8.80	" Buffalo, Lake & Mich. Central R.	16.90
Le Roy	8.90	Rock Island	25.00

G. A. NICOLLS, Sup't P. & R. R. R.
T. McKISSOCK, Sup't C. W. & E. R. R.
HENRY COFFIN, Sup't W. & E. R. R.

Philadelphia, April, 1855.

E. T. HUBBELL, Ticket & Freight Ag't

N. W. Cor. Sixth & Chesnut Sts. Philadelphia.

Brown, Pr., Ledger Buildings, Philada.

THE CALIFORNIA FARMER.

Raspberries	10 — 15
Blackberries, per lb	6 — 8
Gooseberries	6 — 8
California Walnuts, per pound	10 — 12
Almonds, hard shell, per pound	12 — 15
do. soft shell, do.	15 — 20
Foreign Pecan Nuts	15 — 20
Foreign Brazil Nuts	15 — 20
Filberts	15 — 20
Chili Walnuts	10 — 12

Retail Price in the Vegetable Market.

The showing of *Vegetables* now is evidence of our great abundance of these all important culinary wants for the good housewife who knows how to get a good dinner, Peas, Beans, Corn, Asparagus, Cauliflower, Cucumbers, Egg Plants, with blenty of fine Salads make our markets A No. 1, and so say all strangers of our markets.

Asparagus	5 — 6
Artichokes, (French) per doz.	15 — 20
Tomatoes, per lb	3 — 4
Beets, per doz	.. — 25
Broccoli, each,	10 — 12
Cauliflower	10 — 12
Cabbage, do.	8 — 10
Carrots, per doz.	.. — 25
Celery do.	75 — 1 00
Celery Root per dozen	.. — 75
Cress, per dozen bunches	10 — 12
Cranberries, per gallon	75 — 1 00
Corn	8 — 12
Dried Herbs, per doz.	30 — 40
Green Peas, per lb	4 — 6
Lettuce per doz. bunches	12 — 12
Onions per lb.	4 — 5
Horseradish, per lb	12 — 15
Okra, green, per lb	10 — 12
Okra, dried, per lb	— 50
New Potatoes	3 — 5
Choice Potatoes	3 — 4
Potatoes choice, per 100 lbs	2 00 — 2 50
Kidney Potatoes, per lb	4 — 5
Pumpkins	2 — 3
Parsnips, per doz. bunches	.. — 20
Salsify, do. do.	.. — 20
Parsley, do. do.	15 — 20
Pickles, per gallon —	50 — 75
Radishes per doz. bunches	6 — 8
Squash, Marrowfat	2 — 3
do. Hubbard	.. — 4
Lima, Dry	8 — 10
String Beans, per lb	5 — 6
Spinage per lb	— 8
Salsify, per bunch	4 — 5
Turnips, per doz	.. — 20
Garlic	8 — 10
Eschalot	15 — 20

Fish Market.

The *Fish Market* shows as good fish and of as large a variety as any epicure need desire.

We now have the Fish of the Sea, Lake, and River in goodly numbers and at low price.

Salmon ℔ lb	8 — 10
do smoked new	12 — 15
do pickled, ℔ lb	6 — 10
Lake Bigler Trout each	20 — 25
Lake Bigler Trout, extra	20 — 25
Smelts, per lb	.. — 12
Perch do.	.. — 12
Rockfish do.	.. — 12
Codfish, dry, per lb	.. — 10
Herring, fresh, per lb	.. — 5
do smoked, ℔ doz	.. — 25
Tomcod, per lb	— 15
Sardines, fresh, per lb	.. — 10
Solefish, per lb	25 — 30
...erel pickled, each	.. — 25
...er lb	10 — 12
	20 — 25

Grain, Wool, Potato Bags, Etc.

We need not change our report of *Bags and Bagging*, for as the Chinaman say, it is "Alle same as last week."

The *Bag* and *Bagging folks* have t their own way and our grain growers now pay 12½ and 13 cents for bags they could have bought at 8 and 8½ cents last fall, but they thought they would "Hold on"—now they pay for it.

As Messrs. Neville & Co., the proprietors of the large Bag Factory on Clay Street, are not in the "Ring"—and having a good stock of bags on hand and plenty of material to make bags, they can sell their bags as they please without dictation, and the grain growers by trading with Neville & Co., can make quite a saving.

Hand Sewed Bags, Standard, 22 x 36	12½ — 13 cts.
Second Hand, Extra	10 — 11 do.
Machine Sewed, 22 x 36	10½ — 11½ do.
do. do 20 x 36	9 — 10½ do
Barley Bags, 22 x 40	11 — 12½ do
" " 24 x 36	9½ — 10 do
" " second hand	— 9½ do
Wool-sacks, new	45 — 55 do
do. second hand	30 — 40 do
Potatoe Gunnies, Double Sewed	13 — 14 do
do. do. Second Hand	10½ — 11 do
Flour Bags, quarters	6½ — 6½ do
do. halfs, six qualities	9 — 11 do

Staple Home Products.

Our *Home Products* are on the increase in quantity and quality, while we are now exporting largely those products which formerly we imported.

Flax Seed, per lb	2½ — 3¼
Hemp Seed, per lb	6 — 7
Castor Beans, per lb	8 — 8½
Castor Oil No 1 Diamond in cases, per gallon	— 1 10
" " " barrels "	— 1 05
Castor Oil, No. 2 Diamond in cases per gallon	— 1 00
" " " barrels "	— 85
Linseed Oil, Boiled	— 75
do. Raw	— 72
Cocoa Oil	— 55
Hops, California	5 — 8
Alfalfa	12 — 13
Mustard Seed	2 — 2½
English do.	5 — 5½
Canary Seed	6 — 7
Coriander Seed	8 — 10
Broom Corn	4 — 6
Bees Wax	26 — 28
Pea Nuts	5 — 7
Walnuts	8 — 10
Almonds, Soft Shelled	16 — 18
do. Hard do.	10 — 12
Pecans	14 — 16
Filberts	14 — 15

California Leather Market Report.

Hide, Leather and *Tallow*, the Hide market is firm but large sales, Leather do., and Tallow much more active for shippers.

California Sole Leather	— 28
do. Harness do.	— 31½
do. Skirtings,	— 37½
Bridle Leather	4½ — 6½
Rough do. Oak Tanned	18 — 26
Waxed Calf Skins	50 — 1 00
do. Kips do. per dozen	30 00 — 55 00
do. Leather per foot	15 — 17

Wool, Tallow, Hides, Etc.

The *Wool market* is quite dull with declining prices, even choice Oregon Wool is not active, that is also lower in value, and New York reports are not very good.

Wool, Spring Clip,	15 — 18
... Extra	22 — 24
	20 — 25
	15 — 18
	12 — 15
	19 — 22½
	20 — 75
	15 — 10
	7 — 9
	60 — 1 00
	50 — 75
	1 50 — 5 00
	50 — 1 00
	6½ — 7½
	7 — 9

... Prices.

...ity have never been ... better quality, while ...ime past—everybody ...able rate.

	5 — 6½ cts
	4 — 5 do.
	3½ — 4 do.
	6 — 7½ do.
	4 — 5 do.
	5 — 6 do
	5 — 5½ do.
	— 7½ do.

C. P. R. R

COMMENCING

SUNDAY, JUNE 6th, 1875,

AND UNTIL FURTHER NOTICE,

TRAINS AND BOATS WILL LEAVE

SAN FRANCISCO

7:00 A. M., Sundays excepted. Vallejo Steamer, (from Broadway Wharf), connecting at Vallejo with Trains for Calistoga, Knight's Landing and Sacramento; making close connections at Napa with Stages for Sonoma. (Arrive 8:55 P. M.)

8:00 A. M., (Daily) Atlantic Express Train (via Oakland) for Sacramento, Marysville, Redding and Portland, O., Colfax, Reno, Ogden and Omaha. Connects at Niles with Trains arriving at San Jose, 12:35 P. M. (Arrive 5:35 P. M.)

8:00 A. M., Sundays only, Vallejo Steamer (from Broadway Wharf), connecting at Vallejo with trains for Calistoga and Sacramento, and at Napa with Stages for Sonoma. (Arrive 8:55 P. M.)

3:00 P. M., Daily, San Jose Passenger Trains, via Oakland, stopping at all Way Stations. (Arrive 9:35 A. M.)

4:00 P. M., (Daily,) Passenger Train (via Oakland) to Stockton only, connecting at Lathrop with Express Train for Merced, Visalia, Sumner, Caliente and Los Angeles Also at Niles with Train arriving at San Jose 6:55 P. M. (Arrive 12:40 P. M.)

4:00 P. M., Sundays excepted, Vallejo Steamer (from Broadway Wharf), connecting at Vallejo with Trains for Calistoga, Knight's Landing and Sacramento. (Arrive 11:10 A. M.)

4:00 P. M., (Daily) Sacramento Steamer (from Broadway Wharf), touching at Benecia and Landings on the Sacramento River. Taking the Overland Third Class Passengers to connect with Train leaving Sacramento at 9:00 A. M., daily. (Arrive 8:00 P. M.)

OAKLAND AND ALAMEDA FERRY.

FROM SAN FRANCISCO TO OAKLAND.

"Daily"—7:00, 7:30, 8:00, 8:30, 9:00, 9:30, 10:00, and 11:00 A. M.; 12:00, 1:00, 2:00, 3:00, 3:30, 4:00, 4:30, 5:00, 5:30, 6:00 6:30, 7:00, 8:10, 9:20 and 10:30 P. M.
"Daily, except Sundays"—6:10 A. M. and 11:45 P. M.
"Sundays only"—10:30 and 11:30 A. M.; 12:30 and 1:30 P. M.

FROM SAN FRANCISCO TO ALAMEDA.

"Daily"—7:00, 8:00, 9:00, 10:00, A. M.; 12:00, 2:00, 4:00 5:00 6:00 and 10:30 P. M.
"Sundays only"—11:00 A. M., and 1:30 P. M.

FROM SAN FRANCISCO TO FERNSIDE.

"Daily, except Sundays"—7:00, 9:00 and 10:00 A. M.; 5:00 and 10:30 P. M.

FROM SAN FRANCISCO TO BROOKLYN.

"Daily"—7:30, 8:30 and 9:30 A. M.; 1:00, 3:30, 4:30, 5:30, 6:30, 7:00, 8:10 and 9:20 P. M.
"Daily, except Sunday"—6:30, 11:00 A. M. and 11:45
"Sundays only"—10:30, 11:30 A. M. and 12:30 P. M.

FROM BROOKLYN TO SAN FRANCISCO.

"Daily"—6:40, 7:40, 8:40, 9:40, 10:40 A. M. 12:40, 2:40, 4:40, 5:40, 6:40, 7:50, 9:00 and 10:10 P. M.
"Daily except Sundays"—5:10 and 5:50
"Sundays only"—11:40 A. M., and 1:25 P. M.

FROM ALAMEDA TO SAN FRANCISCO.

"Daily"—7:00, 8:03 and 9:00 A. M.; 3:00, 3:58, 5:00, 6:03 and 7:00 P. M.
"Daily, except Sundays"—5:00, 5:40, 11:30, A. M., and 1:30 P. M.
"Sundays only"—10:00, 11:00 A. M., 12:00 and 1:00 P. M.

FROM FERNSIDE TO SAN FRANCISCO.

"Daily, except Sundays"—6:55, 8:00 and 11:05 A. M., 3:50 and 6:05 P. M.

FROM OAKLAND TO SAN FRANCISCO.

"Daily"—6:50, 7:20, 7:50, 8:25, 8:50, 9:20, 9:50, 10:50 and 11:50 A. M.; 12:50, 2:50, 3:20, 3:50, 4:20, 4:50, 5:20, 5:50, 6:30, 6:50, 7:20, 8:00, 9:10 and 10:20 P. M.
"Daily, except Sundays"—5:20 A. M. and 1:50 P. M.
"Sundays only"—10:20 and 11:20 A. M.; 12:20, 1:20 and 1:35 P. M.

T. H. GOODMAN,
General Passenger and Ticket Agent.

A. N. TOWNE,
General Superintendent.

Southern Pacific Railroad.

NORTHERN DIVISION

As shown in this August 28, 1878 issue of The California Farmer, *railroads continued to publish some schedules as advertising in periodicals, but eventually, their periodical advertising would concentrate more on land opportunity announcements, tourism, and train accommodations rather than timetables. Many of these ads closely paralleled and in some cases were identical to material printed in timetables and travel brochures. These advertisements were for the Central and the Southern Pacific Railroads. Very Rare.*

As expansion continued to challenge railroads to advertise effectively, it was necessary to devise new ways to present, to as many potential passengers as possible, schedule information for many trains serving a growing number of towns. That information had to be in a practical format that was easy to read and sized to fit in one's pocket. Schedules also needed to include information on: fares, regions, land availability, towns, and some advertising. In the 1860s, two types had evolved: the folder or *folding brochure*—a single sheet, usually folded into many separate panels to resemble a brochure, and the *stapled pocket booklet* or pamphlet. Both took advantage of the table format of rows and columns and became the most common styles of timetables published.

By the late 1890s most large railroads realized that the stapled booklet format offered more expandability than did the folding brochure style. Booklets also allowed more travel information and advertising, both of which had become very important parts of the timetable.

The stapled booklet was also a more practical format than the folded brochure timetables, which now had evolved to giant sheets of paper—awkward to read, easily caught by the wind, and almost impossible to fold up again. Consequently, the popularity of the stapled booklet increased, its standard format becoming the 8" x 9" center-stapled booklet, folded in half to become 4" x 9." This format is still in common use today.

The folding brochure still was the most practical format for smaller railroads having few listings. It was also the best format for larger roads to use for their condensed, regional, and suburban commuter train schedules. Such timetables were necessitated by the growth of the railroads as lines and schedules expanded. While *general* public timetables showed all trains and all stops, including long distance, local and commuter, *regional* timetables showed only trains serving a specific area. *Condensed* public timetables showed stops of most long distance passenger trains only, in larger towns and cities. *Suburban* timetables showed only commuter and local passenger trains on a specific line. The most popular brochure size folded to 4"x 9."

With 22 separate panels on one side and a full-sized map on the other, this 1885 Chicago, Milwaukee and St. Paul Railway brochure-style timetable's unfolded size is 15 1/2" wide and 41" long—more than three feet! In addition to system schedules, it also included information on steamer lines to San Francisco, China, Japan and India. Rare.

A smaller version also became widely used for suburban commuter schedules and bus lines. Its folded dimensions were 2 3/4" x 4 3/4." These standard formats are still used today by railroads, airlines and bus companies.

Improved Graphic Design

With the establishment of these common formats came the beginning of the most colorful and prolific era in railroad public timetables, starting at the turn of the century and continuing into the 1960s. The nation was covered with a network of steel roads, which reached a peak in 1920, at 252,845 miles. Competing routes and tourism accelerated the public timetable's important role of attracting passengers.

Since cover art was the first thing a prospective traveler saw, the timetable cover was designed to be attractive enough to be chosen before competing timetables in a depot display rack or on a hotel counter. To bring home the sale, it was then up to the timetable's interior design and contents: easy-to-read convenient schedules, popular scenic routes, finest accommodations and on-board services, the latest and most powerful equipment, lowest fares, and accessible train stations in metropolitan areas. AMTRAK timetables still use these elements to appeal to potential travelers.

Frequency of New Timetable Issues

Over the years, a variety of factors affected the frequency of timetable issues. In the 1830s and 40s, the completion of new lines necessitated printing new handbills and broadsides. As railroads expanded and traffic increased through the 1880s, the addition of new trains required frequent timetable printings. Changes in local time also had a significant impact on frequency of issue before Standard Time (See Chapter Three) was adopted in 1883. After the turn of the century, increasing competition intensified the advertising role of public timetables. Travelers frequently saw new timetable issues which updated them on faster schedules, improved dining car services, more comfortable sleeping car accommodations, fare changes, travel tours, route information, and scenery along the way.

Factors Affecting Modern Timetables

Timetable changes are influenced by many factors: Equipment availability, reliability, maintenance,

scheduled replacement, and turnaround locations are very important; track maintenance, capital improvement programs, and seasonal weather changes also have to be considered.

Since operating experience provided information needed to create timetables, annotated copies of current *employee* timetables (See Chapter Three) were used to revise *public* timetables. In this way, additions, changes and adjustments that employees had experienced in the old schedule were reflected in new issues. Federal laws, labor unions, and wage issues effected the availability of train crews, the hours they could work, the conditions they could work under, and where crew changes were made. Also, time was added for schedule makeups, and there was a small margin for error. With all of these things to be factored in, it was amazing that the published times were accurate. The trains usually ran *on time*!

Besides their own employee timetables, many railroad personnel used public timetables in their work. A variety of railroad company employee publications referred to public timetables. As the primary point of contact with the traveling public, the importance of public timetables was always emphasized. The Southern Pacific Company's "MANUAL FOR THE GUIDANCE OF TRAIN PORTERS AND RED CAP STATION PORTERS" of October 1, 1964 included Rule 39 for public timetables and folders:

Train porters while on duty, must carry with them a copy of current timetable Form A. They should familiarize themselves with train schedules, and other information contained therein so that they may be in position to respond to inquiries that may be made by passengers. In the event a passenger requests information that the train porter cannot furnish, the train porter should consult the conductor or other available company representative, in order that the desired information may be supplied.

In the pages that follow, the evolution and variations of public timetables are further illustrated with specific examples.

Producing Twentieth Century Timetables
The April, 1922 edition of the Southern Pacific's employee magazine, *The Bulletin,* offered a rare look at the process of compiling a 20th-century public timetable, illustrating the logistical problems encountered with the updating, printing, and distribution of the many new public issues. The "Divisional Timetables" referred to in the section "When Real Work Begins" are employee timetables. As the railroad's primary organizational and operational tool, the employee timetable was the foundation for all public timetable updating. Form A, referred to throughout the article, is Southern Pacific's complete system-wide public timetable with all the system's schedules combined in one folder.

HOW S.P. TIME-TABLES ARE MADE

Close, Hard Team-Work Necessary in Issuing Over 350,000 Pamphlets of Changes

BY W. G. MADDOX
PASSENGER TRAFFIC DEPARTMENT

"Change of Time, effective February 12, 1922"— Such an announcement to the reader does not carry any thrill—just a commonplace indication of a contemplated change in schedules. But to a considerable part of the Southern Pacific organization it means a stressful period of close application with a seemingly never-ending amount of small detail to be covered, before one can see the light of day on the completed job which is under way.

The Advertising Bureau of the Passenger Traffic Department at San Francisco compiles, publishes and distributes the time-table folders, leaflets and station train cards of Southern Pacific Lines.

The nine folders and eight train cards—effective February 12, 1922—that were printed and distributed on February 8, 9 and 10, and reached all our agents in time to hand the public on the date effective, comprised the following: 75,000 Local Folder Form, being a 42-page complete folder of Pacific System; 15,000 District Folder Form 2 covering Bay Region, Stockton, Sacramento; 35,000 District Folder Form 3 covering Coast Line; 35,000 District Folder Form 4 covering San Joaquin Valley Line; 35,000 District Folder Form 5 covering Sunset Route; 35,000 District Folder Form 6 covering American Canyon Route via Ogden; 35,000 District Form Folder 7 covering Shasta Route;

25,000 Peninsular Folder Form 9 between San Francisco and San Jose; 3,000 San Francisco Train Cards; 2,000 Oakland Alameda-Berkeley Train Cards; 800 Bay Region Train Cards; 2,000 Stockton Train Cards; 1,500 San Joaquin Valley Train Cards; 1,000 Coast Line Train Cards. Also, 75,000 Advance Standard Time Table Form A, sent to our Eastern Agents and to Distributing Companies and Foreign Lines in all the territory beyond Pacific System Terminals.

By experience an average is determined as to the time that will be required to compile and check the schedules; how many men should be called in from the District Offices to assist; also how many days and nights—including a Sunday—will be available in which to complete the work.

When Real Work Begins
The real work on the folders is commenced when the Division Dispatchers are almost ready to print their tables. These Division Time-tables (used by the locomotive engineers and other operating men) are strung, revised and printed at a plant in San Francisco. Here meet the Dispatchers and their assistants—one big family—all interested in developing schedules, as per instructions, that will give the best possible service to the general public. And here, too, is where team work gives the Advertising Bureau its first opportunity to make a start. The men are called in from the various districts; the first bunch of proof sheets have been secured and the whole force "digs in" on the Local Time-table, with about 40,000 corrections or time units, averaging three and a half letters to the unit, to be made and which the printer will re-set in type: there are

eight train cards with seemingly as many figures to correct, and a Peninsular folder covering the local service between San Francisco and San Jose on the "Coast Line" to revise. Then while the printer is loaded with corrected copy and the first proofs are being awaited, pastime, "copy" is started for the Standard Folder Form A, of 56 pages.

All this work has been done from advanced proofs received from the Operating Department and places our folders about sixty per cent to the good in the big rush which will follow when the final check from the printed working time-tables is made.

The entire mass of "copy" is in; the printer has commenced to return first proof; the date effective is so close it seems as if it were tomorrow; we stand up close to our Operating Department; we hear their O.K. given "to print;" we watch the man lock the forms for the press and, approaching the head pressman, request advance sheets without the foreman's O.K. (a print-shop crime); we follow the sheets to the bindery and then to the cutter; in two minutes we are on our way to the General Office Building and then commences the grind of the final check of the 40,000 time-units. We don't wait to be handed the necessary material, nor wait for a messenger to deliver—but for each of the nine divisions affected by the change we repeat the action of standing by the press in order to make good, thus giving us an advantage of about four working days.

On the change of February 12, 1922 time-table corrections for nine out of the ten Divisions were put into folder form for public use. The last page of folder "copy" was closed at noon Monday, February 6, on the Local Folder and two advance copies placed in railroad mail for all agents on the Pacific System, Wednesday afternoon, February 8. The entire issue of 75,999 was distributed in time for use on date effective.

Distribution Problem

One of the most trying jobs common to all large railroad systems is to compile, print and distribute its time-tables by the date on which changes take effect, this on account of the preparatory detail to be worked out before the ten Division time cards

can be officially O.K.'d, and before being passed to the Passenger Department for publication.

In this instance, involving so large a number of changes, the success in reaching terminals with our folders before the effective date of the new time, was due to the close co-operation between Operating and Passenger Departments, and nine out of the ten Divisions were gladly availed of.

The Southern Pacific expends for these time-table forms an average of $150,000.00 annually, and it is most desirable that their publication be prompt and of service to our patrons. The gratifying result in this case was further made possible by the efficient help rendered in revising and checking our time-table folder "copy" rendered by members of our various District Passenger Offices, namely: J.J. Coyle, Sacramento; E.A. Teubner, San Jose; H.R. Greenrose, Oakland; W.A. Holmes, Fresno; B.E. Olmstead, Stockton and H.H. Lord, San Francisco.

Graphic from a 1913 Southern Pacific public timetable cover.

Form 1 - May 1891

THE
MK
AND T
MISSOURI, KANSAS & TEXAS RAILWAY.

TEXAS, MEXICO
AND
CALIFORNIA
FROM
St. Louis, Hannibal
and
Kansas City.

GEO. A. EDDY.   H. C. CROSS,
RECEIVERS.

GASTON MESLIER,
GENERAL PASSENGER AND TICKET AGENT,
SEDALIA, MO.

FORM 1.   POOLE BROS. CHICAGO.   MAY, '91.

This 1891 Missouri, Kansas & Texas Railway timetable exemplifies how the folded size of early brochure-style public timetables had changed slightly to the eventual 4" x 9" (8" x 9" opened) size still in use today by railroads, bus companies, and airlines. Rare.

This 3 1/2" x 6 1/4" booklet timetable — showing 1894 schedules for the Missouri, Kansas and Texas Railway — declared in bold type around the borders of the schedules where stops would be made for meals. Rare.

Missouri, Kansas & Texas Railway
ST. LOUIS TO TAYLOR, HOUSTON, SAN ANTONIO AND GALVESTON.

GOING SOUTH.

Ms	STATIONS.	1 Express Daily.	3 Express Daily.		55 Freight Ex. Sun.
254	Lv. Fort Scott	12 15 AM	1 45 PM		2 20 PM
261	" Ronald	12 29 "	2 05 "		2 55 "
267	" Hiattville	12 41 "	2 17 "		3 25 "
273	" Hepler	12 53 "	2 30 "		3 55 "
281	" Walnut	1 07 "	2 44 "		4 30 "
288	" Osage Mission	1 22 "	2 58 "		5 05 "
295	" South Mound	1 36 "	3 12 "		5 30 "
302	Ar. Parsons	1 50 "	3 25 "		6 00 "
				57	
0	Lv. Kansas City	9 05 AM	10 45 AM	Freight	
137	Ar. Parsons	1 55 AM	3 30 PM	Ex. Sun	
302	Lv. Parsons	2 10 AM	3 40 "	8 00 AM	
311	" Labete	2 29 "	3 59 "	8 30 "	
316	" Oswego	2 41 "	4 11 "	9 10 "	
320	" Chetopa	3 00 "	4 31 "	10 05 "	
332	" Russell Creek	3 12 "	4 43 "	10 43 "	
337	" Welch	3 22 "	5 04 "	11 15 "	
342	" Blue Jacket	3 32 "	5 19 "	11 50 "	
349	" Kelso	3 46 "	5 29 "	12 40PM	
354	Lv. Vinita	3 55 "	5 29 "	1 10 "	
362	" Big Cabin	4 11 "	5 45 "	1 55 "	
370	" Adair	4 25 "	6 00 "	2 50 "	
373	" Perry	4 34 "	6 08 "	3 10 "	
379	" Pryor Creek	4 48 "	6 21 "	3 40 "	
388	" Chouteau	5 09 "	6 42 "	4 20 "	
393	" Mazie	5 19 "	6 55 "	4 45 "	
399	" Lelinetta	5 30 "	7 08 "	5 15 "	
405	" Wagoner	5 42 "	7 18 "	5 55 "	
410	" Gibson	5 59 "	7 32 "	6 30 "	
415	" Wybark	6 12 "	7 44 "	6 45 "	
419	Ar. Muskogee	6 25 "	7 55 "	7 00 "	
419	Lv. Muskogee	6 45 "	8 15 "	4 00 AM	
426	" Summit	6 57 "	8 27 "	4 30 "	
433	" Oak-ta-ha	7 09 "	8 38 "	5 00 "	
440	" Checotah	7 23 "	8 52 "	5 41 "	
445	" Bond	7 34 "	9 02 "	6 05 "	
454	" Eufaula	7 52 "	9 18 "	6 57 "	
463	" South Canadian	8 11 "	9 37 "	7 40 "	
471	" Reams	8 26 "	9 52 "	8 26 "	
480	" McAlester	8 46 "	10 10 "	9 15 "	
482	" South McAlester	8 52 "	10 16 "	9 25 "	
485	" Frink	8 53 "	10 22 "	9 43 "	
490	Lv. Savanna	9 10 "	10 33 "	10 10 "	
498	" Kiowa	9 27 "	10 50 "	10 54 "	
507	" Limestone Gap	9 45 "	11 07 "	11 40 "	
512	" Chili	9 56 "	11 17 "	12 12PM	
518	" Stringtown	10 08 "	11 29 "	12 35 "	
525	" A-to-ka	10 25 "	11 45 "	1 25 "	
529	" Smallwood	10 33 "	11 52PM	1 41 "	
530	" Peck	10 37 "	11 56AM	1 47 "	
537	" Caney	10 00 "	12 08 "	2 18 "	
545	" Caddo	11 07 "	12 27 "	3 10 "	
552	" Armstrong	11 21 "	12 42 "	3 44 "	
557	" Durant	11 30 "	12 51 "	4 16 "	
562	" Cale	11 42 "	1 03 "	4 50 "	
569	" Colbert	11 57 "	1 17 "	5 33 "	
573	" Warner	12 06P.M	1 26 "	6 05 "	
576	Ar Denison	12 15 "	1 35 "	6 30 "	
576	Lv. Denison	12 56 "	2 10 "		
				77 Mixed Daily.	
579	" Ray	1 00 "	2 20 "	7 30 A.M	
585	" Pottsboro	1 12 "	2 33 "	7 44 "	
590	" Hagerman	1 22 "	2 45 "	8 01 "	
592	" Deaver	1 26 "	2 49 "	8 18 "	
598	" Sadler	1 35 "	3 01 "	8 24 "	
602	Ar Whitesboro	1 45 "	3 10 "	8 40 "	
602	Lv. Whitesboro	1 50 "	3 15 "	8 55 "	
608	" Collinsville	2 10 "	3 30 "		
614	" Tioga	2 24 "	3 45 "		

7

(vertical left) Train No. 3, Stops at Hotel Adams, Muskogee, for Supper.

(vertical right) Train No. 1 Stops at Hotel Adams, Muskogee, for Breakfast.

MISSOURI, KANSAS & TEXAS RAILWAY.

NEW DINING STATIONS.

FIRST CLASS SERVICE.

The Dining Stations on this line at Nevada, Parsons, South McAlester, Dallas, Hillsboro and Smithville, are the property of the Missouri, Kansas & Texas Railway System, and are under the immediate supervision of Mr. F. E. Miller, Superintendent of Dining Service. These dining stations are not operated for profit. No expense is spared to supply the table with all the delicacies of the season, prepared by ''chefs'' of acknowledged ability and experience. Any neglect or discourtesy of employes should be promptly reported to Mr. Miller, whose headquarters are at St. Louis, Mo., and the Company will esteem it a special favor to receive this information.

SOUTH-BOUND.

Train No. 1—DINNER AT PORTLAND, 2.35 TO 2.55 P. M.
DINNER AT MOBERLY, 2.05 TO 2.30 P. M.
SUPPER AT SEDALIA, 7.30 TO 7.50 P. M.
BREAKFAST AT SO. McALESTER, 9.00 TO 9.30 A.M.
DINNER AT DENISON, 2.00 TO 2.35 P. M.
SUPPER AT DALLAS, 6.55 TO 7.20 P. M.

Train No. 3—BREAKFAST AT SEDALIA, 8.50 TO 9.10 A. M.
DINNER AT PARSONS, 3.45 TO 4.00 P. M.
SUPPER AT MUSKOGEE, 8.00 TO 8.20 P. M.
BREAKFAST AT DALLAS, 6.50 TO 7.20 A. M.
DINNER AT GRANGER, 1.45 TO 2.05 P. M.

NORTH-BOUND.

Train No. 2—BREAKFAST AT
DINNER AT GRE
SUPPER AT SO.
BREAKFAST AT
DINNER AT MOE
DINNER AT POR

Train No. 4—DINNER AT SMI
SUPPER AT HILL
BREAKFAST AT
DINNER AT PAR
SUPPER AT SED.

All meals served at th
popular price of FIFTY C
La Carte.''

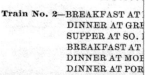

SOLID
FAST VESTIBULED TRAINS
BETWEEN
ST. LOUIS,
CHICAGO,
KANSAS CITY
AND
ALL TEXAS POINTS.

Through Wagner Sleeping Cars.

FREE KATY CHAIR CARS.

MEALS AT COMPANY'S
DINING STATIONS.
.....FIFTY CENTS.

SLEEPING CAR RATES.

HASTY SCHEDULE

WITH

TIME OF TRAINS

AT

IMPORTANT STATIONS

IN EFFECT APRIL 18TH, 1897.

T. C. PURDY, - - VICE-PRES'T AND GEN'L MANAGER,
C. MILLER, - - VICE-PRES'T AND TRAFFIC MANAGER,
A. A. ALLEN, - - ASSISTANT GENERAL MANAGER,
OF THE MISSOURI, KANSAS & TEXAS RAILWAY SYSTEM,
ST. LOUIS, MO.

WOODWARD & TIERNAN PRINTING CO., ST. LOUIS, MO.

So many small towns existed in turn-of-the-century rural America that railroads created "condensed" or, as shown here, "Hasty" timetables listing only the larger towns and cities ("Important Stations"). These timetables generally included only first-class or express trains that were used by through travelers and therefore made fewer stops. Two other important items about this 1897 MK & T Railway timetable: the recently opened "New Dining Stations" and "Arrangement of Wagner Sleeping Cars." Dining cars had been introduced in 1894 but were not yet in common use. George Pullman had yet to corner the market on sleeping car manufacturing and services. Rare.

TRAINS FOR PHILADELPHIA

WEEK-DAYS

Schedule in effect 12.01 A. M., April 19, 1909.

PENNSYLVANIA RAILROAD

PRR

EXPRESS TRAINS
·BETWEEN·
·NEW YORK·
····AND····
·PHILADELPHIA·

W. HEYWARD MYERS   J. R. WOOD   GEO. W. BOYD
General Manager   Passenger Traffic Manager   General Passenger Agent

This 1909 condensed timetable from the Pennsylvania Railroad reverted to the old list format to show only express trains and their equipment between New York and Philadelphia. Rare.

Lv. NEW YORK — W. 23d St. Station	Desb. & Cor. Sts. Stations	Leave Brooklyn	Arrive North Phila.	Arrive West Phila.	Arrive Phila. Broad St. St'n	PARLOR AND SLEEPING CARS
A/M	A/M	A/M	A/M	A/M	A/M	
6.05	6.10	....	8.47	d 8.57	9.01	Accommodation.
7.25	7.30	7.15	d 9.26	d 9.35	9.39	Parlor Car. Dining Car.
7.25	7.30	7.15	9.47	d 9.56	10.00	Accommodation.
7.55	8.00	7.45	b 9.57	b10.06	10.10	Parlor Car. Dining Car.
7.55	8.00	7.45	b10.c8	b10.18	....	Parlor Car. Dining Car.
8.25	8.30	8.15	b10.44	d10.52	10.56	Buffet Parlor Car.
8.55	9.00	8.45	d10.49	d10.56	11.00	Broiler Buffet Parlor Car.
9.25	9.30	9.15	....	11.47		Sleeping Cars. Dining Car.
9.25	9.30	9.15	d11.42	d11.50	11.54	Buffet Parlor Car.
9.55	10.00	9.45	b12.06	d12.15	12.19	Parlor Car. Buffet Sleep. Car.
10.55	11.00	10.45	d12.48	d12.56	1.00	Parlor Car. Dining Car.
10.55	11.00	10.45	b12.52	b 1.01	1.05	Penna. Lim. Extra fare train.
10.55	11.00	10.45	b 1.00	1.08	....	Parlor Car. Dining Car.
10.55	11.00	10.45	1.45	d 1.53	1.57	Accommodation.
11.55	12.00	11.45	d 1.48	d 1.56	2.00	Parlor Car. Dining Car.
11.55	12.00	11.45	2.24	d 2.33	2.37	Broiler Buffet Parlor Car.
12.55	1.00	12.45	b 2.57	d 3.06	3.10	Broiler Buffet Parlor Car.
1.25	1.30	1.15	d 3.43	3.53	....	Par. Car. Slpg. Car. Din. Car.
1.55	2.00	1.45	d 3.48	d 3.56	4.00	Broiler Buffet Parlor Car.
1.55	2.00	1.45	b 3.54			St. Louis Lim. Extra fare train.
1.55	2.00	1.45	b 4.04	b 4.13	4.17	Sleeping Cars. Dining Car.
2.10	2.20	1.45	4.23	d 4.32	4.36	Buffet Parlor Car.
2.55	3.00	2.45	d 5.00	d 5.09	5.13	Broiler Buffet Parlor Car.
3.25	3.30	3.15		5.40		Sleeping Cars. Dining Car.
3.55	4.00	3.45	d 5.48	d 5.56	6.00	Broiler Buffet Parlor Cars.
4.25	4.30	4.15	d 6.24	d 6.33	6.37	Broiler Buffet Parlor Car.
4.25	4.30	4 15	....	6.48		Sleeping Cars. Dining Car.
4.55	5.00	4.45	d 6.48	d 6.56	7.00	Broiler Buffet Parlor Car.
4.55	5.00	4.45	7.08			Chicago Lim. Extra fare train.
4.55	5.10	4.45	7.22	7.30		Parlor Car. Dining Car.
5.55	6.00	5.45	d 7.57	d 8.06	8.10	Parlor Cars. Dining Car.
6.25	6.30	6.15	b 8.33	b 8.44	8.48	Sleeping Cars. Dining Car.
6.55	7.00	6.45	d 8.59	d 9.06	9.10	Broiler Buffet Parlor Car.
6.55	7.00	6.45	10.08	d10.18	10.23	Accommodation.
7.55	8.00	7.45	10.25	d10.34	10.38	Sleeping Cars.
8.25	8.30	8.15	b10.33	d10.42	10.46	Broiler Buff. Par. Car. Sleep. Cars.
8.55	9.00	8.45	d10.58	d11.06	11.10	Buffet Parlor Car. Sleep. Car.
9.25	9.30	9.15	b11.48	d11.57	12.01	Buffet Parlor Car. Sleep. Cars.
9.55	10.00	9.45	12.08	....		Sleeping Cars.
12.10	12.15	11.45	....	b 3.26		Sleeping Cars.
12.10	12.15	11.45	d 3.17	d 3.29	3.34	Sleeping Car. See note.
A/M	A/M	P/M	A/M	A/M	A/M	

"b" Stops only on notice to Conductor to discharge passengers.

"d" Regular stop only to discharge passengers.

SLEEPING CAR for train leaving New York, West 23d Street Station, at 12.10 and Desbrosses and Cortlandt Streets at 12.15 night, daily, will be placed in station at Jersey City, open to receive passengers at 10.00 P. M. Passengers may remain in car until 7.00 A. M.

Note the many stops available on this Wabash Railroad public timetable from October, 1897. Rare.

ARRIVE AT AND DEPART[URE]

WABASH RAILROAD

CHICAGO AND ST. LOUIS LINE.

No. 13. St. Louis Express. Daily.	No. 11. Forrest Accom'dat'n. Daily.	No. 17. St. Louis & Kan.City Ex. Ex.Sun.	No. 15. St. Louis Limited. Daily.	No. 25. Forrest Accom'dat'n. Ex.Sun.	Distance from Chicago.	STATIONS.	No. 12. Chicago Express. Daily.	No. 10. Chicago Accom'dat'n. Daily.	No. 16. Chicago Express. Ex.Su[n.]
						SOUTH-BOUND—READ DOWN / **NORTH-BOUND**			
9.15PM	5.00PM	2.00PM	11.00AM	8.10AM		Lv....Chicago....Ar	7.30AM	9.20AM	2.10
9.25	5.07	2.07	11.07	8.17	1.6	..Archer Ave....	7.20	9.10	2.03
9.40	5.21	2.21	11.21	8.31	6.9	..Englewood....	7.01	8.44	1.49
	f5.25			8.35	8.0	..W. I. June....		f8.40	
	f5.27			8.37	8.9	..Chandler....		f8.36	
	f5.28			f8.39	9.6	..Dewey....		f8.34	
	f5.30			8.40	10.1	..Forest Hill....		f8.32	
				f8.42	10.9	..Landers....		f8.30	
9.57	5.35			8.46	12.2	..Clarkdale Jc..	6.42	8.27	
				f8.50	13.7	..Pleasant Hill..		f8.23	
f10.01	5.41			8.53	14.8	..Oak Lawn..		8.21	
	f5.44			8.56	16.4	..Chicago Ridge..		f8.18	
	5.50	2.45		9.00	17.8	..Worth..		8.16	
	f5.55			f9.05	19.7	..Palos Springs..		f8.10	
	6.02			9.15	23.5	..Orland..		8.03	
	6.09			9.22	26.8	..Alpine..		7.55	
	6.20			9.30	30.4	..Marley..		7.46	
	6.29			9.37	33.5	..New Lennox..		7.32	
	f6.31				33.9	..Steele..		f7.28	
	6.35			9.41	35.2	..Brisbane..		f7.26	
	6.44	3.27	X12.13	9.50	39.9	..Manhattan..		7.18	f12.48
	6.57			10.05	47.3	..Symerton..		7.06	
	7.07			10.18	53.3	..Ritchie..		6.55	
	7.10	3.49	X12.30	10.24	54.8	..Custer Park..		6.52	12.2
	f7.12				55.6	..Horse Creek..		f6.50	
	f7.21			10.38	60.4	..Essex..		6.41	
	f7.27				63.1	..Gronso..		f6.35	
	7.35			10.53	66.7	..Reddick....1		6.27	
	7.48	f4.17		11.04	72.8	..Campus..		6.17	f11.56
	7.58	f4.23		11.14	77.3	..Emington..		6.08	11.4
	8.10	f4.33		11.32	83.1	..Saunemin..		5.56	11.3
	8.20			11.41	88.1	..Wing..		f5.48	f11.2
Ar 12.35 / Lv 12.40	8.30PM	4.50	1.35PM	11.50	93.1	Ar / Lv ..Forrest..2.. Lv / Ar	Ar 3.55 / Lv 3.50	5.40	11.1
		4.53	1.38		100.1	..Strawn..			11.1
		5.07			104.7	..Sibley..			10.5
		5.15	f2.01		109.6	..Garber..			f10.4
1.21		5.30	2.16		112.8	..Gibson..3	3.11		10.3
		f5.37			116.9	..Proctor..			f10.2
		f5.44			120.9	..Foosland..			10.1
		f5.49			124.1	..Howard..4			10.1
		f5.53			125.8	..Osman..			10.0
		f5.57			128.0	..Blue Ridge..			10.0
1.58		6.04	2.49		131.9	..Mansfield..5	2.34		9.5
		6.12			136.7	..Galesville..			f9.5
		6.18			140.0	..Lodge..6			9.4
2.34		6.31	3.14		145.7	..Monticello..7	2.05		9.3
Ar 2.50 / Lv 2.52		6.50	3.30		153.0	Ar / Lv ..Bement.. Lv / Ar	1.45		9.2
		6.55			157.0	..Milmine..			f9.1
f3.09		s	X3.40		161.3	..Cerro Gordo..	f1.29		9.00
		f			165.4	..Oakley..			f8.5
		f			168.2	..Sangamon..			8.5
					172.1	East Decatur			
Ar 3.30 / Lv 3.40		7.17 / 7.20	3.55 / 4.00		173.1 / 173.0	Ar / Lv ..Decatur..8 Lv / Ar	1.05 / 12.55AM		8.4 / 5.2
					187.3	..Blue Mound..			
					193.0	..Stonington..			
4.47		7.59	4.39		202.0	..Taylorville..9	11.52PM		f4.4
					207.0	..Clarksdale..			
					210.0	..Palmer..			
					215.0	..Morrisonville..			
					223.0	..Raymond..			
5.45		8.43	5.23		234.0	..Litchfield..10	10.57		4.1
		X5.35			242.0	..Mt. Olive..	f10.39		
		X5.43			248.0	..Staunton..	f10.27		
		X5.51			254.0	..Worden..	f10.15		
6.37		X9.28	6.07		265.0	..Edwardsville Jc..	9.55		
7.12		10.00			283.0	..East St. Louis..	9.23		3.0
7.32AM		10.15PM	7.00PM		286.0	Ar....St. Louis....Lv	9.05AM		2.4

NOTE.—No. 16 will stop at stations North of Forrest to let off passengers from South and [...]

f Stop on Signal.
X Stop on Signal, Sunday only.

1. Indiana, Illinois & Iowa.
2. Toledo, Peoria & Western.
3. Lake Erie & Western. / Illinois Central.
4. Illinois Central.
5. Big Four.
6. Illinois Central.
7. Illinois Central.
8. Ind'polis, Illinois Ce[ntral], Peoria, D[ecatur], Terre Ha[ute]

WABASH RAILROAD TICKET

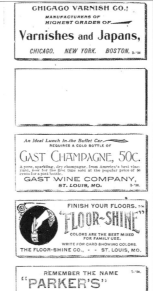

Bordered open spaces on the inside front and back covers of this 1898 Wabash Line timetable beckoned potential advertisers to consider placing ads, a new element afforded by the expandability of the stapled booklet format. This forty-page stapled booklet was the equivalent of an eighty-panel folding brochure timetable, which would have been a practical impossibility! Rare.

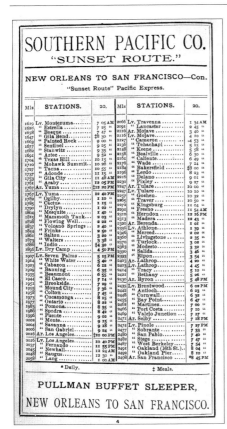

*Although not stated on the cover, this simple and to-the-point booklet-style timetable from 1891 contains schedules for the "Sunset Route" portion **only** of the Southern Pacific from New Orleans to San Francisco. Rare.*

With the standards for public timetables clearly established by 1900, this July 25th edition from The New York Central Lines is an example of the attractiveness and sophistication achieved by timetable makers of this era. This timetable features a glossy cover, a two-color map, illustrations, photographs, and an impressively long list of train schedules. Rare.

General Information

NOTICE. Passengers should apply to the Station Ticket Agent for further information, as these Time Tables are subject to change without notice.

SPECIAL NOTE: TRAINS DO NOT STOP WHERE NO TIME IS SHOWN.

This folder is for public information. The utmost care is taken to keep it revised to date of issue, but perfect accuracy is not guaranteed nor does the railway assume to hold itself responsible for any existing errors. The right is reserved to deviate from or change the figures herein given without public notice.

WHILE THE RAILWAY COMPANY USES EVERY REASONABLE EFFORT TO RUN ITS TRAINS ACCORDING TO SCHEDULE TIME, IT DOES NOT GUARANTEE THAT ITS TRAINS WILL RUN ACCORDING TO SCHEDULE NOR THAT THEY WILL MAKE CONNECTIONS AT JUNCTION POINTS WITH THE TRAINS OF ANY PARTICULAR LINE. ALL TICKETS ARE SOLD SUBJECT TO SUCH DELAYS AS MIGHT BE CAUSED BY THE ELEMENTS OR OTHER UNFORESEEN CIRCUMSTANCES.

1. **REFERENCE MARKS.** *Indicates that train runs daily. †Indicates that train runs daily except Sunday. f Indicates that train stops on signal only. x Meal stations.

2. **MILEAGE.** Distances stated in these time tables are for the information of passengers only and not for use in computing fares.

3. **PURCHASE TICKETS.** Ticket offices in stations are open from thirty minutes to one hour before departure of passenger trains, and passengers are requested to purchase tickets before boarding trains. Extra fare is charged passengers without tickets boarding trains at stations where they are on sale in Kansas, Oklahoma and Texas. Improvements in station facilities are frequently based on passenger revenues collected at that station, consequently it is to your interest to purchase tickets of your home agent wherever possible.

4. **HONORING TICKETS.** All tickets, one-way and round-trip (except where optional routes are permitted, see paragraph 20), are honored via short line only.

5. **TICKETS ON LIMITED TRAINS** Passengers holding tickets to, or desiring stop-over privileges at stations where fast or limited trains are not scheduled to stop, will be carried on said trains only to first regular station stop short of destination or stop-over point, where passenger will leave the train (such stop-over being permitted under the rules) and take the first local train to destination or stop-over point. No agent or conductor has a right to change or vary these rules and regulations.

6. **REDEMPTION OF TICKETS.** Unused tickets should be submitted to ticket agents, who, if they cannot redeem same, will forward to General Passenger Agent for prompt attention.

7. **LIMITED TICKETS.** Through first-class, second-class and round-trip tickets are closely limited as to time. When presented by passengers on trains prior to midnight of date of expiration of limit, all tickets except homeseekers' excursion tickets, will be honored for continuous passage to destination on the M. K. & T. Ry. or M. K. & T. Ry. of Texas.

8. **LOST TICKETS.** The carrier is not responsible for lost tickets. When tickets are lost, take receipt for additional fares paid and if ticket is eventually found, return same unused, together with such receipts, to General Passenger Agent for refund.

9. **COUPON TICKETS.** Tickets from a station on one road to a station on another road are sold at stations designated as coupon stations, on page 4. As passengers frequently save money by purchasing coupon tickets, an intending purchaser at a non-coupon station can secure a through ticket by notifying agent in ample time. At the same time it can be arranged to check baggage through to destination by route of ticket.

10. **CHILDREN.** The lawful fare for children who have passed their fifth birthday, but who have not yet passed their twelfth birthday, is one-half (½) the regular one-way fare charged adults, except that locally within the State of Kansas, children between the ages of six and twelve years will be charged half fare.

The lawful fare for children who have passed their twelfth birthday is the same fare charged adults.

Trouble and annoyance will be saved by purchase of tickets in all cases.

11. **STOP-OVERS.** On the M. K. & T. Lines stop-overs are allowed within limit of ticket, on application to conductor, on tickets as follows:

(a) On one-way tickets reading from stations north of and including Atoka, Okla., to Denison, Tex., or beyond, and vice versa.

(b) On all-year, summer and winter tourist tickets (but not on homeseekers' excursion tickets), on either going or return trip, within transit limit going and within final limit returning.

Always ask the agent for particulars of stop-overs and thus obviate any misunderstanding.

12. **BAGGAGE.** Only 150 pounds of baggage, not exceeding One Hundred Dollars in value, will be checked without charge for each adult passenger, and 75 pounds, not exceeding Fifty Dollars in value, for each child traveling on half ticket.

It shall be the duty of every passenger tendering baggage for transportation to declare the value thereof. Baggage declared to exceed Twenty-five Hundred Dollars in value will not be accepted for transportation in baggage cars.

Unless a greater sum is declared by the passenger, and charges paid for increased valuation at time of delivery, the value of the baggage or articles belonging to or checked for an adult passenger shall be held to have been declared and agreed by him to be, and shall be deemed to be, not in excess of One Hundred Dollars, and the value of the baggage or articles belonging to or checked for a child of half fare age shall be held to have been declared and agreed by him to be, and shall be deemed to be, not in excess of Fifty Dollars.

Time and space will permit of handling only a limited amount of baggage on limited trains. Passengers using either the Limited or Flyer trains are hereby notified that these lines do not undertake to carry their baggage upon said trains, and reserve the right to carry the same on trains following. See also note at bottom of page 17.

To insure prompt forwarding of baggage, passengers should be at the station at east fifteen minutes before the advertised departure of trains.

Passengers should claim baggage immediately upon arrival, as these lines are not liable for loss or damage to baggage after sufficient time has been allowed for removal.

13. **STORAGE ON BAGGAGE.** If not removed within twenty-four hours, storage will be charged on each piece at the following rates: First 24 hours, free; second 24 hours, 25 cents, and each succeeding day or fraction thereof, 10 cents. Baggage checked to a station where there is no agent must be claimed of the train baggageman previous to arrival of train at said station and duplicate check held by passenger surrendered, otherwise baggage will be carried beyond to the first station having an agent.

14. **DOGS.** Dogs are not allowed in coaches. Dogs do not form any part of the baggage allowance. Between stations in Missouri, Kansas and Oklahoma, and for interstate trips—dogs not exceeding twenty-five dollars ($25.00) in value, when not intended for exhibition, bench shows or field trials, if muzzled and provided with properly fitting collar and strong chain, or in crates, and if accompanied by owner or caretaker, will be checked and transported in baggage cars and charge made at regular excess baggage rates for gross weight. The minimum charge for each dog on chain or for each crate containing one or more dogs, will be the regular charge for one hundred (100) pounds of excess baggage between the same points, except that dogs will not be checked beyond junction points where wagon transfer is required.

Between stations in Texas—a charge of 25 cents for each dog, any distance under fifty miles and one-half cent per mile for distance over fifty miles, not to exceed one dollar for the trip.

15. **BICYCLES, TRICYCLES, BABY CARRIAGES AND GO-CARTS** will be checked and charge made at excess baggage rates for gross weight, minimum charge the same as for fifty pounds of excess baggage. Motorcycles will not be checked.

16. **PARCEL ROOMS.** Parcel rooms will be found at principal stations where packages, hand baggage, etc., may be checked and cared for at a nominal charge.

17. **CORPSES.** A full fare, regardless of the age of the deceased, must be paid

In buying a ticket to Oklahoma or Texas say "Katy" to the Agent; he will understand.

3

Public timetables included general information for the passenger's use. Material in this 1915 MK&T timetable suggests what train travel was like during this time. Rare.

Free "Farm Opportunity Books" about Zone of Plenty States—Send for them

These are eight "worth-your-reading" books, [
gration Department of the Great Northern R[
you want to know" about the unusual opportunitie[
farmer in Northern Minnesota, North Dakota, Montan[
Oregon. Opportunities in general farming on "lands for[
opportunities in "corn, alfalfa and cows", opportunities[
orcharding; opportunities "for the man of moderate[
dependably described.

Any, or all, of these books are yours for the asking—ch[
the coupon below and mail the coupon to

E. C. LEEDY, General Immigration Agent, Great Northern

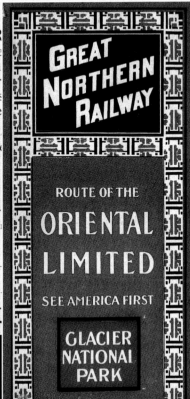

This 1917 Great Northern public timetable included two full-page advertisements for travel and farming opportunity publications offered free or at a small cost by the railroad. Rare.

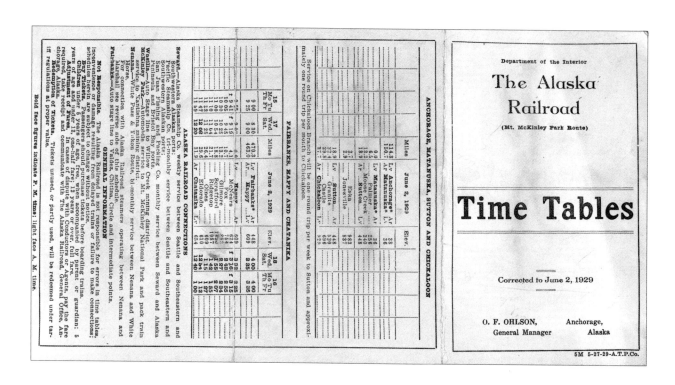

The folding brochure timetable remained a popular and practical public timetable format for smaller railroads. This 1929 example is printed on medium card stock. The Alaska Railroad was the only railroad ever owned and operated by the Department of the Interior. It now belongs to the State of Alaska. Rare.

*Many large railroads printed separate public timetables for specific divisions or regions of their systems. Southern Pacific's 1937 Form E included schedules for the Overland Route **only** in a separate timetable folder. Form F for 1938 covered their Sunset and Golden State Routes. Form A was Southern Pacific's system-wide public timetable. Common.*

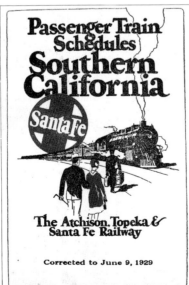

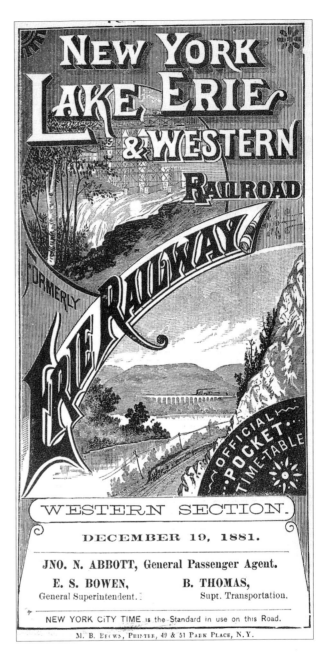

Examples of regional schedules published in smaller
brochure-style folders: 1934 Chicago, Milwaukee, St.Paul
and Pacific Railroad; 1881 New York, Lake Erie &
Western Railroad; 1929 Atchison, Topeka & Santa Fe
Railway. Rare.

Dinner in the diner became an American social icon. No meal tasted better than one served on the train. Ads for dining car service, as shown in this 1936 Missouri, Kansas & Texas Railway example, were part of almost every public timetable. Common.

As shown in this 1936 Santa Fe "Superchief" schedule, many railroads stayed with the practice of stopping at eating houses for meals, as opposed to purchasing and equipping dining cars. Railroads also provided hotel services in lieu of or in addition to sleeping cars. The most famous railroad eating houses and hotels in American history were those provided to the Santa Fe Railroad under contract by entrepreneur Fred Harvey. Common.

Santa Fe Meal Service
Fred Harvey

All through passenger trains which do not carry dining cars are scheduled to stop at dining stations placed at convenient points along the line, and indicated in time tables thus —*. Ample time is allowed for meals.

These dining stations offer special train meals—breakfast, 40c, 35c and 25c; luncheon, 45c, 40c and 35c; dinner, 55c, 45c and 40c. Other club breakfasts, 40c to 65c; plate luncheons, 50c to 75c; plate dinners, 60c to 90c. Also extended a la carte service at reasonable prices.

Dining car service on trains 17 and 18 (The Super Chief) and trains 19 and 20 (The Chief) is a la carte. Trains 3 and 4 (California Limited) and 23 and 24 (Grand Canyon Limited) between Chicago and Los Angeles, trains 9 and 10 (The Navajo) between Chicago and Kansas City, and trains 5 and 6 between Chicago and Texas points, offer extensive a la carte service, as well as table d'hote meals—breakfast, 50c, 65c and 75c; luncheon, 90c; dinner, $1.25.

All Santa Fe-Fred Harvey dining cars are now air-conditioned the year round.

Supplementary meal service from dining car is available for tourist sleeper, chair car and coach passengers not wishing regular dining car meals. Light refreshments are procurable at reasonable prices on the following trains:

Trains 9, 10 and 23 between Chicago and Kansas City.
Trains 5 and 6 between Chicago and Fort Worth.
Trains 49 and 50 between Kansas City and Tulsa.
Trains 13 and 14 between La Junta and Denver.
Trains 27 and 28 between Oklahoma City and Fort Worth.
Trains 42 and 47 between Ash Fork and Phoenix.
Train 24 Los Angeles to Needles.
Trains 23 and 2 between Barstow and San Francisco.

The restaurants and lunch rooms in the terminals at Chicago, Kansas City, Houston, Galveston and El Paso are also under Fred Harvey management, offering both table d'hote and a la carte service at moderate prices.

LUNCH ROOMS

LUNCH ROOMS	SEATING CAPACITY	LUNCH ROOMS	SEATING CAPACITY	LUNCH ROOMS	SEATING CAPACITY
Albuquerque, N. M.	124	Ft. Worth, Tex.*	.	Purcell, Okla.*	.
Amarillo, Tex.*	51	Gainesville, Tex.*	.	Rincon, N. M.*	.
Arkansas City, Kan.*	.	Gallup, N. M.	97	San Bernardino, Cal.	48
Ash Fork, Ariz.*	128	Galveston, Tex.	66	San Diego, Calif.*	.
Bakersfield, Calif.	.	Grand Canyon Ariz.	222	Seligman, Ariz.	48
Barstow, Calif.	52	Guthrie, Okla.*	.	Slaton, Tex.	46
Belen, N. M.	45	Houston, Tex.	91	Somerville, Tex.	50
Brownwood, Tex.	33	Hutchinson, Kan.	48	Sweetwater, Tex.*	.
Canadian, Tex.	42	Kansas City, Mo.	394	Temple, Tex.*	.
Chanute, Kan.*	.	Kingman, Ariz.	38	Topeka, Kan.	24
Chicago, Ill. (Dearborn Sta.)	34	La Junta, Colo.	64	Vaughn, N. M.	42
Clovis, N. M.*	.	Lamy, N. M.	34	Waynoka, Okla.	37
Colo. Spgs., Colo.	47	Las Vegas, N. M.	24	Wellington, Kan.	67
Dodge City, Kan.	101	Los Angeles, Calif.	48	Wichita, Kan.*	.
El Paso, Tex.	104	Merced, Calif.*	.	Williams, Ariz.	53
Emporia, Kan.	44	Needles, Calif.	104	Winslow, Ariz.	124
		Newton, Kan.	35		

* Temporarily closed.

Hotel Accommodations are provided at:

	GUEST ROOMS		GUEST ROOMS		GUEST ROOMS
Albuquerque, N. M.	119	Grand Canyon, Ariz.	79	Seligman, Ariz.	19
Ash Fork, Ariz.	21	Hutchinson, Kan.	80	Somerville, Tex.	14
Barstow, Calif.	29	La Junta, Colo.	44	Syracuse, Kan.	15
Clovis, N. M.	35	Lamy, N. M.	8	Vaughn, N. M.	10
Dodge City, Kan.	41	Las Vegas, N. M.	36	Wellington, Kan.	19
Emporia, Kan.	7	Needles, Calif.	29	Williams, Ariz.	37
Gallup, N. M.	71	Rincon, N. M.	11	Winslow, Ariz.	65

At those hotels operated on the European plan the rates for rooms are generally $1.50 a day and up. Those operated on the American plan are $4.75 a day and up, except at El Tovar, where the rate is $5.50 per day and up.

The most noteworthy of the Santa Fe hotels are:

	Capacity of DINING ROOMS	Number of GUEST ROOMS
THE BISONTE, at Hutchinson, Kansas	110	70 E
EL VAQUERO, at Dodge City, Kansas	80	41 E
THE GRAN-QUIVIRA, at Clovis, New Mexico	98	35 E
THE CASTANEDA, at Las Vegas, New Mexico	75	36 E
EL ORTIZ, at Lamy, New Mexico	12	8 E
LA FONDA, at Santa Fe, N. M.	360	147 E
THE ALVARADO, at Albuquerque, New Mexico	120	121 E
EL NAVAJO, at Gallup, New Mexico	108	71 E
LA POSADA, at Winslow, Arizona	.	67 E
THE FRAY MARCOS, at Williams, Arizona	.	37 E
EL TOVAR, at Grand Canyon Arizona	200	80 A
BRIGHT ANGEL LODGE AND CABINS, at Grand Canyon, Arizona	222	134 E
EL ESCALANTE, at Ash Fork, Arizona	.	21 E
EL GARCES, at Needles, California	.	26 E
THE CASA DEL DESIERTO, at Barstow, California	111	29 E

E— European Plan. A—American Plan. * Temporarily closed.
▲ Coffee Shop.

DINING ROOMS

DINING ROOMS	SEATING CAPACITY	DINING ROOMS	SEATING CAPACITY	DINING ROOMS	SEATING CAPACITY
Albuquerque, N. M.	120	El Paso, Tex.	69	Purcell, Okla.*	.
▲Amarillo, Tex.	88	▲Emporia, Kan.	104	▲San Bernardino, Cal.	26
Arkansas City, Kan.*	.	Ft. Worth, Tex.*	.	▲Seligman, Ariz.	100
Ash Fork, Ariz.*	.	Gallup, N. M.	108	Syracuse, Kan.*	.
▲Barstow, Calif.	111	Grand Canyon, Ariz.	200	Temple, Tex.*	.
▲Belen, N. M.	60	Hutchinson, Kan.	110	▲Topeka, Kan.	55
Brownwood, Tex.*	.	Kansas City, Mo.	104	Vaughn, N. M.*	.
▲Canadian, Tex.*	.	▲Kingman, Ariz.	42	▲Waynoka, Okla.	60
Chicago, Ill. (Dearborn Sta.)	76	La Junta, Colo.	76	▲Wellington, Kan.	72
Clovis, N. M.*	.	Lamy, N. M.	12	▲Williams, Ariz.*	.
Colorado Spgs., Colo.*	.	▲Las Vegas, N. M.	78	Winslow, Ariz.*	.
▲Dodge City, Kan.	80	Merced, Calif.*	.	▲ Coffee Shop.	
		Needles, Calif.*	.	* Temporarily closed.	
		▲ Newton, Kan.	80		

THE *Super* CHIEF

New Lower

MEAL PRICES

Meals of typical Fred Harvey quality, famous for 60 years, offering complete and attractive menus at NEW LOW COST. These low-cost meals are available for passengers on certain Santa Fe trains stopping at those conveniently placed and attractive Harvey dining stations, where ample time is allowed for meals.

TYPICAL

45¢

LUNCHEON

Chicken Pot Pie
Mashed Potatoes   New Beets
Pineapple Sherbert
Assorted Bread   Rolls
Coffee   Tea   Milk

Boiled Frankfurters,
Hot Potato Salad, Rolls
Coffee, Tea or Milk, **40c**

Chicken Salad
Bread and Butter Sandwich
Coffee, Tea or Milk, **35c**

BREAKFAST
40¢   35¢ and 25¢

DINNER 55¢
45¢ and 40¢
A la carte service as well

Also lower dining car prices on the CALIFORNIA LIMITED and the GRAND

LOCAL
Time Tables

Effective November 1, 1936

The
Atchison, Topeka & Santa Fe
AND
Panhandle & Santa Fe
Railway Companies

Advertisement for Fred Harvey meals in a 1936 Atchison, Topeka & Santa Fe public timetable presages fast food value meals by almost sixty years. Check the amount of food a train passenger received for forty-five cents. Common.

Railroad companies issued joint public timetables when it was advantageous to all parties involved. These from the 1967 Southern Pacific/Santa Fe and 1956 Spokane, Portland and Seattle/ Northern Pacific/ Great Northern Railroads are examples. Common.

WE SELL SLEEP

Via the Noiseless Route

We sell sleep as well as transportation. Lack of noise all the way spells sleep all the way, pleasant dreams, complete rest.

Our route is through quiet Illinois farmlands. No noisy station stops—no big cities with their disturbances. Only the soothing click of the big steel rails to sing you to sleep.

SPIRIT OF PROGRESS *Midnight Flyer*

Individual bedrooms, drawing-room compartment sleepers, club-lounge (radio), serving midnight supper and breakfast. Valet service. Free reclining chair cars.

SOUTHBOUND		NORTHBOUND	
Lv. Chicago · · 11:55 p. m.		Lv. St. Louis · 12:00 midnight	
Ar. St. Louis · · 7:21 a. m.		Ar. Chicago · 7:25 a. m.	

CENTURY OF PROGRESS 6½ hours

Fast as the Fastest. Observation drawing-room parlor car. Club-lounge (radio). Delicious luncheon at surprisingly low price. Free reclining chair cars.

Air Conditioned—Clean—Quiet—Comfortable

SOUTHBOUND		NORTHBOUND	
Lv. Chicago · · 11:25 a. m.		Lv. St. Louis · · 12:04 p. m.	
Ar. St. Louis · · 5:55 p. m.		Ar. Chicago · · 6:34 p. m.	

Ask about the *New Low Cost of Railroad Tickets* —coach and sleeping car—one-way and round-trip.

(All time shown is Central Standard Time)

TO PLEASE—
TO BE OF SERVICE—
is the constant aim of the C & E I. Our regular patrons realize this—our occasional patron is imbued with the spirit — we bespeak the opportunity to serve others for we know a trial will be convincing.

Our service begins with the inquiry for information, tickets or reservation.

CHICAGO & EASTERN ILLINOIS RAILWAY
E. H. Batchelder, General Passenger Agent
760 McCormick Building, Chicago

C & E I TRAINS
depart and arrive
at
DEARBORN STATION
Polk and Dearborn Sts.
CHICAGO
and
UNION STATION
ST. LOUIS

Between Chicago - St. Louis

The soothing "clickity clack" sound of the steel wheels running over joints between rails and the train's gentle rocking motions were extolled in this 1934 Chicago and Eastern Illinois Railroad public timetable advertisement. Common.

Some railroads were better than others at presenting conventional timetables in a readable, more attractive fashion. In this 1936 example from the Cotton Belt Route, drawings depicting regional life-styles, commerce, and history illustrate the schedules. Common.

Special-event timetables similar to those published as handbills in the 1840s were still issued occasionally in the 1960s. This 1965 Santa Fe Railroad flyer offering two special trains to the Big Red game is an example. Common.

It was the exception rather than the rule for railroads to provide intermodal combined service schedules as in this 1937 Maine Central Railroad timetable. Railroads traditionally competed fiercely with highway and air travel, as this 1968 Rio Grande Railroad timetable ad illustrates. Rare and Common.

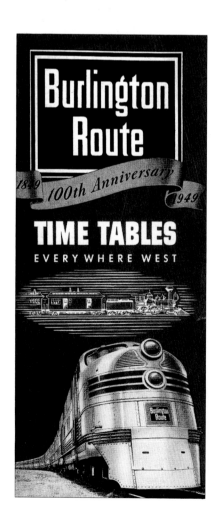

Timetable covers often depicted railroad heritage and anniversary themes such as this 1949 Burlington Route's Centennial. Common.

TIME TABLE

THE ATCHISON, TOPEKA AND SANTA FE RAILWAY CO.

Santa Fe

708

CONDENSED SCHEDULES
OF PASSENGER SERVICE
Issued: July 1, 1970

The last timetable issued by the Santa Fe Railroad in 1970, prior to the nationalization of most passenger service by AMTRAK, was a traditional sixteen-panel folding brochure, a format in use for over 100 years. Common.

Delicious food from a wide menu selection is a regular treat for travelers on Santa Fe.

The Turquoise Room for private dining and the Champagne dinner are two of the deluxe features of the famous Super Chief.

room travel accommodations that range from single rooms to spacious suites.

Super Chief travelers enjoy a complimentary "Wake-up Cup" of coffee.

Santa Fe's passenger fleet remains America's most relaxing ride. Even in the jet age.

It's fun to travel—take time to enjoy it aboard the Super Chief and El Capitan between Chicago and Los Angeles . . . San Francisco Chief between Chicago, Texas, San Joaquin Valley points and San Francisco . . . Texas Chief between Chicago and Houston.

Schedules, equipment and other information on our passenger trains are contained in this timetable.

Santa Fe offers a choice of services and accommodations: spacious private rooms in the sleeping cars or relaxing stretch-out chair car seats, cheery lounge areas, and excellent dining at reasonable prices.

You can charge all of your Santa Fe travel costs, too, with Master Charge, an Interbank card, or BankAmericard.

Pick the train that fits your travel plans best. Then let your travel agent or nearest Santa Fe ticket office give you full details on the One-Price Ticket arrangement. It saves money for individual travelers and families—covers all major travel expenses while aboard Santa Fe trains.

All 60 seats in El Capitan's Hi-Level Lounge offer a panoramic view of the countryside from big two-tier windows.

Hi-Level cars on El Capitan and San Francisco Chief put travelers at the scenic level for daytime enjoyment, and offer a quieter, smoother ride day and night.

Santa Fe chair cars feature stretch-out seats and leg rests for fine riding comfort day and night. Big picture windows too.

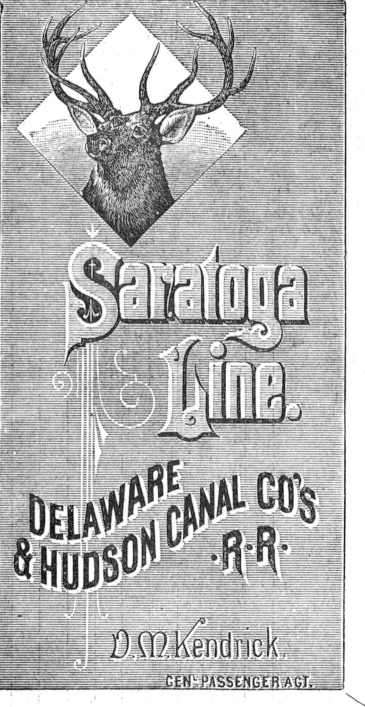

SEPTEMBER 25th, 1882.

Saratoga Line.

DELAWARE & HUDSON CANAL CO'S ·R·R·

D. M. Kendrick.

GEN. PASSENGER AGT.

PEOPLE'S RY. GUIDE PRINT.

This fine 1882 example of an early suburban
timetable is from the Saratoga Line of the Delaware
& Hudson Canal Company Railroad. Rare.

CHAPTER TWO
SUBURBAN TIMETABLES

IT IS THE 1880s and you have found the good life in suburbia. As you stand on the station platform waiting for the train, you reflect that you are one among thousands who have left crowded cities to live pleasantly in surrounding communities. Railroad lines spread from the hub city like spokes of a wagon wheel, connecting the many new towns. You look down the list of stations in the current suburban timetable and appreciate how the many trains running every day on this line have made it easy and practical to live in all these places and still work or shop in the city.

The depot in every large or small town is the center of activity. Mail, milk, money, and Mom all ride the local trains. You ride commuter trains every day to your job in the city. On weekends, special excursion trains offer outings in the country or shopping trips to the city. Any day of the week can bring the tools you ordered for your business or the parts to repair your plow. The railroad carries to market the corn you harvest and brings the letters you receive every day. Fresh milk from your dairy leaves by train early every morning and the daily newspaper arrives by train every evening. The local train brings the dress you have saved for, hardware for the shed you are building, cocoa for baking, lumber for your house, the new ice box for the kitchen, a seat for the commode in the outhouse, bricks for the streets, the toy train and doll you dreamed of. Anything you want can be ordered from the big catalog houses in the city at the end of the rail line. Everything and everyone comes and goes by train in the 1880's.

This 1886 Chicago, Rock Island and Pacific Railway suburban timetable included forty-two trains in both directions on the line between Chicago, Blue Island, and Joliet, Illinois. The ornate cover notes the inclusion of commutation ticket rates as well as schedules. Rare.

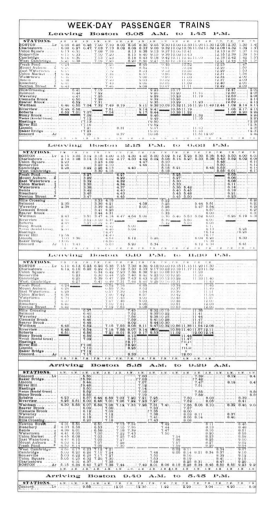

In 1894, the Fitchburg Railroad took advantage of the folding brochure format, oriented vertically, to show suburban train schedules between Boston and Concord. Rare.

This 1951 New York, Susquehanna & Western Railroad schedule typifies suburban timetables of the 1940s and 50s. Rare.

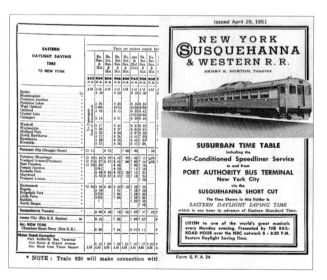

Commuter Trains / Suburban Growth

America's railroads helped create hubs of commercial activity. By the 1880s, great centers of commerce had been established, their locations dictated by the needs of geography and trade. Chicago, New York, New Orleans, Boston, St. Louis, Kansas City, and San Francisco had all become capitals of free enterprise in a thriving democracy. As these cities grew and became more crowded, people migrated to surrounding areas. By providing frequently scheduled train service, the same railroads that made these cities prosper also made it practical to live in communities nearby.

Commuter trains and locals became an integral part of rural American life as they stopped in every town along their way. Thousands rode commuter trains daily to jobs in the cities. Local trains carried everything that industrial and agricultural America produced. These trains affected everyone, for they were the lifelines of the community.

In 1951, the Illinois Central Railroad celebrated its 100th anniversary with a commemorative booklet, *The Building of Mid-America*, which included "20 railroad stories as told by a fifth-generation member of an Illinois Central family." One of these recounts how suburban train service on the IC brought Hyde Park into being.

Chicago's South Side Grows Up

Paul Cornell was a Chicago lawyer a hundred years ago and sharper than a tack. He and my great-great-grandfather met when the Illinois Central surveying crew crossed 300 acres of land that Cornell owned six miles south of town along the lake shore. That's around Fifty-third street now, and built up solid, but in those days Chicago had only 34,000 people and ended at Twenty-second street.

Lawyer Cornell called his land Hyde Park. He figured Chicago would eventually grow out to there, but railroad service would speed the process. When the surveyors showed up, he sold the railroad the right of way and a few extra acres as a sweetener. And he got a promise of eventual daily passenger service to Hyde Park.

In 1856 he subdivided his property for sale, and Illinois Central scheduled four daily round trips. Great-great-grandpa said the first Hyde Park Special carried nary a passenger.

After a year hard times hit, and the railroad needed to reduce service. Cornell staved this off by paying about $25.00 a month until traffic caught up with the expenses. He came out ahead, too. By 1880 Hyde Park had 16,000 people, and the Illinois Central was operating 36 week-day trains.

After the Chicago Fire of 1871, thousands of families moved to the suburbs, and the Illinois Central extended suburban service fifteen miles to the south. The railroad kept adding extra tracks and branch lines as new neighborhoods built up. It designed double-ender locomotives and side-door coaches to speed up the service.

Chicago grew like a weed, but the South Side grew even faster then the rest. That was because of the Illinois Central suburban service.

Fast freight advertisement from a 1932 Illinois Central Railroad suburban timetable. Rare.

The Illinois Central Railroad listed several hundred trains in their complete electric suburban schedules for 1932. This thirty-two-page stapled booklet had a folded size of 3 1/2" x 7." Rare.

By the 1930s, 2 1/2" x 5" folders, as exemplified by the 1936 Sacramento Northern Railroad timetable, had become a common size for suburban timetables. Note that the content of suburban timetables had changed little over the years, giving only schedule, fare, and bus/train connection information. Rare.

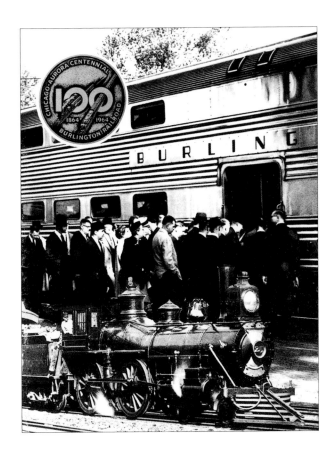

night carry their residents to and from business much more pleasantly, much more quickly, and always more promptly on time than residents within the city are carried one fifth the distance on streetcars. In the city we have dusty streets, manure bestrewn alleys, dirty yards, stifling air in the pokey little flats or tenement houses and with grimy smoke and dust on everything. At the end of half an hour's journey on the train, nay, even in half that time, one sees copiously sprinkled avenues and boulevards, houses surrounded by trees and well kept lawns, pure air."

At this point the narrative goes on to point out the shortcomings of commuting within the city by street cars, which, except for other suburban lines, were the only competition for early commuter trains.

Another special commemorative booklet, published by the Chicago, Burlington, and Quincy Railroad in 1964 (above, Common), celebrated 100 years of existence for the Chicago-Aurora suburban line. In a section called "The Good Life in Suburbia," it quotes from a booklet published in 1895 by the railroad's passenger department and promoting the advantages of suburban living. The communities referred to were along the suburban lines of other, competing railroads.

"Out of reach of the smoke and grime and dust, and yet completely in touch with the city, are hundreds and hundreds of beautiful homes along the Chicago, Burlington & Quincy Railroad. Nearly all of the suburban districts in which these homes are located are, in point of time, nearer to the business part of the city than Lake View, Hyde Park, Englewood, Holstein, or Humbolt Park. Trains that run to and from them during the day and

SACRAMENTO NORTHERN TRAIN SERVICE

Corrected to January 1, 1941

EASTBOUND Read Down	12 Daily	6 Daily	28 Daily Except Sun. & Hol.	32 Daily Except Sun. & Hol.	36 Sun. & Hol. Only	40 Sun. & Hol. Only
	AM	PM	PM	PM	PM	PM
San Francisco—East Bay Terminal	7 30	1 20	4 40	5 20	8 00	10 00
Oakland—40th and Shafter	6 23	1 47	5 03	5 40	8 22	10 23
Oakland, College and Shafter	6 26	1 52	5 10	5 53	8 27	10 25
St. Mary's College	6 51	2 13	5 31	6 15	8 51	10 51
Lafayette	8 58	2 19	5 30	6 24	8 58	10 58
Walnut Creek	9 05	2 26	5 44	6 31	7 05	11 04
Concord	9 15	2 38	5 59	6 45	7 18	11 15
Port Chicago	9 39	2 56			7 29	11 34
Pittsburg	9 45	3 05			7 43	11 40
	AM	PM	PM	PM	PM	PM

LEAVE SAN FRANCISCO THIRD STREET	Moun- tain View	ARRIVE		
		Sunny vale	Santa Clara	San Jose
6 00 Ex. Sun.	7 19	7 25	7 34	7 40
7 00 Daily	8 14	8 20	f 8 28	8 35
8 20 Daily	9 31	9 36	9 44	9 50
10 30 Sun. & (a)	11 46	11 50	11 58	12 05
11 15 Ex. Sun. & (a)	12 39	12 45	12 53	1 00
12 10 Sat. only (f)	1 14			1 30
12 25 Sat. only (f)	1 41	1 46	1 54	2 00
1 15 Sat. only (f)	2 21	2 27		2 40
1 35 Daily	2 53	2 59	3 09	3 15
2 15 Sat. only (f)	3 30	3 35	3 43	3 50
3 05 Ex. Sun.	4 24	4 30	4 38	4 45
b 4 00 Daily				b 4 59
4 05 Ex. Sun. & (a)	5 14	5 19		5 35
4 05 Sun. & (a)	5 24	5 30	f 5 38	5 45
4 20 Ex. Sun. & (a)	5 39	5 44	5 54	6 00
4 37 Ex. Sun. & (a)	5 43	5 50		6 05
4 40 Sun. & (a)	5 59	6 05	f 6 13	6 20
4 45 Ex.Sa.Su.&(a)				6 10
5 00 Ex.Sa.Su.&(a)	6 00		6 13	6 20
5 00 Sat. & (a)	6 22	6 27	6 34	6 40
5 21 Ex.Sa.Su.&(a)		6 17		6 31
5 25 Ex.Sa.Su.&(a)	6 19		6 29	6 45
5 25 Su.Su.&(a)	6 43	6 48	6 57	7 05
5 29 Ex.Sa.Su.&(a)		6 30	6 38	6 44
5 33 Ex.Sa.Su.&(a)	6 33			6 50
5 37 Ex.Sa.Su.&(a)		6 47		7 02
5 45 Ex.Sa.Su.&(a)	6 58			7 15
6 00 Ex. Sun. & (a)		7 11	7 18	7 25
6 35 Daily	7 51	7 56	f 8 04	8 10
#7 05 Daily				8 20
7 20 Daily	8 30	8 35	f 8 43	8 50
8 20 Daily	9 34	9 39	9 49	9 55
9 45 Daily	11 00	11 05	f11 13	11 20
11 00 Daily	12 16	12 21	f12 28	12 35
12 30 Daily	1 46	1 51	1 59	2 05

Fares between San Francisco and	One- way Fare	10 Day Round- trip	Week Pass	Month (Ex. Sun.)
Mountain View	*$0.81	*$1.20	$3.60	$12.88
Sunnyvale	*.88	*1.35	3.85	13.86
Santa Clara	*.99	*1.35	4.40	15.78
San Jose	*1.05	*1.65	4.65	16.77

*—15% Federal Tax not Included.

For explanation of characters, see other side.

SOUTHERN PACIFIC

Small pocket cards such as these, issued by the Southern Pacific Railroad in 1941 and the Sacramento Northern Railroad in 1945, were an important part of the commuter's daily life. Common.

Suburban Timetable Formats

The practical need for suburban timetables grew out of the rapid increase in the number of commuter and local trains by the 1880s. Even though these trains were included in the through-schedules of large, system-wide public timetables, smaller condensed versions were needed for local use. Commuters found the smaller versions more convenient because of their size and because they included only the schedules needed for a specific commute.

The most common suburban timetable formats were pocket cards and folders. *Pocket card* sizes ranged from 2 1/2" x 4 or 5" to approximately 3" x 5 1/2," with the latter dimensions being the most common. *Pocket folder* sizes ranged between the two most common—approximately 2 3/4" x4 3/4" or 4" x 8." A 4" x 9" folder was also common, being the same size folded as a stapled-booklet format public timetable.

Suburban timetables usually included only the schedules for a specific line and its branches. Ex-

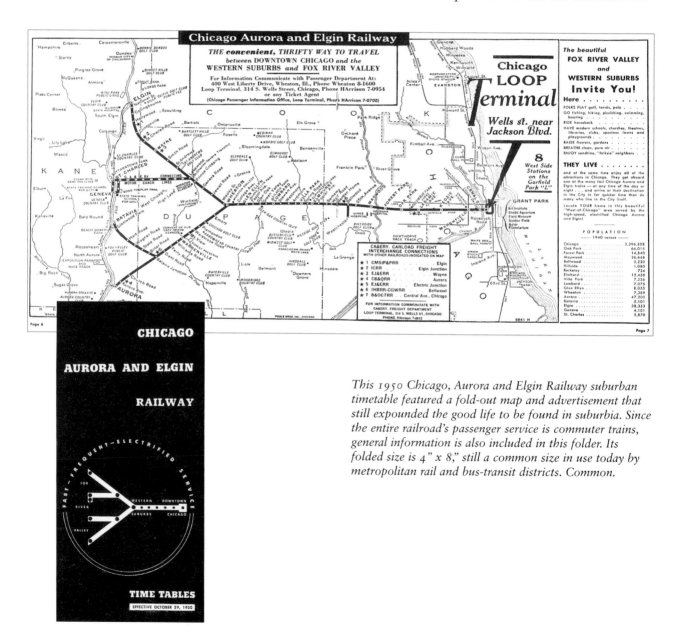

This 1950 Chicago, Aurora and Elgin Railway suburban timetable featured a fold-out map and advertisement that still expounded the good life to be found in suburbia. Since the entire railroad's passenger service is commuter trains, general information is also included in this folder. Its folded size is 4" x 8," still a common size in use today by metropolitan rail and bus-transit districts. Common.

cept for their covers, very few graphics were used. Since early suburban coaches had spartan seating, woodstove heat, gas lighting and windows that opened, information on train equipment and accommodations was not included. Any additional information was about connecting trains and fares.

The importance of publishing suburban train schedules separate from long-distance schedules has not diminished in modern times. As cities grow and suburbs expand, the need for suburban timetables that are pocket-sized and easy to use is greater than ever. Today's AMTRAK suburban service is featured in a number of separate timetable issues, as are the lines of many metropolitan rail, light-rail, and bus-transit districts.

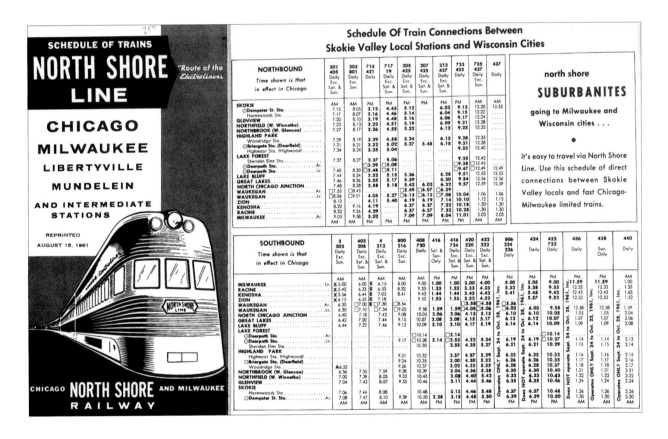

This 1961 Chicago, North Shore and Milwaukee Railway timetable's unfolded size is 6 1/2" by 3' and lists over 200 trains. Common.

CHICAGO & NORTH-WESTERN RY.

WISCONSIN DIVISION.

No. 153 TIME TABLE No. 153

Takes effect Sunday, April 17, 1892,

At 12 O'clock Noon.

FOR THE GOVERNMENT AND INFORMATION OF EMPLOYES ONLY.

J. M. WHITMAN,
General Manager.

W. A. GARDNER,
Superintendent.

S. SANBORN,
General Superintendent.

J. C. STUART,
Assistant Superintendent.

A classic example of an early "horse blanket" employee timetable. These yield a wealth of historical information and stand alone as vignettes of life on the railroads of the time. A map of the Wisconsin Division on the Chicago & North-Western Railway is shown on the cover of this 1892 issue. Very Rare.

CHAPTER THREE
EMPLOYEE TIMETABLES

IT'S A CLEAR, cold morning, in November, 1867, as you stand next to the train, ready for work. You're a second generation railroader, son of a man who worked for this line from day one. You've been a brakeman for five years, time enough to earn the seniority to work on passenger trains.

It's 8:20 A.M. according to the station's "standard" clock. You note that your watch is more than two minutes slow, although it has been adjusted for cold weather and was keeping good time yesterday.

"Chas," you yell to the conductor, "my watch is no good."

"Great, we leave in five minutes," he yells back, barely audible over the loud steam hiss of the locomotive.

He finishes his conversation with the engineman and walks quickly over to you.

"How slow?" he asks.

"Over two minutes."

"That will never do. Here, use my old one. Remember I told you I always carry a spare. If you ever want to be a conductor, then you will too!"

He hands you the watch and you thank him. Out of habit, you both look again at the station's clock, then at each other's watches.

"Hey," you smile, "I'm learning."

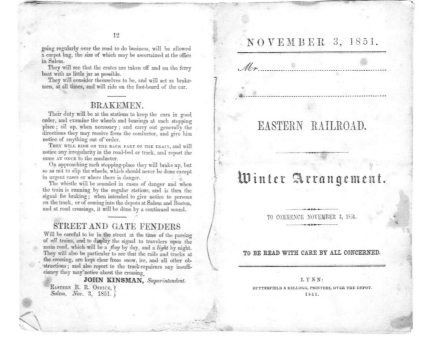

This unusual 1851 "Winter Arrangement" booklet for employees of the Eastern Railroad included timetables, lists of conditions for organizing the movement of trains to and from Boston and for two branch lines, rules and regulations, and considerations unique to specific occupations on the railroad—material which gives insight into the daily operations of early trains. Very Rare.

The Importance of Timing

Running many trains on *one* pair of rails had, early on, mandated a meticulous system of organization. The very first railroads ran two or four trains a day. One or two left in the morning and then returned that night. The first train going back could not leave until another arrived. That was simple enough until one didn't show up. Then: Where was it? The train or trains going back had to know, for fear they might meet the missing train broken down on a blind curve.

Because the safe operation of railroads depended upon uniform and precise timing, nothing was more important to railroad employees than their watches, rule books, and employee timetables. These were the basic operational tools of the trade. The schedules and rules printed in the employee timetable were the foundation of the system. Employee watches, synchronized with one another and with the railroad's standard clock, brought life to the timetable, making the system workable and safe.

As early railroads evolved they developed more ways to deal with problems of timing, meeting and passing. The use of sidings, double track and standard time zones were some solutions, all of which were reflected in the various elements making up employee timetables.

Passings

As early railroad lines became longer and more crowded, sidings were built so trains could pass each other. Sidings, also called "side tracks" or "turnouts," were usually just a little longer than the longest trains that normally ran on the railroad. For a siding to do its work, a train had to be there at the right time. Since there were no telegraph, radio, or telephones to communicate, timing had to be nearly perfect or accidents could result. Employee timetables gave the times that trains were to leave stations and when they were to be in sidings ("stopping-places") so that "passings"—also called "meets"—could occur. Timetables also contained rules, which were operational considerations employees needed to follow to assure safety.

Since junctions between, or of the same, railroads were almost always at stations, early sidings were most often located there as well, allowing stationmasters to monitor the progress of train movements. This was favored over having sidings in remote areas where the exact status of a passing train could not be observed. Even with sidings, it became increasingly difficult to schedule the growing number of trains on single tracks.

More trains required even more monitoring of train movement and passing. If any one of the many trains operating on the line had problems

Western R. R.—TIME TABLE—Dec. 21, 1841.

TIMES WHEN TRAINS ARE TO LEAVE STATIONS.

WESTERN TRAINS.

LEAVE	Springfield to Greenbush.			Greenbush to Springfield.		
	1st Pass'r.	2d Pass'r.	Freight.	1st Pass'r.	2d Pass'r.	Freight.
Springfield,	7.00 A.M.	1.00 P.M.	5.30 A.M.	12.30 P.M.	6.30 P.M.	4.30 P.M.
West Springfield,	7.05	1.05	5.34	12.25	6.25	4.15
Westfield,	7.25	1.25	6.12	12.07	6.07	3.42
Chester Village,	7.55	1.55	7.25	11.37	5.37	2.51
Chester Factories,	8.20	2.20	8.20	11.19	5.19	2.20
Becket,	8.54	2.54	9.25	10.47	4.47	1.19 P.M.
Washington,	9.10	3.10	9.56	10.31	4.31	12.51
Hinsdale,	9.21	3.21	10.24	10.26	4.22	12.30
Dalton,	9.33	3.33	10.46	10.09	4.06	12.01 M
Pittsfield,	9.52	3.52	11.30	9.52	3.52	11.30
Shaker Village,	10.02	4.02	11.50	9.35	3.35	10.48
Richmond,	10.13	4.13	12.25	9.22	3.22	10.13
State Line,	10.27	4.27	12.50	9.13	3.13	9.53
Summit,	10.41	4.41	1.08	8.57	2.57	9.30
Chapman's,	11.01	5.01	1.36	8.37	2.37	8.51
Chatham,	11.28	5.28	2.17½	8.17½	2.17½	8.17½
Kinderhook,	11.43	5.43	2.57	7.47	1.47	7.14
Schodack,	12.07	6.07	3.35	7.23	1.23	6.20
Greenbush,	12.25	6.25	4.15	7.00 A.M.	1.00 P.M.	5.30 A.M.

* 1st. Pass. T. to Greenbush passes 1st Ft. T. to Greenbush at C. Factories at 8 20.
† 1st. Pass. T. to Greenbush passes 1st Pass. T. to Springfield at Pittsfield at 9 52.
‡ 1st. Pass. T. to Greenbush passes 1st Ft. T. to Springfield at Richmond at 10 13.
** 2d. Pass. T. to Greenbush passes 1st Ft. T. to Springfield at C Factories at 2 20.
§ 2d. Pass. T. to Greenbush passes 2d. Pass. T. to Springfield at 3 52.
‖ 1st. Pass. T. to Springfield passes 1st Ft. T. to Greenbush at Hinsdale at 10 22.
†† 1st. Ft. T. to Greenbush passes 1st Pass. T. to Springfield at Pittsfield at 11 31.
§ 2d. Pass. T. to Springfield passes 1st Ft. T. to Greenbush at Chatham at 2 17.
‡‡ 1st. Pass. T. to Springfield passes 1st Ft. T. to Springfield at Chatham at 8 17.

This 1841 example—the earliest found, by the author, of an employee timetable—controlled movements for three trains in each direction, for a total of six per day on the Western Rail Road line in Massachusetts. Only departure times are listed. Very Rare.

CONNECTICUT RIVER RAIL ROAD.

TIME TABLE.

On and after Monday, MAY 7, 1855, Trains will run as follows:

No Train will be allowed to leave a station before its time, as specified in this Time Table.

Whenever one Passenger Train takes the precedence over another, that Train shall allow three minutes for the Variation of Watches, but the Train that is behind Time shall not use the over time allowed by the other Train.

Dist.	LEAVE	Springfield to S. Vernon.			Northampton Special-up.		Greenfield Freight.		Northampton Special Down.		South Vernon to Springfield.		
		1st Pass'r.	2d Pass'r.	Freight.	1st.	2d.	UP.	DOWN.	1st.	2d.	1st Pass'r.	2d Pass'r.	Freight.
	SPRINGFIELD,..	7.30, A. M.	1.45, P. M.	6.30, A.M.	12.00 M.	9.15, P. M.	1.10, P.M.	10.55 A.M.	10.00 A.M.	4.30, P.M	11.50, A. M	6.50, P. M.	6.40, P.M.
3.2	CHICOPEE,......	7.40, "	1.55, "	6.45, "	12.10, P.M.	9.25, "	1.25, "	10.35, "	9.50, "	4.15, "	11.40, "	6.40, "	6.25, "
6.6	WILLIMANSETT,.	7.50, "	2.05, "	7.00, "	12.20, "	9.35, "	1.40, "	10.20, "	9.40, "	4.00, "	11.30, "	6.30, "	6.10, "
7.5	HOLYOKE,......	7.55, "	2.10 E "	7.30, "	12.25, "	9.40, "	2.10 E	10.10, "	9.35, "	3.55, "	11.26, "	6.26, "	6.00, "
12.5	SMITH'S FERRY,	8.08 A "	2.23, "	8.08 A "	12.38, "	9.53, "	2.40, "	9.35, " C	9.20, "	3.40, "	11.12, "	6.12, "	5.30, "
16.8	NORTHAMPTON,..	8.23, "	2.38, "	{ 8.30 Ar. C / 8.55 Le. }	12.50, "	10.05, "	3.10, "	{ 8.55 Ar. / 8.33 B }	9.10, "	3.30, "	11.03, "	6.03, "	5.10, "
21.4	HATFIELD,......	8.33 B "	2.48, "	9.20, "			3.30, "	8.33 B			10.51, "	5.51, "	4.38, "
25.9	WHATELY,......	8.43, "	2.58, "	9.40, "			3.50, "	8.00, "			10.42, "	5.42, "	4.18, "
28.1	S. DEERFIELD,..	8.48, "	3.03, "	10.00, "			4.08 G	7.45, "			10.37, "	5.37, "	4.08 G "
32.5	DEERFIELD, ...	9.00, "	3.13, "	10.25 D "			4.30, "	7.15, "			10.25 D "	5.25, "	3.43, "
35.8	GREENFIELD,...	9.13, "	3.23 F "	10.50, "			4.45, "	7.00, "			10.15, "	5.15, "	3.23 F "
42.4	BERNARDSTON,..	9.29, "	3.39, "	11.20, "							10.00, "	5.00, "	2.40, "
50	SOUTH VERNON,	9.45, "	3.55, "	11.50, "							9.45, "	4.45, "	2.00, "

A. 8.08, A. M. Smith's Ferry. Passenger Train passes Freight Train.
B. 8.33, A. M. Hatfield. Passenger and Freight Trains meet. But all Freight Trains will keep entirely out of the way of all Passenger Trains in all cases whatever.
C. 8.55, A. M. Northampton. Freight Trains meet.
D. 10.25, A. M. Deerfield. Passenger and Freight Trains meet.
E. 2.10, P. M. Holyoke. Passenger Train passes Freight.
F. 3.23, P. M. Greenfield. Passenger and Freight Trains meet.
G. 4.08, P. M. S. Deerfield. Freight Trains meet.

If the 7.30 A. M. Train from Springfield cannot reach S. Vernon at 9.45 A. M., it will keep out of the way of the down Train from S. Vernon at 9.45 A. M., which will have the track to Springfield until 7.30 P. M.; then it will keep out of the way of the 7.15 Chicopee Falls and the Northampton Evening Trains.

The 4.45 P. M. Train from S. Vernon will not leave until the Train due from Springfield at 3.55 has arrived; then it will have the track to Springfield until 7.30 P. M. But if it cannot reach Springfield at 7.30 P. M., it will keep out of the way of the Chicopee Falls and Northampton Evening Trains. All other than the above mentioned Chicopee Falls and Northampton Trains will keep entirely out of the way of the through Passenger Trains.

All Trains detained over night will keep out of the way of all regular Trains whatever.

ASHUELOT RAIL ROAD.

Dist.	LEAVE	Keene to So. Vernon.	S. Vernon to Keene.
	KEENE,.........	7.15, A. M.	6.15, P. M.
5.4	SWANZEY,........	7.30, "	6.00, "
7.9	WESTPORT,.......	7.45, "	5.45, "
13.3	WINCHESTER,.....	8.05, "	5.25, "
15.5	ASHUELOT,.......	8.15, "	5.15, "
19.	HINSDALE,........	8.30, "	5.00, "
23.7	SOUTH VERNON,....	8.45, "	4.45, "

LEAVE	SPRINGFIELD TO CHICOPEE FALLS.				
Springfield	7.30, A.M.	10.20, M.	12.00, P.M.	1.45, P.M.	7.15, P.M.
Chicopee,	7.40, "	10.35, P.M.	12.10, "	1.55, "	7.30, "
Ch. Falls,	8.00, "	10.50, "	12.30, "	2.15, "	7.45, "

LEAVE	CHICOPEE FALLS TO SPRINGFIELD.				
Ch. Falls,	9.25, A.M.	11.00, P.M.	1.30, P.M.	3.50, P.M	7.55, "
Chicopee,	9.50, "	11.15, "	1.50, "	4.15, "	8.05, "
Springfield	10.00, "	11.30, "		4.30, "	8.15, "

..... Holyoke, Deerfield, or South Vernon Bridges, should be one minute.

As traffic increased, the list of "meets" grew longer. This early Connecticut River Rail Road employee timetable from 1855 typifies such lists at this time: the meets are shown in the schedules with bold type. Very Rare.

CAPE COD BRANCH RAILROAD.

RUNNING TIME FOR PASSENGER AND FREIGHT TRAINS.

To take Effect May 29th, 1848.

FROM AGAWAM.				FROM MIDDLEBORO'.			
	1ST PASS.	FREIGHT.	2D PASS.		1ST PASS.	FREIGHT.	2D PASS.
To Leave	A. M.	A. M.	P. M.	To Leave	A. M.	P. M.	P. M.
Sandwich . . .	5.40	11.45	2.55	Middleboro', . .	8.20	2.50	5.44
Scusset	5.47	12.00	3.02	Rock M. House .	8.33	3.10	5.57
Herring River .	5.51	12.08	3.06	So. Middleboro' .	8.41	3.23	6.05
Monument . . .	6.00	12.25	3.15	Tremont I. Works	8.51	3.44 m. P.	6.15
Cohasset Narrows	6.04	12.32	3.20	Burbank's . . .	8.55	3.53	6.19
Agawam . . .	6.12	12.45	3.27	Wareham . . .	9.00	4.04	6.25
Wareham . . .	6.20	12.51	3.35	Agawam . . .	9.08	4.19	6.33
Burbank's . . .	6.25	1.02	3.40	Cohasset Narrows	9.16	4.35	6.41
Tremont I. Works	6.29	1.12	3.44 m. F.	Monument . . .	9.20	4.43	6.45
So. Middleboro' .	6.39	1.31	3.54	Herring River . .	9.30	4.58	6.55
Rock M. House .	6.47	1.40	4.02	Scusset	9.34	5.06	7.00
Reach Middleboro'	7.00	2.00	4.15	*Reach* Sandwich .	9.40	5.20	7.05

GENERAL RULES.

1st.   No Train will leave a Station before the card time.

2d.   Freight Trains will not leave the Station next preceding a Station, when a Passenger Train is expected—unless they have the *full* running time specified in the table.   All Freight Trains must be kept out of the way of Passenger Trains, as Passenger Trains *will not* wait for Freight Trains.

3d.   Gravel Trains will avoid *all* Regular Trains, and not run to a Station where it is expected to meet a Regular Train, unless it can arrive *full ten minutes before* the Regular Train is due.

4th.   All persons employed on the road will be particular to give notice by the red flag, of any obstructions on the road.

5th.   Every Engineman, on approaching a road or switch, should *see* that the way is clear before he reaches it.   If the switch cannot be seen to be right, *halt*, until perfectly sure of its position.   The bell must be rung eighty rods before crossing a road, and rung until it is passed.

6th.   In cases of any uncertainty as to the occupation of the track, a man must be sent ahead and one back, and be kept at least half a mile distant, until the danger is over.

7th.   In cases of uncertainty, *always* take that course which is *safe*.   Be careful always.

8th.   A white flag displayed from an Engine is a signal that the Engine may be expected in its return immediately.

9th.   Trains or Engines, at night, must have a good light behind and in front.

10th.   If the Train breaks down or stops, send a man a mile back, and one as far forward, to warn any Train that may approach.

11th.   When two Engines are running in the same direction, in immediate succession, the first will display a red flag.

LUTHER HAVEN, *Sup't.*

Sandwich, May 26th, 1848.

By 1848, a general format was already in place for employee timetables and the operating rules they would contain, as shown in this very rare 1848 Cape Cod Branch Railroad example:

1. This first and most important rule gave the timetable its authority.

2 .Rule 2 restricted a train that was running late from leaving a station unless the "run" to the next station would not interfere with another train.

3. In the early years of rapid growth, construction trains were a daily part of railroad operations. This rule clearly established their low priority, and added a ten-minute margin of safety for their slow movements. This was probably due to the use of older equipment prone to breakdowns, and the heavier weight of their cars causing very slow starts.

4. "Flagging" rules were extremely important, since they provided standards for warning other trains approaching from the front or the rear of a train in distress on the main line.

5. This rule combined two considerations of great importance to the engineer. First, switches into or out of a siding had to be in the proper mechanical position or the train would either go into the siding when it did not intend to, or would derail at the rail merge point coming out of a siding. Second, the use of whistles was restricted because they would frighten horses, so ringing the bell at road crossings was the preferred warning at this time.

6. If the crew thought there was any danger of a train approaching too close from ahead or behind, a crew member was required to walk or run along ahead of or behind it for protection.

7. This rule reminded train crews that if there was ever any doubt, it was better to err on the side of safety.

8. An engine running as a helper or "light" would display a white flag so the station would know it would return before another train could leave.

9. The requirements for headlights was an early consideration.

10. If a train was standing still on the main line, broken down or ahead of schedule, this rule required men to "protect" the front and rear by flagging until the situation could be corrected.

11. Unique to this road's operation, the leader of two engines running together was required to carry a red flag. Very Rare.

meeting the schedule, its only chances to recover were those outlined in the list of passings, allowed by the rules, or considered in the notes of the employee timetable. Otherwise, special arrangements would have to be made for its movement. Without the benefit of telegraphic communication, this was very difficult.

Sometimes a serious mechanical failure caused a train to run "out of time" and have to "drop out of the schedule." Infrequently, special arrangements could be made, but usually the train had to wait up to twenty-four hours to operate "back in schedule" again. A paragraph in the conductor's rule section of an employee timetable clearly emphasizes this crucial procedure:

Conductors
They will never allow the train to proceed beyond its regular station for meeting, Until the Arrival of the Next Train Due, unless certain advice that it will not come, or written instructions to the contrary, be received from the Superintendent. On this point there is to be No Discretion *and this regulation is to be obeyed at all events, and under all circumstances.*

Double Track Meets
The introduction of double track provided the means of accommodating increased rail traffic. It simplified operations by allowing multiple trains to run in each direction on lines designated specifically for that purpose, thus eliminating many of the constant timing concerns necessary for clearing single-track main lines at sidings. This was a more efficient system, but also more expensive. Traffic had to be enough to warrant the large capital expenditures necessary to double-track, and it took some time before many railroads could afford to build them.

Double track meets were noted on early employee timetables. The progress of trains on double track had to be followed in order to efficiently space out trains on the designated line. Timetable information helped train crews coordinate trains from or back onto a single main track if the double track did not start or end at a terminal point.

Sun and Local Times

The standard for all timetables, time itself, also presented problems which interfered with safe, efficient train operation. For most people in the early 1800s, time was a simple matter of the location of the sun, and local or "sun" times prevailed. A 1951 informational brochure titled "Standard Time in America" explains what it was like for early travelers without a system of standard time:

Sun Time
Before the introduction of the railroads, the quickest means of transportation was by stage coach or post rider. It took a person the greater part of two days to travel between New York and Philadelphia, a distance of only ninety miles. Then and for centuries before, each community of any importance used what was known as "Sun Time;" that is when the sun showed high noon at the town hall or at some other important place, it was noon all over town and its surrounding area. It is estimated that over 100 local times were in use in the United States in 1883. This custom was deeply rooted in the lives of the people.

All these differences in time, often for towns only a few miles apart, became very troublesome with the increased speed of travel brought about by the railroads and the invention of the telegraph. Each railroad overcame this problem in

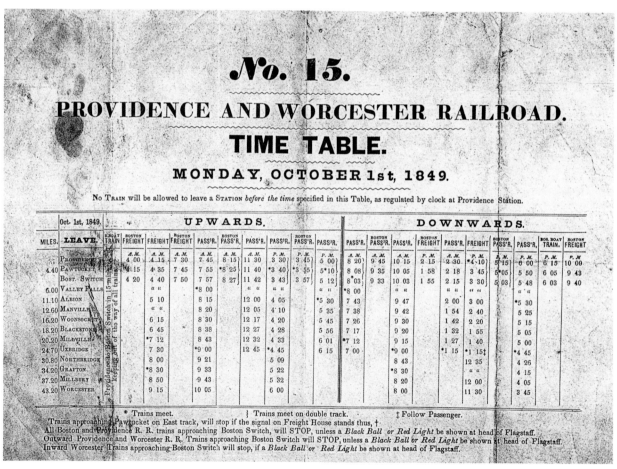

As this 1849 Providence and Worcester Railroad timetable shows, some railroads included only a few important operating rules on their timetables. Informational rules "pamphlets" were published separately. Very Rare.

5

...aces for Trains.

..., 15, 18, 19, 20, 21, 2?, 23, 24, 25,
...nd 43 will stop at special as well as

...stop at Wilmington Junction.

No. 2 will not stop between Boston and Lawrence.

Nos. 7, 11, 14, 26, 30 and 32 will not stop between Boston and
Reading.

No. 10 will not stop between Boston and So. Reading Junction.

No. 17 stops only at Andover, So. Lawrence, Haverhill, Exeter,
and Dover.

No. 22 will stop at So. Reading Junction to take passengers.

Nos. 6, 15, 31, 37, and 41 will stop at all regular stations including Stoneham.

No. 27 will not stop between So. Reading Junction and Boston.

No. 31, will stop at Wyoming.

No. 33, will stop only at Andover between Lawrence and
Boston, excepting to leave way passengers from East of Haverhill.
at Reading for Train No. 34. No. 42, will stop only at Andover
between Lawrence and Boston, excepting to leave passengers from
East of Haverhill.

No. 40 will stop to leave passengers only between South Reading
and Boston.

No. 44 stop only to leave passengers.

Nos. 3, 7, 10, and 16, leave, and Nos. 25, 29, 36, and 38, take cars
from the S. R. Branch Railroad.

If cars from South Reading Branch Railroad are left by the train
which should take them, the train following must stop for them.

The Special Stations are Charlestown, Wyoming and Greenwood.

Nos. 1, 5, 8, 9, 12, 13, 19, 20, 22, 28, 35, and 36, ONLY,
will stop at Edgeworth.

Nos. 13, 19, and 22, will stop at Oak Grove.

The special stations and the following regular stations are target
or red-flag signal stopping places, viz:—Somerville, Wilmington,
Atkinson, Plaistow, Newton, East Kingston, and Madbury All
others are stopping places without signals excepting as to above trains.

☞ Freight Trains must *keep out of the way* of Passenger Trains
and must not *leave* any station ahead of the time fixed by the Time
Table ; but after leaving a station, they may *arrive* at the next station as early as they can with a speed of 12 miles per hour.

They will, however, never leave any station unless they can reach
the next station and be out of the way of a passenger train, at least
eight minutes before a passenger train is due there, from either direction. The Great Falls Freight Trains will pass each other at
Plaistow Brick Yard. The Portland Freight Trains pass at South
Berwick Junction.

The South Berwick Junction Freight Trains which run OUTWARD
on Monday, Wednesday, and Friday, and INWARD on Tuesday,
Thursday and Saturday, and will keep out of the way of the regular
Great Falls and Portland Freight Trains.

*so as to bring them on the time of
the Great Falls Freight Trains, they will
keep out of the way of the Passenger Trains.*

*The Eastern Railroad pub-
lished this string-tied employee timetable and rules booklet in 1870 under the title "Rules and Regulations for Running Trains, Etc." Bold type warned all who possessed it to "Destroy All Former Time Books." Very Rare.*

Boston & Maine R. R.

LOWELL SYSTEM.

SOUTHERN DIVISION.

Departure and Arrival of Trains at Boston Station.

Time-table in Effect Oct. 7, 1889.

FOR EMPLOYEES ONLY.

DEPART, WEEK-DAYS.

No.		
1	Through Freight	12.15 A.M.
5	Nashua Way Freight	4.05 "
611	Central Mass. Freight	4.35 "
7	Stoneham Freight	5.00 "
9	Lexington Pass.	6.00 "
17	Lowell Pass. (via B. & B.)	6.45 "
19	Wilmington Pass.	6.55 "
23	Bedford Pass.	7.05 "
617	Wayland Pass.	7.15 "
29	Concord R. R. Local	7.30 "
31	Woburn Pass.	7.32 "
621	Northampton Pass.	7.45 "
39	Middlesex Cent. Pass.	7.50 "
41	Lawrence Pass.	8.00 "
45	Stoneham Pass.	8.10 "
49	Lexington Pass.	8.20 "
53	Cent. Vt. and Keene Express	8.30 "
59	Lowell Pass.	8.35 "
61	Canadian Pacific Express	9.00 "
67	Stoneham Pass.	9.05 "
69	Lexington Pass.	9.10 "
631	Hudson Pass.	9.20 "
73	Woburn Pass.	9.35 "
79	Through Freight	9.40 "
87	Lowell Pass. (via B & B.)	10.00 "
91	Stoneham Pass.	10.15 "
93	Lowell Freight (from Mystic Jct.)	10.30 "
101	Lexington Pass.	10.50 "
101	Lawrence Pass.	11.00 "
113	Stoneham Pass.	11.30 "
641	Wayland Pass.	11.40 "
121	Concord and Wilton Pass.	12.00 M.
127	Woburn Pass.	12.10 P.M.
131	Lexington Pass.	12.20 "
133	Through Freight	12.25 "
145	Montreal and Chicago Express	1.00 "
140	Lawrence Pass.	1.10 "
151	Milk Train (from Mystic Jct.)	1.20 "
153	Middlesex Cent. Pass.	1.15 "
647	Northampton Pass.	1.30 "
157	Middlesex Cent. Pass.	1.35 "
161	Stoneham Pass.	1.40 "
167	Lowell Pass.	2.00 "
179	Stoneham Pass.	2.30 "

Without an effective means of immediately communicating exceptions to the times published in employee timetables, complexity of meets continued to grow. This 1868 Boston and Maine employee timetable includes the railroader's own notes penned in the extensive list of passings. Very Rare.

By 1889, the Boston and Maine had so many trains arriving and leaving Boston that it published this four-column quick-reference card for their employees. Yet the B&M was only one of many railroads serving Boston. Very Rare.

part by adopting, for operating and time-table purposes, the time of some important city or cities along the line which it served. However, this was not satisfactory. As for illustration, it was necessary for a traveler to change his watch three times during the journey from New York to Boston just to keep the correct railroad time. He would ignore the local time of each town at in-between stops en route unless he happened to leave the train at one of these points. As a result of conditions existing in 1883, the railroads in the United States and Canada found it necessary to operate under some fifty different standard times.

For safe operation, railroads could not use more than one local time. Times for operating trains had to be standardized. Railroads arbitrarily "declared" the local time for one large city on the line as their standard time. This important declaration almost always was printed after the date at the top of the employee timetable. Train crew members and some other employees were required to set their watches to the standard time mandated by the timetable's declaration and its other time-related rules. Watch-setting rules were very important, and it was mandatory that watches were regularly inspected and adjusted by railroad-certified watch inspectors.

For example, a New Haven, Hartford and Springfield Railroad timetable declared the clock at the "Station House in Hartford" to be its standard time. All employees were required to set their watches regularly to this clock. In addition to this standard time, employees of this railroad also had to follow the standard times of two other roads, since all their trains came together at shared junctions or stations. Adopting local times as standards for railroad operations was not without confusion.

Early Employee Timetable Format

The first employee timetables were similar in size and format to early public timetable handbills (flyers). They were a *single page,* printed on both sides, with schedule information and a list of meets on the front, followed by rules on the back.

Meets were shown in bold type. Each new issue was sequentially numbered and dated—an important feature, since all employees needed to begin using the same timetable simultaneously. Two different sizes of single sheets were common: 7" x 9" and a larger 10" x 14," with slight variations. Surviving examples show they were often printed on colored linen stock, with yellow and blue being the most popular.

Because the amount of information needed by employees soon exceeded the limits of the single page printed on two sides, a *string-tied booklet* format followed. Its sizes generally ranged from 4" to 5" by 7" to 8." In addition to schedules, these employee timetables contained operating or "running" rules, notes, lists of meets, and regulations.

Change Orders and Bulletins

Any variety of operational adjustments could occur during the time between timetable issues, including changes in scheduled times, train additions and deletions, special trains, addition or deletions of track, stations and siding, and introduction of or changes to signaled track areas. Such changes from the times, rules or notes published in a current employee timetable issue needed to be communicated as quickly as possible. This was the job of "general orders," later called Timetable Bulletins. A variety of terms for general orders were used. With few exceptions, orders and bulletins were issued by the superintendent's office, as single- or multiple-page forms, and became effective immediately. They were given directly to operating employees and posted on bulletin boards to assure that all employees had seen them.

Supplements

On occasion, a newly printed employee timetable had major errors or gross omissions. Rather than issue a corrected timetable, supplements containing the corrected information would be printed and distributed. They might take the form of single pages to be pasted over incorrect ones, or insert pages to be added as an addendum, or several pages bound separately in the same format as

BOSTON & MAINE RAILROAD.

Superintendent's Office, Eastern Division.

ORDER No. 1.

BOSTON, July 1, 1890.

ON JULY 4, 1890, the following freight trains will be cancelled: —
Nos. 141, 149, 227, 235, 239, 241, 243, 249, 253, 257, 146, 158, 230, 240, 242, 244, 250, 254, 262.

Also Freight Train No. 256, of SATURDAY, JULY 5, will be cancelled.

Freights Nos. 199, 200, 237, 238, 245, 246, 247, 248, 251, 252, 255, 236, 256, 481 and 482 of JULY 4th, will run as usual.

W. T. PERKINS.
Superintendent.

JAS. T. FURBER,
General Manager.

the timetable being corrected. Supplements were also used to make major schedule updates in order to lengthen the life of current timetables. This allowed railroads to delay the cost of new issues for as long as possible.

Format Changes

In the 1880s, the number of stations and the trains serving them were still growing at a rapid rate. Since employee timetables showed *all* trains, both freight and passenger, the small page size of the early string-tied booklet format had schedules spread over many pages, making the timetable somewhat difficult to use. For the large schedules of some railroads, this booklet format became impractical. An obvious solution was to increase the page size to print a larger and more readable schedule format. This was the beginning of *large-format* employee timetables, which were later called *"horse blankets."* These, if they had many pages, were staple-bound.

Usually measuring from 10" to 12" by 13" to 15," the advantages of this large, rectangular format were quickly realized, and it soon became the preferred style, used by many midwestern and western railroads up to the 1950s. Their fall from popular use may have been due to reduced operations and cost-cutting measures implemented by railroads after World War II. Many small railroads that had adopted this format continued to use it, however, since the amount of information they needed to print could easily be contained on a large piece of paper printed on one or both sides on from one to four unbound pages.

Divisional Timetables

As they grew, railroads needed to divide their systems into logical operating "divisions" with each issuing a separate employee timetable. This division of crews, equipment, and other resources into specific groups allowed the more efficient movement of trains over large railroad systems. The divisions were delineated by "points," which were usually terminals in large towns or cities. (Terminal facilities included switching yards,

freight houses, locomotive and car maintenance facilities, and large, joint-use passenger stations, which several railroads cooperated to build in major cities they served.) Division points could also be major junctions where railroads came together and "interchanged" freight cars, or even whole trains, between them.

In the western states, it was often necessary to place division points at small remote "boom towns" to accommodate crew changes and equipment maintenance on long stretches of the line. (Boom towns came into existence during the construction of railroads. Most did not last, but ones situated in certain remote areas survived in their roles as division points, growing to provide homes for railroaders.) Division points were the only places for which employee timetable information would overlap.

Each division also included the many branch lines that were connected to trunk or main lines between large towns and cities. Where the larger early railroads needed only two or three divisions, later railroads had up to fifteen or twenty divisions on some very large roads. Separate timetables, with maps, usually were issued for each division. Creation of new divisions or changes in the boundaries of existing ones were cause for additional employee timetable issues.

Other Factors Affecting Employee Timetables

The period of the early 1880s through the 1920s saw a number of significant technological changes in American life and in the railroad industry itself. These changes were reflected in employee timetables. They included the adoption of one standard time, the telegraph, rule books, block signals, and centralized traffic control on railroad lines.

National Standard Time

Railroads had adopted more than fifty different local times by 1883. In Pittsburgh, for example, railroads used six different local times for the arrival and departure of trains. The use of these various local times had always made it confusing for passengers to correctly interpret timetables and

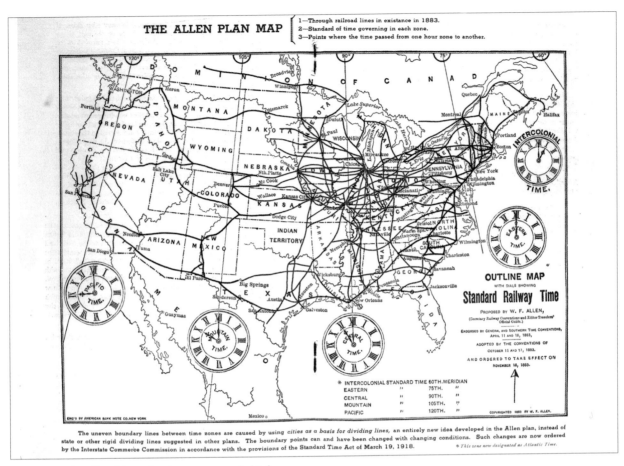

*Known as The Allen Plan after its creator and chief
proponent, William F. Allen, this map shows the plan for
Standard Railway Time adopted by the railroads on
October 11, 1883, to take effect November 11, 1883. Rare.*

catch connecting trains. This adoption of different
local times by railroads in the same area also
made it very difficult to coordinate train movements at crossings and interchanges with connecting lines. Railroads that ran over long distances
sometimes had to use two or more standard times,
further increasing the chances of an accident-caus-
ing error. To eliminate the confusion and difficul-
ty of using local times, railroads—and the nation—adopted a system of Standard Time in
October, 1883. North America was divided into
four time zones one hour apart, with the minutes
always the same in each. Only the hours varied
between time zones, with a one-hour to four-hour

difference. Standard time greatly increased the
efficiency of not only the railroad industry, but
American commerce as a whole.

Telegraph
The use of the telegraph allowed railroads to
immediately communicate and act upon exceptions to the scheduled times printed in employee
timetables. Telegraphic train orders could be
issued which anticipated and altered the circumstances that might come about when trains were
delayed and operating out of schedule. They could
then operate inside the schedules of other trains
without interfering. Information telegraphed to

other trains passing stations along the line let them know what was going on. Extra trains not in the timetable could operate this way too. Such train orders were also used to communicate other operational activities: speed restrictions for track in need of or under repair ("slow orders"), extra stops, and special trains.

The increased level of communication the telegraph provided was very important, for it allowed greater flexibility, safety, and efficiency in the movement of trains. By the 1880s, most railroads were using telegraphic train orders to assist in the movements of trains under the employee timetable/watch system. Telegraphic train order rules were included in employee timetables and rule books.

Block Signal Systems

Safety and efficiency of train movements were further increased with the introduction of the "block" signaling system in the 1890s. Such railroad signal systems were the subject of many promotional brochures explaining to the public the safety advantages gained by their use. This was the first automatic trackside signaling system widely adopted by the industry. Sections of track were divided into "blocks" one to three miles long. One of the most common versions of the system ran battery current through the rails in the block to form a closed circuit. This current controlled a relay that energized a small electric motor holding a signal arm on a trackside mast at a thirty-degree inclined position to show the green or "proceed" signal. When a train entered the block, the signal current was short-circuited by the wheels and axles of the engine and cars. The current loss caused the signal arm to fall to its weighted horizontal default position, indicating red or "stop." The engineer of a train following another in a block, or a train facing the block, saw the red indication for as long as a preceding or opposing train occupied the block.

However, a short circuit and stop signal could also be caused by an "open" or fouled switch. "Open" switch was the term used for a switch positioned so the train would go from the main line onto the siding. A switch is normally "closed" to the main line. A switch was "fouled" if a car was positioned on the siding so close as to obstruct the passing of trains on the main line. Mechanical problems—including disruption in the continuity of the rail, such as a broken rail or washout, crossed or broken wires, and signal battery power failure—also caused interruption of the circuit and gave a red signal indication at both ends of the block. In sum, block signaling was a simple and reliable system which greatly increased operating safety.

Railroad intersections at grade were also protected by block signals. Their electrical interconnection was such that conflicting signals could never be shown. Called "interlocking," this prevented the possibility of collisions.

Those sections of track controlled by block signals were noted in employee timetables. Illustrations of signal positions were used to show how the indications or "aspects" looked. The railroads adopted many new rules when block signal systems came into use. For the many railroads that were still printing rules in employee timetables, the addition of block signaling rules caused them to begin publishing "rule books" separately. Most were doing so by 1910.

Rule Books

As railroads became bigger and their operations more complex, additional rules were needed. New rules for safety, signals, and running, and rules specific to occupations, continued to be added and printed on the back pages of employee timetables. Soon employee timetables included several large pages of rules in very small print. This format was hard to read. Yet even though some railroads had been printing separate operating-rule pamphlets since the 1840s, most roads, by the 1890s, were still printing rules in their employee timetables. The need increased for a companion publication separate from the timetable, and during the early 1890s the first railroad "Rule Books" appeared. These small booklets could contain all the rules, printed in a more readable format, yet they easily fit into the railroader's pocket or grip.

Employee timetables now included a statement in bold print on the last page referring the user to

AUTOMATIC SIGNALS.

DESCRIPTION OF AUTOMATIC BLOCK SIGNALS

Signals are of the Semaphore and Disc Pattern.

The HOME SEMAPHORE SIGNAL having a blade with a convex end painted red with a circular white stripe on the governing side indicates "STOP," when the arm is extended at right angles to the post by day or when a red light is displayed at night. (Fig. 1).

The HOME SEMAPHORE SIGNAL indicates "CLEAR," "PROCEED," when the arm is inclined at an angle of sixty degrees by day or when a green light is displayed at night. (Fig. 2).

Semaphore signals.

AUTOMATIC HOME

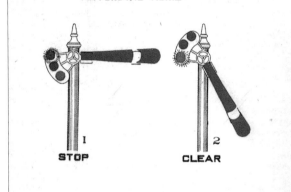

1
STOP

2
CLEAR

These rules and illustrations for Automatic Block Signals were part of the 1909 Santa Fe Railroad book of "Rules and Regulations of the Operating Department." Rare.

RULE 290.

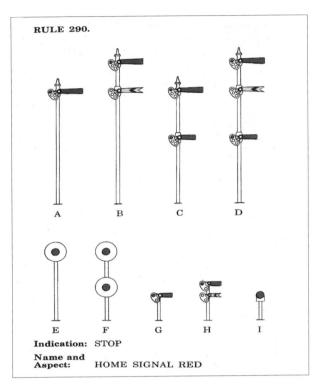

A   B   C   D

E   F   G   H   I

Indication: STOP

Name and Aspect: HOME SIGNAL RED

C.T.C./Block signal indications for "stop" are shown in Rule 290 of this 1960 Southern Pacific Company rule book. Common.

This page, reproduced from a 1910 Union Pacific Railroad booklet on "Railroad Signaling," shows block signals. Rare.

the rules "issued in book form." Only special rules that were unique to operations on a division, and changes to general rules since the last rule book was issued, continued to be printed in employee timetables. By the turn of the century, most railroads were using the standardized rules set forth by The General Time Convention held by the railroads in 1889. Railroad members of this convention continued to meet regularly to update and standardize operating rules industry-wide. Every rule that was adopted had a history of operating practices that led to it.

Cab Signals and Centralized Traffic Control (C.T.C.)

Two other important signaling systems—cab signals and Centralized Traffic Control (C.T.C.)—were adopted by railroads during the 1930s, 40s and 50s, greatly improving operating safety and efficiency. These systems were included in employee timetable schedules, special rules and instructions, and rule book issues.

Panel lights in the locomotive cab were developed as a necessary adjunct to block signal systems. Panel lights confirmed for the engineer the current block signal indication and the distant signal "aspect" (or indications) for the next block. On some railroads, relays connected these cab signals to brake equipment that would stop the train automatically if it passed a red signal.

Eventually, trackside signals and switch positions were monitored and controlled remotely by dispatchers at central locations. This system, called Centralized Traffic Control, was pioneered on the New York Central Railroad in 1927. By the 1940s, C.T.C.'s use was rapidly being instituted in high-traffic areas on major railroads. C.T.C. allowed constant monitoring of train positions, so that decisions about train passings could be even more flexible. The dispatcher sat at a large display panel/desk with a diagram of the track and sidings he controlled. Small colored lights on the panel board indicated the positions of trains. Signal indications were also shown. The dispatcher could closely follow the progress of all trains on the line, make decisions, and route trains onto sidings for passings more efficiently than by using telegraphic train orders.

Under C.T.C. trackside signals evolved from semaphore arms with lights, to lights only. Combinations of lights communicated different messages regarding current track occupancy, condition of the track ahead, position of dual control switches—manipulated remotely by the dispatcher or manually by the train crews—and which indication to expect at the next signal. The system was made even more efficient with track-side phones and train two-way radios for crew members to talk with the dispatcher.

Those portions of the railroad operating under

This Norfolk and Western Railway freight timetable illustration from 1962 shows the C.T.C. dispatcher at work. One person in a central location making prompt decisions and taking immediate actions regarding train movements made dispatching via C.T.C. a very powerful tool that greatly increased operating efficiency. This high-stress decision-making job was developed by many good dispatchers into a true art form. Common.

C.T.C.—known as C.T.C. "territory"—were indicated in the schedules of employee timetables. Rules covering all aspects of train movements under C.T.C. were included in rule books and special rules sections of employee timetables. For clarity, most rules included color illustrations of signal aspects (indications). Currently, many large railroads operate with a combination of C.T.C., block, and manual signaling under the employee timetable/watch/rule book system. Some railroads operate entirely under Centralized Traffic Control, being completely train-order-free. Very small railroads continue to rely only on manual signaling, employee timetables, and VFH radios for their day-to-day operations.

The Southern Pacific Company General Auditor's Bulletin No. 538 from January 15, 1952 gives the definition of a timetable as:

Authority for the movement of regular trains subject to railway train rules, with a schedule that prescribes train classification, direction, identification, and movement. Timetable schedules usually are in effect for 12 hours after their time at each station, and a train behind schedule for more than the prescribed time limit can proceed only as authorized by train order. Timetable authority may be superseded by rules providing for block signals and interlocking signals.

Employee Timetable Content
Throughout their history, employee timetables have included a wide variety of necessary information:

Freight and passenger train names.

Mileage from terminals.

Distance between stations.

Mileposts - Mileage markers used as references for indicating exact train positions, areas of track in need of repair or under slow orders, etc.

Yard limits.

Bulletin board locations - General orders and timetable bulletins were posted at locations where employees would see them immediately when they came to work.

Train speed restrictions - Depending on the condition of the track, vicinity to populated areas, and for other reasons, train speeds were restricted.

Speed tables - Gave time / distance calculations for different speeds so train crews could better plan their movements.

Siding capacities - Originally given in number of freight cars a siding would hold, later given in feet.

Locomotive speed restrictions - Safe mechanical operating speed limits for different types of locomotives.

List of company physicians - Employees were to call them first if injured on the job.

Engine tonnage ratings - Weights of trains on different lines that locomotives were capable of pulling, depending on the "tractive effort" of the locomotive and hills on the line.

Train weight restrictions - Primarily on branch lines that were not constructed or maintained as well as main lines.

Watch inspectors - Employees took their watches only to company authorized watch inspectors for checks and repairs.

Flag stops - For the boarding and discharge of passengers.

First-aid instructions.

Locating placarded cars in trains - Cars containing certain hazardous materials cannot be next to others that would create a hazard.

"Hot box"/dragging equipment locations - Electronic trackside sensors detect problems with equipment, preventing a possible derailment.

Tunnel/bridge clearances - Some locomotives and cars were restricted on lines because of their size.

Other Employee Timetable Formats
Many large railroads still preferred the smaller—string-tied and, later, staple-bound—booklet-style employee timetable and continued to use and evolve this format. The page size was enlarged to 8" to 9" by 10" to 11" which became the standard approximate sizes used. Creases were added to facilitate folding them in half to fit into hip pockets. Bright orange covers were used so that crew members could be seen more easily when giving hand signals while holding the timetable. This stapled-booklet size was commonly referred to as a *magazine-style* timetable. By the 1950s, most railroads still using horse blankets had switched

Movement of Trains by Telegraph.

Safety demands that all persons connected with the movement of Trains by Telegraph should use the utmost care and watchfulness.

80. **An Operator having an order** for a train or engine will immediately upon the receipt of it, display a RED FLAG by day, or a RED LIGHT by night, on the signal-post erected for this purpose, which signal must be immediately taken in upon the delivery of the order, but not before.

81. **All orders for the movement of trains** by telegraph will be addressed to the Conductor and Engineer. and written by the receiving operator on "manifold" paper; three impressions being made. The Conductor addressed shall read the order carefully, and if understood, shall sign it for himself and Engineer. It will then be repeated back to the sender, over their signatures, and if found correct, he will reply "O K," which will be endorsed upon the order by the receiving operator, with the exact time "O K" is received, and countersigned by him. The operator will file one copy, and give two copies to the Conductor, who will retain one and deliver one to the Engineer, who must invariably read it before starting the train.

82. **After the receipt of an order,** should the line cease to work before the "O K" is received, the operator will destroy the order, and inform the Conductor and Engineer of the fact. They will then be governed by the Time Table regulations. Conductors and Engineers will keep a sharp lookout for train order signals at all telegraph stations, and when running behind time, will inquire of operators if any orders.

83. **When a train has been ordered to run regardless** of a SPECIFIED TRAIN, it gives the train under such orders no right over another train. All special orders for moving trains are only for persons to whom they are directed, AND NO OTHER PERSON SHALL USE SUCH ORDERS AS AUTHORITY TO MOVE THEIR TRAINS.

84. **Should a Train having right to the Road** be directed not to leave a Station until a specified time unless another train has arrived, the train so held will wait the usual FIVE MINUTES AFTER SAID SPECIFIED TIME, FOR SAFETY, BEFORE PROCEEDING, if the train does not arrive by the time specified.

85. **Should a train be held** over 30 minutes at a telegraph station where there is no Night Operator, the Conductor will call the Day Operator into the office to get orders for him.

86. **When Operators relieve each other,** the one going off duty must carefully call the attention of the one coming on to orders still in effect, and get his understanding of the same.

86½. **Should a Train have an order** to hold at any Station for orders, such order must be recalled before proceeding.

87. **Operators must keep on hand** at all times the necessary signals to carry out these instructions, viz.: One RED FLAG, and one RED LANTERN, and will have them convenient and in order for immediate use when occasion requies.

GENERAL RULES.

88. **Any Employe** who may be cognizant of default in duty by another employé, and fails to report the same to the Superintendent, becomes equally censurable with the defaulter.

89. **No person will be employed** who is in the habit of using intoxicating drinks as a beverage.

90. **Should anyone using this Card** have any doubts as to the meaning of any part of it, it is the duty of such person to apply to the Superintendent for the proper explanation.

91. **All former Rules** that conflict with this card are abolished, and all former Time Tables are to be destroyed.

The "Signals and Rules" section of Time Table No. 31 from the Chicago, Milwaukee and St. Paul Railway of 1887 includes a section titled "Movement of Trains by Telegraph." Rare.

over to this larger booklet format. It remains one of the most common formats still in use today.

Another popular booklet format that had evolved by the 1960s is still commonly used for today's employee timetables. These are staple- or glue-bound booklets measuring approximately 4" to 5" by 9" to 11," the same size as the magazine style folded in half.

Computer-Generated Timetables

The newest form of employee timetables reflect modern computer technology. Whole employee timetables are composed and edited on desktop computer systems. Proofs are generated by laser printers, and rule books and employee timetables are issued in standard three-ring binders. Edits are easy to make. Changes are as simple as having revised pages printed and distributed for insertion in binders, and some railroads now transmit timetable changes via FAX machines. The effect of computers on the railroad industry will be further evidenced as the content of timetable pages appears on locomotive cab computer displays, whole divisions become automated with trackside sensors, and trains move under computer control.

New Issues

There were a variety of reasons to issue new employee timetables, including all those mentioned in Chapter One for public timetable issues. After an employee timetable was issued, general orders, supplements, and bulletins related to its use began to accumulate in the superintendent's office. The changing needs of the marketing and traffic departments also had to be accommodated. Decisions from the board of directors, president's office, motive power and maintenance of way departments required integration into current schedules and resulted in the creation of a new employee timetable.

An article, appearing in the December, 1954,

Examples of 1950s and 1960s magazine-style employee timetables. Common.

Examples of 1950s and 1960s booklet-style timetables. Common.

GENERAL RULES AND REGULATIONS

GOVERNING

Employes of the Operating Department

ARE ISSUED IN BOOK FORM.

———◆———

The following exceptions, additions and explanations are made to said Rules:

Rule 14. Minors may be employed, after proper release is given by their parents.

40. When the Number of Train is changed on New Time Table of Trains on the road, then get orders.

65. When Train following a White Signal meets Train carrying White Signal, the Train following a White Signal cannot proceed without orders.

96. When a Train is 12 hours late at *any station,* it must be fully understood that it has lost all rights to the road.

102. Where for want of space time table does not show clearance time for freight trains, ahead of, following or against, trains of superior class, clearance time is provided, and Rule No. 102 must be obeyed.

103. Passenger Trains running in sections or moving in same direction will be governed by rule 103, page 26, book of rules and regulations, except that they will keep five minutes apart.

106. Passenger Trains are excepted where they do not stop.

128. South Bound Freight Trains are excepted passing Waukegan, and North Bound Freight Trains passing Palatine, Cary and Granville.

136. Passenger Trains that do not stop at Des Plaines, Lake Bluff and South Milwaukee may register by using Blank C.

143. Work Train orders must specify which track they are to use when working within limits of double track.

209. Trains need not stop for clearance as follows: Passenger Trains on double track; North-bound Freight Trains at Palatine, Cary and Granville; South-bound Freight Trains at Waukegan and Woodstock. Conductors and Engineers must keep sharp lookout for signals at points above named.

220. Train receiving this order will not wait 5 minutes for the Train they receive orders against.

223. May be added to Rules No. 217 or 220.

354. Does not apply to Passenger Conductors of suburban trains while on double tracks.

A "General Rules and Regulations" section was included on the last page of a Chicago and North-Western Railway Wisconsin Division timetable of 1892. Changes and additions to the last rule book printed were shown in the employee timetable until a new book of rules was published. Rare.

Missouri-Kansas-Texas Railroad employee magazine, illustrates this process:

How to String a Time Card
They're "stringing a time card" in the Katy superintendent's Office at Denison right now.

In railroad parlance, this means a new Employees' Time Table is in the process of preparation. Actual issuance date has not yet been determined.

G.I. Stricklin, Katy Assistant Superintendent at that point, was kind enough to give us some particulars of just how the new "working time card" is compiled. Part of the job is the actual stringing of a board that corresponds to the card itself.

It seems that whenever a change in operating procedures calculated to improve service is put into effect, a new Employees' Time Table must be issued for each Katy Division affected.

First, times of arrival and departure for various terminals, having been determined by heads of Operating and Traffic Departments, are furnished to the Division supervisory officials. These men then go to work to make up a "dummy" time table folder or worksheet incorporating all new times over the line between various points, inserting necessary adjustments. Various factors are considered: that no train is scheduled faster than the permissible maximum speed; whether or not a train is to stop at certain stations; need to gauge the length of time necessary to perform station work—loading and unloading of passengers, mail, express, etc.

Once the new, apparently satisfactory, schedules are penciled in, the man in charge, Stricklin at Denison, for example, gets down his board and starts stringing, the purpose being to see that times as listed on the worksheets are feasible.

The boards at Denison, one for each Katy Sub-Division, are sizeable easel-like affairs. Tacked onto each is a sheet of heavy paper, roughly 3 ft. by 6 ft., ruled off horizontally at 5-minute intervals (midnight to midnight), and vertically by mileage. Various stations and sidings are spaced to scale with accurate mileage indicated thereon. Ordinary, garden variety string is used to represent the trains. Red lengths of string with small red cards attached are the passenger trains, black strings with green tags, the freight. Each tag bears a train number.

6 LOS ANGELES DIVISION   **SECOND DISTRICT**

WESTWARD   EASTWARD

TIME TABLE NO. 116 — Sept. 7, 1941

Second Class 37 Freight (Leave Daily)	Second Class 35 Freight (Leave Daily)	First Class 7 Fast Mail Express (Leave Daily)	First Class 19 The Chief (Leave Daily)	First Class 3 California Limited (Leave Daily)	First Class 17 Super Chief (Leave Monday and Thursday)	First Class 1 The Scout (Leave Daily)	First Class 21 El Capitan (Leave Monday and Thursday)	Mile Posts	STATIONS	First Class 42 MOTOR (Arrive Daily)	First Class 20 The Chief (Arrive Daily)	First Class 22 El Capitan (Arrive Tuesday and Friday)	First Class 4 California Limited (Arrive Daily)	First Class 18 Super Chief (Arrive Tuesday and Friday)	First Class 2 The Scout (Arrive Daily)	First Class 8 Fast Mail Express (Arrive Daily)
PM 1.10³⁰	AM 1.00	6.20	9.50	9.35	7.30	6.06³¹	6.00¹	81.3	SAN BERNARDINO	PM 12.35	PM 1.10³⁷	PM 3.00	PM 9.00	PM 9.30	PM 10.00	AM 12.45
1.25	1.15	6.28	9.59	9.45	7.36	6.16	6.06	84.9	RIALTO	s12.25	1.03	2.53	8.51	9.23	9.52	12.36
1.35	1.25	6.32	10.05	9.51	7.41	f 6.23	6.11	88.8	FONTANA	12.18	12.59	2.49	8.46	9.19	9.46	12.31
1.42	1.32	6.35	10.10	9.55	7.44	6.30	6.14	92.5	WADE	12.12	12.55	2.45	8.42	9.15	9.42	12.27
1.44	1.34	6.37	10.11	9.57	7.45	f 6.32	6.15	92.7	ETIWANDA	f12.10	12.54	2.44	8.41	9.14	9.41	12.26
1.52	1.42	6.41	10.16	10.02	7.49	f 6.40	6.19	97.7	CUCAMONGA	12.03 PM	12.50	2.40	8.36	9.10	9.36	12.21
2.00	1.50	6.45	10.21	10.07	7.52	s 6.46	6.22	100.9	UPLAND	s11.57	12.46	2.36	8.32	9.06	9.32	12.17
2.08	1.58	6.50	10.27	10.13	7.57	6.53	6.27	105.9	CLAREMONT	s11.47	12.41	2.31	8.27	9.01	9.26	12.12
2.14	1.54	6.52	10.29	10.15	7.59	6.56	6.29	106.7	POMONA	s11.41	12.39	2.29	8.25	8.59	9.24	12.10
2.17	1.57	6.53	10.31	10.17	8.00	f 6.59	6.30	107.9	LA VERNE	s11.37	12.37	2.27	8.23	8.57	9.22	12.08
2.24²²	2.02	6.56	10.34	10.20	8.03	f 7.03	6.33	110.2	SAN DIMAS	s11.30	12.34	2.24³⁷	8.20	8.54	9.19	12.05 AM
2.35	2.10	7.01	10.39	10.25	8.07	7.11	6.37	114.4	GLENDORA	s11.20	12.28	2.19	8.14	8.49	9.13	11.59
2.40	2.15	7.04	10.42	10.28	8.09	f 7.15	6.39	116.9	AZUSA	s11.13	12.25	2.16	8.11	8.46	9.10	11.57
2.42	2.17	7.06	10.43	10.29	8.11	7.18	6.41	118.0	KINCAID	11.08	12.23	2.15	8.09	8.45	9.08	11.55
2.47	2.22	7.08	10.45	10.31	8.13	7.22	6.43	120.2	BUTLER	11.03	12.21	2.13	8.06	8.43	9.05	11.52
2.52	2.27	7.10	10.48	10.34	8.15	f 7.25	6.45	122.4	MONROVIA	f10.58	12.19	2.11	8.03	8.41	9.02	11.50
2.57	2.32	7.12	10.50	10.37	8.17	f 7.28	6.47	124.2	ARCADIA	f10.55	12.17	2.09	8.01	8.39	9.00	11.48
3.01	2.36	7.14	10.52⁴²	10.40	8.19	7.32	6.49	125.9	SANTA ANITA (S. Madre)	f10.52¹⁹	12.15	2.07	7.59	8.37	8.58	11.46
3.05	2.40	7.16	10.55	10.44⁴⁷	8.21	7.35	6.51	127.3	CHAPMAN	10.44³	12.13	2.06	7.57	8.36	8.56	11.44
3.07	2.42	7.17	10.57	10.47	8.22	7.37	6.52		LAMANDA PARK	f10.37	12.09	2.05	7.56	8.35	8.55	11.43
3.20	2.55	7.28	s11.18	s11.05	s 8.35	s 8.00	s 7.05	131.7	PASADENA	s10.25	s12.01 PM	s 1.55	s 7.45	s 8.25	s 8.45	s11.30
3.27	3.02	7.33	11.24	11.12	8.40	f 8.07	7.10	133.7	SOUTH PASADENA	f10.10	11.50	1.48	7.36	8.18	8.34	11.19
3.29	3.04	7.35⁴	11.25	11.13	8.41	8.08	7.11	134.2	OLGA	10.08	11.49	1.47	7.35⁷	8.17	8.33	11.18
3.37	3.12	7.41	11.29	11.18	8.45	f 8.13	7.15	135.9	HIGHLAND PARK (Union Pacific R. R. Crossing)	f10.04	11.46	1.43	7.30	8.13	8.29	11.14
3.47	3.22	7.48	11.36	11.26	8.52	8.20	7.22	138.7	WATER STREET (Union Pacific R. R. Crossing)	9.57	11.39	1.36	7.23	8.06	8.22	11.07
3.50	3.25	7.50	11.37³⁰	11.28	8.54	8.21	7.24	139.4	BROADWAY	9.55	11.37¹⁹	1.35	7.21	8.05	8.20	11.05
3.53 PM	3.28 AM	7.52 PM	11.40 AM	11.30 AM	8.55 AM	8.23 AM	7.25 AM	162.1	MISSION TOWER	9.54 AM	11.34 AM	1.34 PM	7.19 PM	8.04 PM	8.19 PM	11.04 PM
		8.00 PM	11.50 AM	11.40 AM	9.00 AM	8.30 AM	7.30 AM		LOS ANGELES (Union Station) (50.6)	9.50 AM	11.30 AM	1.30 PM	7.15 PM	8.00 PM	8.15 PM	11.00 PM
4.00 PM	3.40 AM							141.1	FIRST STREET							
Arrive Daily (21.1)	Arrive Daily (22.1)	Arrive Daily (33.6)	Arrive Daily (29.7)	Arrive Daily (28.6)	Arrive Monday and Thursday (39.6)	Arrive Daily (34.7)	Arrive Monday and Thursday (39.6)	Average speed per hour	(59.7)	Leave Daily (21.6)	Leave Daily (35.6)	Leave Tuesday and Friday (39.6)	Leave Daily (33.9)	Leave Tuesday and Friday (39.6)	Leave Daily (33.9)	Leave Daily (33.9)

Except as otherwise provided, first class trains, inferior by right or direction, must clear the time of Nos. 17, 18, 21 and 22 not less than five minutes. Second class and extra trains and yard engines must clear the time of Nos. 17, 18, 21 and 22 not less than ten minutes.

This page from a 1941 Santa Fe Railroad "horse blanket" shows one reason why they are so popular with collectors today. The schedules for several very famous passenger trains appear together on the same page. Common.

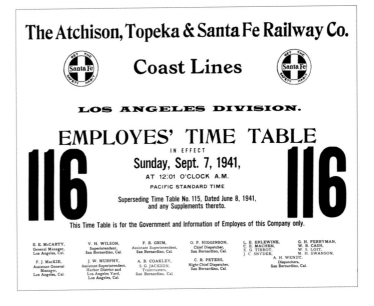

The Atchison, Topeka & Santa Fe Railway Co.

Coast Lines

LOS ANGELES DIVISION.

EMPLOYES' TIME TABLE

116 IN EFFECT
Sunday, Sept. 7, 1941,
AT 12:01 O'CLOCK A.M.
PACIFIC STANDARD TIME
Superseding Time Table No. 115, Dated June 8, 1941, and any Supplements thereto. **116**

This Time Table is for the Government and Information of Employes of this Company only.

E. E. McCARTY, General Manager, Los Angeles, Cal.
V. H. WILSON, Superintendent, San Bernardino, Cal.
F. B. GRIM, Assistant Superintendent, San Bernardino, Cal.
O. F. HIGGINSON, Chief Dispatcher, San Bernardino, Cal.
L. E. ERLEWINE, C. E. MACHEN, E. G. TIBBOT, J. C. SNYDER, Dispatchers, San Bernardino, Cal.
G. H. FERRYMAN, W. B. CASH, W. S. LOIT, M. H. SWANSON

F. J. MacKIE, Assistant General Manager, Los Angeles, Cal.
J. W. MURPHY, Assistant Superintendent, Harbor District and Los Angeles Yard, Los Angeles, Cal.
A. B. COAKLEY, S. G. JACKSON, Trainmasters, San Bernardino, Cal.
C. R. PETERS, Night Chief Dispatcher, San Bernardino, Cal.
A. H. WENDT, Dispatchers, San Bernardino, Cal.

The string representing the train under scrutiny is fastened to the chart at the train's point of origin at its scheduled hour of departure and started off in the proper direction.

As the string is extended upward or down (depending on the direction, southward trains down and northward trains upward) indicating distance traveled, it also moves at a vertical angle to indicate time elapsed between stations. Another pin anchors the string at its time of arrival and departure from each station. It is carried down (or up) along its schedule route until a "Foreign" string crosses to indicate its meeting or passing another train.

If this original string represents an "inferior" train, the inferior train must take siding and wait for the "superior" train. When two times (arriving and departing) are assigned a train at a station, the string is stretched horizontally to denote lapse of time while it waits for a scheduled departure. Then another pin is fastened, and the train is on its way.

Sound complicated? It is.

But this is the purpose of the board—a visual demonstration of where and when trains will meet and pass as per schedule on the "dummy" time table.

An example taken from the Dallas Sub-Division board:

The Dallas connection of the Katy Komet, No. 281, is scheduled to leave Ray Yard at 5:45 p.m. according to worksheets. On the board, the black string representing this train crossed the red string of train No. 5, the southbound Katy Flyer, at Whitewright. Our No. 281 also crosses the red string for No. 2, the northbound Texas Special, at that same point. No. 281, then is required to let No. 5 pass at Whitewright (it's a "superior" train), and then must also remain at this point until No. 2 has passed. Because of the lapse of time involved in this operation, Stricklin stretches the string representing No. 281 horizontally across the board for the duration of time that train remains in the siding at Whitewright, then it resumes its downward course.

Incidentally, a time card must be strung in strict accordance with the company's Book of Rules, and it is imperative that the schedules be prepared

in such manner that all rules can be faithfully observed.

Once the board is strung and the worksheets okayed, the "dummy" is off to the printer and shortly thereafter the job of checking begins: the time table proofs are read and reread.

In the back portion of the "working time card," under the heading of "Special Instructions," are pages of information pertinent to the operation of the Division.

There's information concerning tonnage ratings for various diesels, impaired clearance data, listings of stations where General Order Books are located, etc. Stricklin admits the finished product represents a "considerable amount of time and effort."

Although plain and utilitarian in appearance, employee timetables tell the story of life on the railroad. The schedules, towns, miles, trains, and rules therein paint a picture of the long hours, hard work, scenic country, wild weather, powerful locomotives, and smooth operations—the lifetime experiences of running the trains. They offer vignettes of railroad history, the locales they served, and still serve, and of a part of life in America. Take some time to browse through them.

Nᵒ 6735

THIS BOOK

IS THE PROPERTY OF

The Atchison, Topeka & Santa Fe Ry. System,

AND IS LOANED TO

NAME	EMPLOYED AS
W. A. Beak	

Who hereby agrees to return it to the proper officer when called for, or upon leaving the service, or pay for same.

Hall 2 09 30M 2557

"Santa Fe."

The Atchison, Topeka & Santa Fe Railway System.

RULES AND REGULATIONS

OF THE

OPERATING DEPARTMENT.

1909.

Inside cover, with employee's signature opposite title page of 1909 Santa Fe "Rules and Regulations for Operating Trains." Very Rare.

FREIGHT

BETWEEN

BOSTON & NEW YORK

VIA FALL RIVER LINE.

FREIGHT between BOSTON and NEW YORK, via Old Colony & Fall River Railroad and Bay State Steamboat Company, will be forwarded daily (Sundays excepted). Freight Train leaves Boston at 2 o'clock, P.M., arriving in New York the following morning. Freight from New York arrives in Boston the following morning after shipment, at 11.50 A.M.

All Freight shipped by this line will be forwarded without delay, and no commission charged.

For the convenience of shippers and others, an office has been taken at

No. 75 STATE STREET,

(Corner of Kilby and State, over the Maverick Bank,)

where all desired information in relation to the subject will be freely communicated.

Notice of non-delivery of Goods will be promptly attended to.

☞ Freight taken for NEW BEDFORD, NANTUCKET, MARTHA'S VINEYARD, and all Stations upon Old Colony & Fall River, Cape Cod, Fairhaven and South Shore Railroads.

FREIGHTS AS LOW AS BY OTHER LINES.

☞ *Your patronage is particularly solicited.* ☜

JOHN O. PRESBREY, Agent.

☞ Office No. 75 State Street, and at the Old Colony & Fall River R. R. Freight Depot, Cove St.

BOSTON, FEB. 16, 1858.

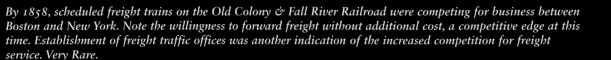

By 1858, scheduled freight trains on the Old Colony & Fall River Railroad were competing for business between Boston and New York. Note the willingness to forward freight without additional cost, a competitive edge at this time. Establishment of freight traffic offices was another indication of the increased competition for freight service. Very Rare.

CHAPTER FOUR
FAST FREIGHT SCHEDULES

"I NEED TO BE SURE my carloads will be there on time," Bob said to Joe. "Last year was a disaster."

Bob is a tomato grower in the San Joaquin Valley of California. Joe is a freight-traffic representative for a different railroad than Bob has used in the past. Joe heard Bob was not happy with the service he had been receiving and phoned him to see if they could get together and talk.

Bob was recounting last year's bad shipping experience to Joe. At harvest time he had ordered his freight cars early, loaded them quickly, and had them ready for pickup at the scheduled times. They left without any problems, but several cars did not make it to their destination until well after the times published in the freight schedules. The high-quality tomatoes they carried spoiled. Since they usually sold at top dollar, the loss hurt Bob financially and marred his reputation as a quality grower/supplier with one of his best customers. He was still angry.

"We will provide service you can count on," said Joe. "If we don't deliver, you don't stay in business, and neither do we."

Bob liked Joe's comment and smiled. "All I ask is my tomatoes get there on schedule. If something comes up and the schedules change, I need to know ahead of time so I can plan accordingly."

Joe handed Bob the current season's fast freight timetable for perishables. "If there are any changes, I'll let you know immediately," Joe said. "Otherwise we'll deliver at the times shown here or before."

"OK, then, I'll try you guys this year," said Bob. "I'll call you next Tuesday with my car order."

"Great," said Joe, "I appreciate the opportunity to serve you. You will not be disappointed."

With that, both men shook hands and said good-bye. They had work to do.

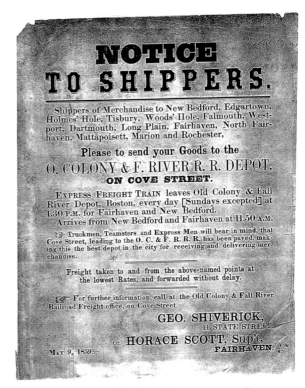

NOTICE TO SHIPPERS.

Shippers of Merchandise to New Bedford, Edgartown, Holmes' Hole, Tisbury, Woods' Hole, Falmouth, Westport, Dartmouth, Long Plain, Fairhaven, North Fairhaven, Mattapoisett, Marion and Rochester,

Please to send your Goods to the

O. COLONY & F. RIVER R. R. DEPOT,

ON COVE STREET.

EXPRESS FREIGHT TRAIN leaves Old Colony & Fall River Depot, Boston, every day [Sundays excepted] at 1.30 P.M. for Fairhaven and New Bedford.
Arrives from New Bedford and Fairhaven at 11.50 A.M.

Truckmen, Teamsters and Express Men will bear in mind, that Cove Street, leading to the O. C. & F. R. R. R. has been paved, making this the best depot in the city for receiving and delivering merchandise.

Freight taken to and from the above-named points at the lowest Rates, and forwarded without delay.

For further information, call at the Old Colony & Fall River Railroad Freight office, on Cove Street.

GEO. SHIVERICK,
11 STATE STREET.
Or **HORACE SCOTT, Sup't,**
FAIRHAVEN.

MAY 9, 1859.

As with any successful advertising campaign, "no stone is left unturned." In this 1859 ad, "cobblestones" are the advantage offered to potential customers. The paved road to the Old Colony & Fall River Rail Road freight depot made it more accessible. Very Rare.

63

Early Freight Service
On the very first railroads, freight and passenger service were considered one and the same. Cars or "carriages" carrying freight and passengers were mixed together in the few trains that operated each day. As a matter of course, timetable flyers included schedules, fares, and freight rates for the combined services they offered.

Demand for both services increased rapidly, and as passengers became a priority a practical distinction developed between freight and passenger services. By the early 1840s, most railroads recognized these two different classes of service and were operating separate freight and passenger trains.

The great success of these early railroads encouraged many entrepreneurs to build lines in populated areas in hope of easy profits. Since many lines were serving the same towns and cities, competition was fierce. With competition came increased advertising. Many public timetable flyers of the 1840s made reference to both passenger and freight service, but by the 1850s, the majority of railroads were printing separate flyers for freight service.

Freight Timetable Formats
The *single-page flyer* format used in early public timetables was also used for the first freight schedules (timetables). And, like public timetable flyers, fast freight schedules soon could not hold enough information. They, too, were replaced with the *folding brochure* (folder) format. Folded or closed sizes were approximately 4" by 9." A small, *stapled booklet* style also evolved. Both formats easily fit into a busy shipping clerk's pocket, and became the most common formats used.

The style and content of fast freight schedules also are similar to that of public timetables. The schedules were designed for ease of reading by clearly showing the symbol names of each railroad's fast freight trains, along with their departure and arrival times. Also included was important information on various routings (interchanges) available to major cities off the line. The primary purpose of freight schedules was and is to provide shipping information to businessmen,

farmers, and shipping clerks, not to the general public. For this reason, their design has remained relatively plain throughout most of the 19th and into the 20th century.

By the 1920s, passenger train travel and revenues began a slow decline as automobiles became more common and highways improved. Freight traffic, however, continued to increase as the nation's population surged.

Truck freight service began to compete for the shipment of manufactured goods. Although railroads continued to carry the majority of these products, they shifted their advertising emphasis toward raw materials. Railroads began to profit from their ability to carry large volumes much more efficiently than did trucks. By the 1950s, manifest fast-freight service for agricultural commodities and raw materials had become the most profitable aspect of the railroad business.

Competition Initiated Design Changes
As a response to highway truck competition and freight services offered by other railroads, more colorful, attention-getting freight schedules were printed. Their goal was to sell shippers on the freight services of their particular railroad. Many had color photos of new locomotives and freight cars. Maps were included, showing major routes and freight rate territories. Fast freight schedules advertised the latest modern operating features of the railroad, including communications, signal systems, classification yards, seaport facilities, truck terminal connections, electronic data-processing and traffic sales offices. For a while, even advertising about streamlined passenger service was included.

For years, railroads were locked in a fierce battle with highway trucks for the shipment of manufactured goods. This brochure (opposite) illustrates how the Union Pacific was competing for business in 1939. See color section for cover of this brochure. Rare.

An Unbeatable Combination!

● Union Pacific recently announced new, fast Merchandise Freight schedules from jobbing centers to their territorial markets. To this it added free pick-up and store-door delivery service by responsible trucking companies in local communities at practically all points on the entire railroad. The result — a Superior Less-than-Carload and Package Merchandise service, combining the outstanding advantages of rail and truck in their respective fields — a truly unbeatable combination. This new, complete service assures shippers of fast, dependable, on-time deliveries by a reliable organization which assumes complete responsibility for package merchandise, large or small, between shipper's platform and receiver's door.

· · · AND TO MAKE IT MOST EFFECTIVE · · ·

UNION PACIFIC HAS CONSTRUCTED 100 NEW SPECIALLY DESIGNED Challenger Merchandise Cars!

These cars are specially designed — with double size doors for most efficient handling of merchandise, and equipped with high-speed trucks for smooth-riding operation on the fast train schedules now in effect.

The Union Pacific organization is at your service anywhere — any time.

THE PROGRESSIVE
UNION PACIFIC RAILROAD

8-39-300
PRINTED IN U.S.A.

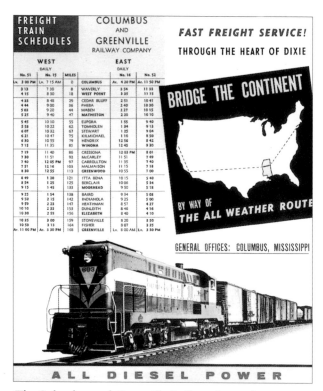

The attractive covers of these fast freight schedules advertised priority freight trains of the Southern Pacific and New York Central Railroads in the 1950s. Rare.

The Columbus and Greenville Railway featured new Baldwin Diesel-Electric locomotives for fast freight service in this early 1950s brochure. Rare.

Typical condensed fast freight schedules from the Great Northern Railway and the Northern Pacific Railway in the 1950s illustrate the two most popular formats, public timetable-sized folders and small, stapled booklets. Rare.

ATLANTIC
COAST LINE
RAILROAD

SCHEDULES

for

Fruits and Vegetables

from

FLORIDA

via

ACL RAILROAD
and CONNECTIONS

Season 1960-1961

J. J. Peacock
General Superintendent Transportation.

R. C. McLemore
Freight Traffic Manager.

Jacksonville, Florida

J&B-33957

SEABOARD
AIR LINE RAILROAD COMPANY

Schedule
— OF —

**Advance and Regular
Service**

• —

Fast Dependable
Freight Service

— FOR —

FRUITS and VEGETABLES

— FROM —

FLORIDA

— TO —

Eastern Northern and Western
Points

SEASON 1960-61

CENTRAL OF GEORGIA RAILWAY CO.

DAILY
FAST FREIGHT

PERISHABLE SCHEDULES

FROM

FLORIDA AND CUBA

TO

SOUTHEASTERN - WESTERN

and

MID-WEST MARKETS

**CENTRAL
GEORGIA**

SEASON 1958-59

1958-1959 SEASON

SHIP
FLORIDA FRUITS
AND
VEGETABLES
via

THE SOUTHERN
SR
SERVES THE SOUTH

SOUTHERN
RAILWAY SYSTEM

TRAIN SCHEDULES INSIDE

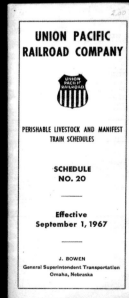

UNION PACIFIC
RAILROAD COMPANY

PERISHABLE LIVESTOCK AND MANIFEST
TRAIN SCHEDULES

SCHEDULE
NO. 20

Effective
September 1, 1967

J. BOWEN
General Superintendent Transportation
Omaha, Nebraska

*A sampling of seasonal
schedules from the 1950s
and 60s illustrates the
commitment by railroads
to provide timely services
in the shipment of perishables. Each shows differ-
ent connections shippers
can make at interchanges
with the fast freight trains
of other railroads. Rare.*

Santa Fe's Fashions in Freight

It takes nearly 100 different types of rail freight cars, Piggy-Back trailers and containers to fill the needs of our shippers. Here is a quick look at the Santa Fe fleet. Ask your Santa Fe representative for our freight equipment folders that give complete details on all equipment.

Box Cars:	Number of Cars
40' DF and SL Appliance	606
40' Load Divider Appliance	37
40' XF Food Cars	123
40' Flour Box	267
40' Common Box	11,701
50' P D Type	160
50' 4 Belt DF–2	1,075
50' 5 Belt	3
50' 8-9 Belt SD—DF	2,342
50' 8-9 Belt SL—2	40
50' 11 Belt DF–2	8
50' 17 Belt SL—1	21
50' 19 Belt SD—DF—1	4
50' 19 Belt SD—DF—2	3
50' 18-19 Belt DD—DF	214
50' Fully adjustable DD-DF	13
50' Insul. Air-Pak Load Dividers	807
50' Insul. Load Dividers SW Fillers	2,885
50' Non-Insul. Air-Pak	8
50' Hi-Cube Appliance	43
50' Airplane Parts	12
50' Auto Parts & other Equipped Box	29
50' Common Box	6,107
60' Auto Parts & other Equipped Box	739
60' Hi-Cube Appliance	4
60' Insul. Air-Pak Load Dividers	484
60' Non-Insul. Air-Pak Load Dividers	34
60' Insul. Load Dividers, SW Fillers	693
60' Insul. SL	143
86' Box	414
Total All Box Cars	**29,019**

(11,298 cars have special interior features) DF= Evans Damage Free, SL=Transco Safe Loaders, SD=Single Door, DD=Double Door, Insul.=Insulated, PD=Perforated Side Wall. SW=Side Wall

Flat Cars:	Number of Cars
53'6" Plain	732
60' Plain	225
44'6"—TOFC	69
85'—TOFC	328
88'—TOFC	50
89'—TOFC & COFC	452
88' Mark 5 Container Loading	30
60'0"—COFC	2
53'6" Chain Tie-down Equipment	187
60'6" Chain Tie-down Equipment	295
89' Chain Tie-down (Fork lift trucks)	2
Articulated	70
Heavy Duty & Depressed	19
Wallboard	603
Lumber	62
Copper Anode	22
Tri-Level Auto-Veyor	834
Special Enclosed Tri-Levels	26
Bi-Level Auto-Veyor	515
Tandem Saddle truck loading	62
89' Auto Frame Loading	41
Auto, Airplane, Parts & Other Equipped Flats	36
Total Flat Cars, all types	**4,662**

COFC=Container on flat car
TOFC=Trailer-on-flat car. TTX=Trailer-Train

Gondola Cars:	Number of Cars
Drop Bottom	1,735
Solid Bottom Low Side (Except 65')	4,116
High Side, 42' Solid Bottom	31
High Side, 53' Solid Bottom	1,160
Solid Bottom (100-ton) Coal	101
65' Low Side, Solid Bottom	622
65' High Side, Solid Bottom	199
Coil Steel	30
Ore	268
Sulphur	6
Covered Gondolas	222
Other special equipped gondolas	487
Total Gondolas	**8,977**

Hopper Cars:	Number of Cars
Open Top	2,561
Open Top Longitudinals	1,364
Open Top Cross Hopper 100-Ton	1,044
Total Hopper Cars	**4,969**

Covered Hoppers (LO Type)	
2 Comp. 2000 Cu. Ft. 70-Ton	2,567
3 Comp. 2900 Cu. Ft. 70-Ton	571
3 Comp. 3200 Cu. Ft. 70-Ton	389
3 Comp. 3500 Cu. Ft. 100-Ton	50
2 Comp. 2900 Cu. Ft. 100-Ton	#169
3 Comp. 3390 Cu. Ft. 100-Ton	#24
3 Comp. 4000 Cu. Ft. 100-Ton	574
3 Comp. 4427 Cu. Ft. 100-Ton	8,079
3 Comp. 4460 Cu. Ft. 100-Ton	396
3 Comp. 4500 Cu. Ft. 100-Ton	491
3 Comp. 4600 Cu. Ft. 100-Ton	995
3 Comp. 4650 Cu. Ft. 100-Ton	#19
3 Comp. 4750 Cu. Ft. 100-Ton	995
4 Comp. 5000 Cu. Ft. 100-Ton	2
4 Comp. 5250 Cu. Ft. 100-Ton	61
Airslide 2600 Cu. Ft.	307
Airslide 4180 Cu. Ft.	55
Granu-Flow	2
Total Covered Hoppers	**15,746**

#=Center flow "Teardrop" Design.
Comp.=Compartment. Cu. Ft.=Cubic Feet

Refrigerator Cars:	Number of Cars
MTC (Mechanicals)	4,500
(Includes 4,218 SFRC's; 282 SFRP's	
RS type	348
40' SFRB, DF	21
50' SFRB, DF	1,245
50' SFRE, Load Dividers, SW Fillers	31
50' SFRE, Load Dividers	208
Refrigerated Covered Hoppers	100
Total Refrigerator Cars	**6,453**

MTC=Mechanical Temperature Control. RS= Bunker refrigerator for chunk ice with or without means of ventilation. SFRB=Insulated box car equipped with cross bars and gates. No bunkers. SFRC=Mechanical refrigerator equipped with load dividers. SFRE=Insulated box car with load dividers, some cars have side wall fillers. No bunkers. SFRP=Mechanical Refrigerator without load dividers.

Piggy-Back Trailers	Number
40'—open top—flat bed	432
40' x 12'6"—484 non-refrigerated, 1,000 refrigerated	1,484
40' x 13'6"—1,549 non-refrigerated, 716 refrigerated	2,265
Total Piggy-Back Trailers	**4,181**

Containers	
24' Containers	99
40' Flexivan Type Closed—Mail	70
28' Chassis—Mail	119
Total Containers	**288**

Equipment in service October 1, 1974

Super Freight Schedules

zipping across the Santa Fe

Santa Fe

Major Santa Fe freight schedules including

"Super C"

world's fastest freight train

December 1, 1974

The Santa Fe offered Super Freight Schedules in their 1974 folder, including a list of freight cars available to customers. Rare.

Fast Freight Services Offered

In their history of competing for freight business, railroads have offered a variety of freight services to shippers of agricultural commodities, raw materials, and manufactured goods, including:

Perishable schedules—Special high priority trains were operated seasonally to accommodate harvest commodities.

Overnight and high-speed service—Offered to all shippers using the latest and most powerful locomotives running on the fastest and best-maintained routes with the highest freight train operating priority on the railroad. Destination terminals were strategically located in major metropolitan areas. Special boxcars designed for ease of loading/unloading merchandise were used exclusively on these trains.

Truck trailer on flat car service (known as "T.O.F.C." or "Piggyback")—Offered as above with destinations at special T.O.F.C. terminal facilities. This service grew out of the need to interface train and truck freight traffic without reloading between modes of transportation.

Intermodal container on flat car service (known as "C.O.F.C.")—Also offered as above, this is the most efficient system currently in use. Shippers can load commodities, raw materials or manufactured goods in standard-sized containers that are compatible with all modes of transportation on land, sea and rail. Intermodal facilities are offered by railroads, trucking lines, and shipping firms at strategic locations in major metropolitan areas.

Fast freight schedules give collectors and the general reader or rail passenger an interesting look at railroads from a perspective usually available only to businesses. They are hard to find today because they were specialized and plain in appearance, were printed in small numbers, and had limited distribution, mostly to businesses which might use the service. Thus, not many were saved.

The Illinois Central Railroad listed T.O.F.C. options available to shippers in the 1970s. Schedules are for T.O.F.C. and C.O.F.C. trains only. Rare.

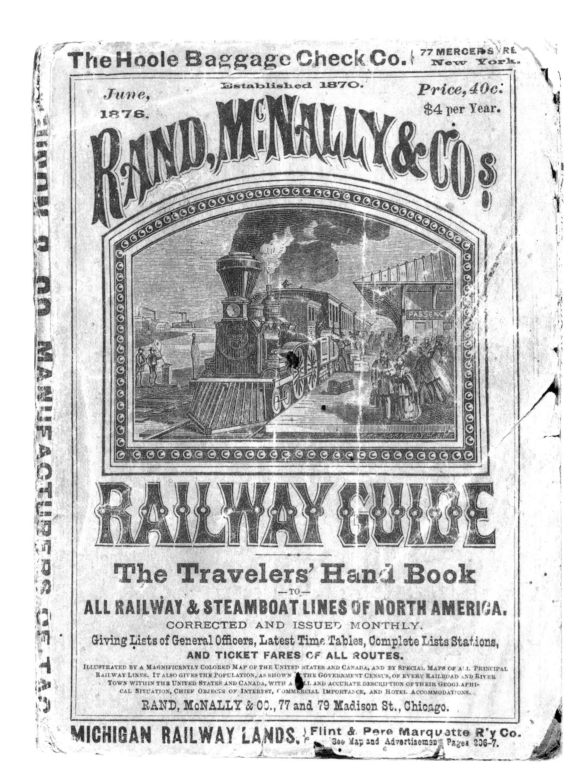

June, 1876.

Established 1870.

Price, 40c: $4 per Year.

RAND, McNALLY & CO's

RAILWAY GUIDE

The Travelers' Hand Book

— TO —

ALL RAILWAY & STEAMBOAT LINES OF NORTH AMERICA.

CORRECTED AND ISSUED MONTHLY.

Giving Lists of General Officers, Latest Time Tables, Complete Lists Stations,

AND TICKET FARES OF ALL ROUTES.

ILLUSTRATED BY A MAGNIFICENTLY COLORED MAP OF THE UNITED STATES AND CANADA, AND BY SPECIAL MAPS OF ALL PRINCIPAL RAILWAY LINES. IT ALSO GIVES THE POPULATION, AS SHOWN IN THE GOVERNMENT CENSUS, OF EVERY RAILROAD AND RIVER TOWN WITHIN THE UNITED STATES AND CANADA, WITH A FULL AND ACCURATE DESCRIPTION OF THEIR GEOGRAPHI-CAL SITUATION, CHIEF OBJECTS OF INTEREST, COMMERCIAL IMPORTANCE, AND HOTEL ACCOMMODATIONS.

RAND, McNALLY & CO., 77 and 79 Madison St., Chicago.

Rand McNally & Co.'s Railway Guide, June, 1876. Very Rare.

CHAPTER FIVE
TRAVEL GUIDES

EQUIPPED with only her courage, a little money, and a travel guide, Mary's greatest adventures were yet to unfold as she began her journey from New York City west to the Mississippi by train in the 1860s. Mary was a young Irish-born woman on her way to a Missouri town called St. Louis.

"What time is it, please?" she asked the ticket agent in the station.

"Clock's on the wall," was his reply.

"Is that the time here in New York City or the time on your timetable in this book?" She placed the railway travel guide on the counter.

"That clock is our railroad's standard time, the same as in your travel guide" he said. "You see, Miss, every railroad has a standard time. It's usually the same as local time in most big cities. Local times in smaller towns, though, will be a few minutes different from railroad time. Keep that in mind when you're traveling."

"That's confusing," Mary replied.

"Yes it is," said the agent, "but the times for most of the train connections you'll make will not be close enough to worry about."

Mary was excited about her cross-country train trip. Her future husband was waiting for her. He had sent her the money to come all the way from Ireland, where they had grown up together and fallen in love. He had come to the United States to work and build a future for them, finding a good job as a teamster. After not seeing him for over a year, she was less than a week away. With the travel guide she had just bought, detailing train times and routes, Mary was confident of getting there without too much trouble.

"I am going to look at this a bit more and then I'll be back to buy my ticket," Mary said.

"That's a good travel guide to use," said the agent. "Next please!"

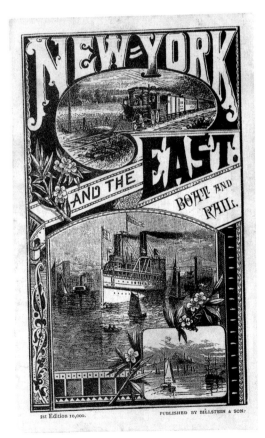

New York and the East. Boat and Rail, 1850s.
Very Rare.

Title page and advertisements from Dinsmore's American Railway Guide, 1856. Included is an ad for the "companion guide" (see pages 73 and 74) to this travel guide. Very Rare.

Need for travel guidance

Planning rail travel in the 1870s was a challenge if you were traveling long distances on several different lines. Travelers did not know exactly where they could go via railroad, what various routes they could take to get there, or how they could make connections for all the railroads they would need to travel. There were no comprehensive, national timetables such as those available today. Each railroad produced its own timetables.

The larger railroads distributed these within the local areas they served, but it was too expensive to distribute them to the public nationwide. Many ticket agents received copies, but not all agents had timetables for every railroad. Travelers going to the same destination might receive different routing from two different ticket agents. These routes may not have always been the most direct, or the least expensive possible, but an agent could only sell tickets by referring to whatever current public timetables he had available.

Travel Guides

Ticket agents and the public did have another option, *travel guides: independently published* compendiums of timetables for railroads throughout the United States. The earliest, mid-19th century, railway travel guides usually contained nothing but timetables, solicited from railroads by independent publishers. The publisher would then reproduce these with a minimum amount of editing. Sometimes maps of railroad lines were included. This system was a practical alternative for those railroads that could not afford to print and distribute timetables to ticket agents on all the railroads across the nation.

Early Guides

The reliability of early independently published guides varied, so users were often reluctant to trust them. Sometimes ticket agents were prohibited from using them, with railroad rules allowing only the use of timetables published by the railroads. Nevertheless, such travel guides continued to be used as a resource for ticket agents and the public. They gave railroads the opportunity to be noticed and patronized for a small fraction of what it cost to print large quantities of public timetables.

While their main content was their collections of timetables for different railroad lines, for a short period in our history, many early travel guides also included limited information and advertising related to the regions and locales they covered. Usually, however, tourist or traveler's information, and advertising about specific regions and their cities, towns and geographical features, appeared in railroad advertisements placed in local periodicals. (Some independent publishers of early travel guides printed such regional advertising and information in *tourist guides*. Discussed fully in Chapter Six, these were designed to be used as *companions to travel guides*. Only condensed, or portions of, timetables, if any, were included in tourist guides.)

Unfortunately, the 1840s through the 1860s saw many inaccurate travel guides come into existence. Often, they were duplications of outdated previous editions from other publishers. It was difficult for the public and ticket agents to know who was printing the latest accurate schedules. With so many guides in existence, each claiming to be the most accurate, many tickets were sold for trips that ended in confusion.

Several travel guides did stand out, however, either because of hard work, diligence and fairness in their solicitations of schedules and advertisements from railroads, or, their blatant plagiarism and strong marketing. The descriptions of the guides that follow offer a nostalgic look at this relatively obscure venture in American publishing history. Major guides—which the collector is most likely to find—are discussed, and examples are given of many of the other national and regional travel guides, each similar to the others, that were published over the years.

Early Travel Guides 1850s - 1880s

These were independently published books of national or regional timetables, used by ticket agents.

Dinsmore's American Railway Guide

First published in 1850, Dinsmore's *American Railway Guide* was one of the first and most successful railroad travel guides in America. Monthly editions contained "Correct Tables For Time Of Starting From All Stations, Distances, Fares, Etc. On All The Railway Lines In The United States; Together With A Complete Railway Map." The large foldout map was of the eastern half of North America, including almost all of the United States and Canada. The small 3 1/2" by 5 1/4" booklet also contained advertising pages inside the front and back blue card covers. Ads included products such as furnaces, hotels, padlocks, photographs and daguerreotypes, pianos, prostheses, salves, safes, sewing machines, snuff, surgeons' tools, yeast and remedies. The stuff of life in the 1850s!

Dinsmore also published a *Railroad and Steam Navigation Guide and Companion*, which included "a new feature never before published" giving "principal Terminal Stations" and "Roads over which you go—when you start—through time—" along with a "Railroad Gazetteer" section "with general information of interest to Tourists—the principal Hotels, etc."

By the 1860s, *Dinsmore's American Railway Guide* was being published as *Batterman's American Railway Guide*, which by proprietary succession from Mr. Batterman ultimately became the *Travelers' Official Railway Guide* in June, 1868.

Appletons' Railway & Steam Navigation Guide

Appletons' Railway and Steam Navigation Guide, which began publication in July of 1857, is a little-deserved success story. Appletons' first issue was plagiarized from the November, 1856, issue of *Batterman's Railway Guide*. Appletons' ability to quickly overshadow existing travel guide competition was due to its then-modern mass-printing, sales, marketing and distribution capabilities. (One clue to Appletons' distribution network is a small note in the July, 1860, issue stating the *Companion Hand-Book* "Can be obtained of the boys who sell Appletons' Railway Guide upon the principal Railways throughout the United States and Canada.") Appletons' enjoyed enormous success, which lasted until the late 1860s, claiming itself as the "Only Railway Guide."

Appletons' lead in travel guide sales made it an essential publication for railroads to use to announce their schedules. Advertisers also had to be in Appletons'. Taking advantage of their success, the fees charged to railroads for the publication of maps and schedules were rapidly increased. Appletons' even went so far as to chastise, in the editorial pages of their guide, those railroad officials who elected not to pay these exorbitant fees. Only token, abbreviated schedules from these roads were printed. By knocking out most of their competition, Appletons' also eliminated any monitoring of accuracy in the schedules they printed.

As further proof of their success, Appletons' attempted to protect the content of their guides under copyright laws. They tried to stop other publishers from printing the same schedules. Since these schedules remained the property of the railroads that had submitted them, Appletons' claim was denied. Undaunted, they went on to argue that they were the sole originators of the travel guide format in general, and that no one else had the right to copy this style. They eventually failed in this as well.

Railroad officials and ticket agents were forced to take action against Appletons' monopoly. By 1866, the National Association of General Passenger and Ticket Agents (NAGPTA)—which later became the American Association of Passenger Ticket Officials—moved to establish an official publication of their own. In March of 1868, editor Edward Vernon, a former railroad ticket agent, gained enough endorsements from member railroads to begin publication of the association-sponsored *The Travelers' Official Guide of the Railways*, which became the symbol of accuracy in travel guides. Eventually, *The Travelers' Official Railway Guide* acquired Appletons,' and ended its publication in 1885.

Despite its questionable reputation, *Appletons' Illustrated Railway Guide* provides a stimulating look at the United States in the 1850s and 60s. Like its predecessors, it included advertisements for many of the products and services used by Americans during this time. It also included an "Index to Railways and Their Terminal Stations," a "Counting House Calendar," news of "Railways and Their Progress," "Anecdotes and In-

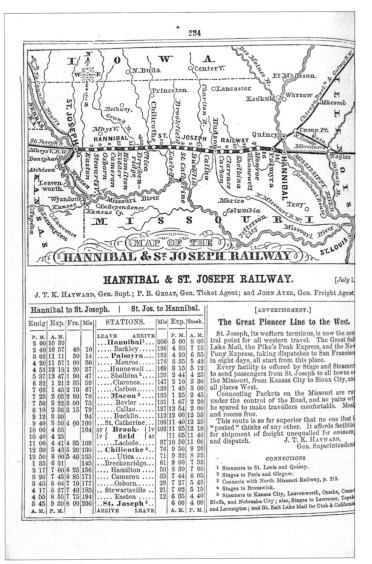

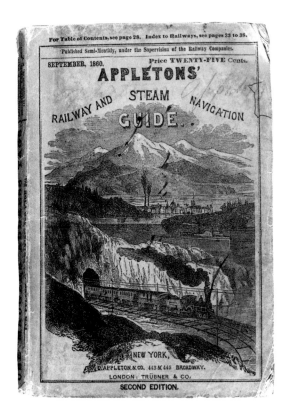

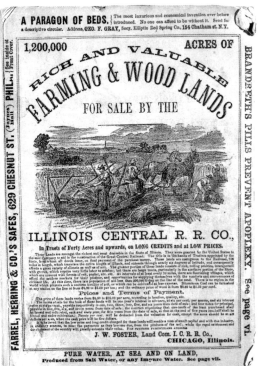

Covers and map with timetable from Appletons' Railway Guide, September, 1860. Very Rare.

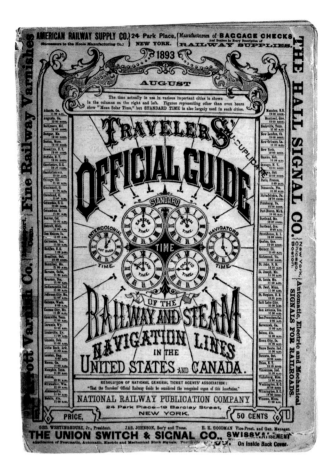

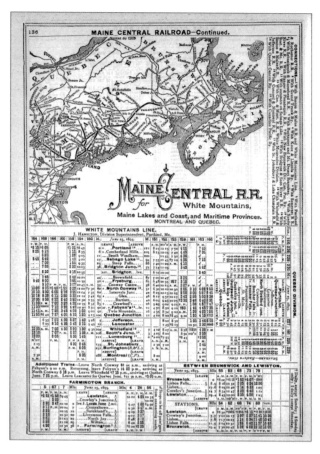

Cover, map and timetable pages and advertisments from the Travelers' Official Railway Guide, 1893. This book is more than one inch thick! Rare.

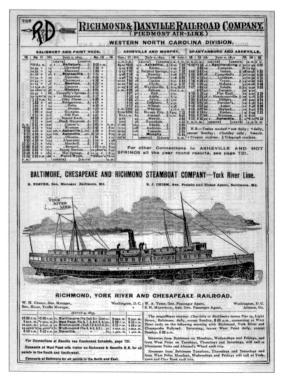

cidents of Travel," and a brief "Tourist's Guide of The Principal Watering Places, Springs, and Places of Fashionable Resort in the United States."

Appletons' also published a *Companion Hand-Book of Travel* which "contains a full description of the principal Cities, towns, and places of interest: together with Hotels, and Routes of Travel throughout the United States and Canada—With colored Maps—It contains nearly 300 pages." This latter was another early example of a tourist guide (See Chapter Six) published independently of railroads and local periodicals.

Travelers' Official Railway Guide of The United States and Canada

First published in June of 1868, *The Travelers' Official Railway Guide* signaled a new era in the publication of accurate and respected travel guides. Officially endorsed by NAGPTA member railroads and published by the National Railway Publication Company as their officially sanctioned guide, it soon became a valuable tool for ticket agents throughout the nation and the preferred reference by the majority of the traveling public.

The *Official Guide*, as it became commonly known, published schedules and maps of railroads at no charge to the railroads. Advertisements were accepted at a very reasonable rate, which was the same for all railroads, no matter their size. Revenues came primarily from the sale of subscriptions. No other travel guide of the era could compete with such a publication, including Appletons'. The *Travelers' Official Railway Guide* quickly became the standard.

Publication of the *Official Guide* ended the problems caused by inaccurate travel guides. Railroads knew their schedules would be correctly reproduced in "The Guide." Ticket agents and the public gained a new confidence as the guide made railroad travel easier, playing a significant role in the speed and efficiency with which people could travel throughout the growing nation.

The *Travelers' Official Railway Guide* format was similar to that of earlier travel guides. It was based primarily on the original Dinsmore guide, the format of which editor Edward Vernon had obtained permission to use.

A typical monthly *Official Guide*, from 1893 included: an "Index to Advertisers," "General Index of Railroad and Steamship Lines," advertisements for hand cars, artificial limbs, steamship lines, European and American Railroads, cast iron pipe, locomotives, sleeping cars, train order signals, wheels, axles, car seats, locomotive driving wheels, farm tools, rails, and railway supplies. There was a section of "General Railway Information" containing railroad news, railroad news releases and editorial comments, an "Official List of Names of the General Ticket, Passenger Agents, and Officers Connected with the Passenger Department of the Principal Railways &c," a list of "Dividing Points" for "Standard Time Sections" in the United States, an important railway map section printed on pink pages, and the "Official Railway Time-Tables" of all railroads in the United States. For the ticket agent and traveler, no greater resource could be found!

The format of the *Official Guide* was a brown card-cover book measuring 5" by 7 1/2." By the 1880s, its size increased to 7" by 10." The standard time clock's graphic and the bold *"Official Guide"* lettering on the cover made it immediately recognizable. Over the years, it increased in thickness, reaching its largest size in the early 1930s, with each monthly edition containing more than 1,800 pages of schedules and maps for American railroads and steamship lines. These editions were almost three inches thick!

The slow decline of passenger service brought changes to this respected travel guide. As passenger trains were discontinued and shipping lines became fewer, the guide's pages were also reduced in number. By the 1960s, the guide was a ghost of its former self, containing only a few hundred pages. It continues publication today, however, in its role of providing AMTRAK timetables and fast freight schedule information to shippers.

GREAT NIAGARA FALLS ROUTE!

BETWEEN NEW YORK, BOSTON,

PHILADELPHIA AND CHICAGO.

GREAT WESTERN RAILWAY OF CANADA.

READ!

TOURISTS and pleasure-seekers should travel by this Railway, and every visitor to the

UNITED STATES OF AMERICA

Should not fail to see the great Suspension Bridge which connects that wonderful country with the

DOMINION OF CANADA.

From this marvelous bridge, which extends 800 feet across the great Niagara river, the

FALLS OF NIAGARA

can be seen in all their beauty.

This railway, with the New York Central, Boston & Albany, and the Michigan Central Railways, form the shortest route between

and has running over it the magnificent Parlor, Drawing Room, Dining and

PALACE SLEEPING CARS

for which this continent is so famous. All its stock is of the best description, fitted with Westinghouse Air Brake, Miller Platform and Coupling, and every other requisite for the safety and comfort of travelers. There are also first class REFRESHMENT ROOMS on the route. The line passes through the Garden of Canada, a portion of the road running through scenery that is termed by travelers

"THE SWITZERLAND OF CANADA,"

And situated upon it are the cities of Toronto, Hamilton, and London, and its western terminus is the beautiful city of Detroit.

Passengers can travel also by the Erie Railway from New York, and connect closely with all Express Trains on this line at Suspen-

Railroad listings and map from Rand McNally & Co.'s Railway Guide, June, 1876. Very Rare.

Rand McNally Co's Railway Guide

Rand McNally & Co. was an early American cartography and printing firm engaged in creating maps for railroads. It was natural that the firm would also publish an independent travel guide. In 1870, Rand McNally began publication of *The Travelers' Hand Book to All Railway & Steamboat Lines of North America*. Its size and format were similar to other guides of the era. Like the early *Official Railway Guide*, it was printed monthly as a card-covered book measuring approximately 5" by 7 1/2." Its popularity was based on exquisitely detailed and accurate maps of railroads, including the regular feature of a large fold-out railroad map of the United States. On occasion, special colored maps were also printed. The June, 1876, edition included a colored map of Fairmont Park in Philadelphia, touting the nation's upcoming Centennial celebration.

Rand McNally's distinguished itself from other travel guides by including a pink-paged "Travelers' Hand Book Section" in each monthly issue. This section contained brief descriptions of principal cities along railroad lines, including location, population, railroads serving them, hotels, business interests, and public halls. Ads for local hotels and businesses were also included. This was the kind of information other travel guides printed separately, in companion tourist guides.

Other Early Guides 1850s - 1880s

The Mackey ABC Guide, "Issued Every Monday" by the ABC Guide Co. of New York City. Established in 1862, this weekly pamphlet-style travel guide included schedules for railroads, steamboats and steamship lines serving New York City.

New York and the East: Boat and Rail, an early, very rare travel guide published by Billstein and Son of New York in the 1850s.

Three additional guides known to the author but for which no examples could be obtained were:

Disturnell's Railroad, Steamboat and Telegraph Guide, an eastern regional guide established in 1846.

Doggett's Railroad Guide and Gazetteer, an eastern regional guide established in 1848.

Lloyd's American Guide, established in 1857.

Regional Travel Guides 1880s - 1940s

These were independently published books of regional public timetables with local hotel or merchant advertising.

Later Rand McNally Publications

In the 1890s, Rand McNally focused its mapmaking and printing efforts on providing railroads with travel brochures, route guides, tickets, and elaborate timetables, becoming one of the most popular railway printing firms in the United States. Many of the finest surviving examples of these types of publications are those produced by Rand McNally. Publication of *Rand McNally & Co's Railway Guide* was continued after the turn of the century by The American Railway Guide Company as the "Western Section" of the *Travelers Railway Guide*.

Travelers Railway Guide — Western Section

By the turn of the century, NAGPTA's *Travelers' Official Guide of the Railways* had become a large, detailed book of schedules used primarily by railroad and steamship ticket agents. The general public still needed a travel guide that could be easily carried and referred to. This void was filled with publications like *Travelers Railway Guide*. Formerly published as *Rand McNally's Railway Guide*, the *Travelers Railway Guide, Western Section* was published by The American Railway Guide Company of Chicago, as a "Sectional Edition of the Official Railway Guide." It was a condensed regional edition printed by arrangement with The National Railway Publication Company, publishers of the industry-endorsed *Official Guide*, an arrangement attesting to its accuracy and to the fact that by this time in history, no other travel guide was competing.

The *Travelers Railway Guide, Western Section* was published as a card-covered booklet measuring 6" x 8." It ceased publication in the 1930s.

Travelers Railway Guide — Eastern Section

The *Travelers Railway Guide, Eastern Section* was published by the Knickerbocker Guide Company, and had formerly been published as *Appletons' Railway Guide*. Reflecting the transition that had

308

Entered according to Act of Congress in the year 1894, by THE A B C GUIDE Co., in the office of the Librarian of Congress at Washington, D. C.

The MACKEY  GUIDE.

ESTABLISHED 1862.   PUBLISHED BY   REORGANIZED 1892.

ISSUED EVERY MONDAY.   THE ABC GUIDE CO. [INCORPORATED]

OFFICE 48 & 50 DUANE ST. N.Y. PRICE $6.00 PER. YEAR IN ADVANCE. THO'S. A. O'KEEFE, PRES.

Vol. 40.   For Week Ending MAY 25, 1895.   **No. 2.**

Official Closing of Foreign Mails at the New York General Post Office.

MONDAY. 20

MAILS for COLON and PANAMA, (specially addressed only), per Steamer ALLIANCA, close at Nine-thirty (9.30) a.m. SUPPLEMENTARY MAIL TO 10.30 A.M.

MAILS for CENTRAL AMERICA (except Costa Rica) and SOUTH PACIFIC Ports, and specially addressed for Guatemala, (via Colon), per Steamer NEWPORT, close at Ten (10) a.m. SUPPLEMENTARY MAIL TO 11 A.M.

MAILS for PROGRESSO, also specially addressed for other parts of Mexico, per Steamer CIUDAD CONDAL, close at Ten (10) a.m.

MAILS for BELIZE, PUERTO CORTEZ and GUATEMALA, (via New Orleans), close at Three (3) p.m.

MAILS for JAMAICA, per Steamer BARNSTABLE (via Boston), close at Nine (9) p.m.

TUESDAY. 21

MAILS for GERMANY, DENMARK, SWEDEN, NORWAY and RUSSIA; also specially addressed for other European countries, per Steamer LAHN, close at One (1) p.m. SUPPLEMENTARY MAIL IS RECEIVED AT G. P. O. TO 2.30 P.M., AND ON DOCK, SECOND ST., HOBOKEN, UNTIL 3.50 P.M.

MAILS for FORTUNE ISLAND and HAYTI, per Steamer ATHOS, close at Ten (10) a.m. SUPPLEMENTARY MAIL TO 10.30 A.M.

MAILS for COSTA RICA, (via New Orleans); also BLUEFIELDS (via Mobile), close at Three (3) p.m.

MAILS for NEWFOUNDLAND, (via Halifax), close at Eight-thirty (8.30) p.m.

Mails via San Francisco close on dates given at New York Post Office at 6.30 p.m., as follows: For China, Japan and East Indies, May 28th, June 9 17 and 27th. For Hawaiian Islands, June 9th. For Australia, (except those for West Australia, which are forwarded via Europe), New Zealand, Hawaiian, Fiji and Samoan Islands, May 24th For Society Islands May 25th. These mails close at San Francisco six days later.

WEDNESDAY. 22

MAILS for EUROPE, per Steamer NEW YORK, close at Eight (8) a.m. SUPPLEMENTARY MAIL AT G. P. O. TO 10 A.M., AND ON DOCK, FULTON ST., N. R., TO 10.50 A.M.

DIRECT MAIL for BELGIUM, (specially addressed), per Steamer FRIESLAND, close at Ten (10) a.m.

MAILS for EUROPE, per Steamer MAJESTIC, close at Twelve (12) noon. SUPPLEMENTARY MAIL AT G. P. O. TO 1.30 P.M., AND ON DOCK, W. 10TH ST., TO 2.50 P.M.

MAILS for GRENADA TRINIDAD, TOBAGO, DEMERARA and PARAMARIBO, per Steamer GULF OF AKABA, may close on this date at Twelve (12 noon.

MAILS for NASSAU, N. P., (specially addressed only), per Steamer ANTILIA, close at One (1) p.m. SUPPLEMENTARY MAIL TO 1.30 P.M.

MAILS for CUBA, per Steamer VIGILANCIA, close at One (1) p.m.

MAILS for PUERTO CORTEZ, (via New Orleans); also BOCAS DEL TORA, (via Mobile), close at Three (3) p.m.

MAILS for PORT ANTONIO, per Steamer ETHELRED (via Boston), close at Nine (9) p.m.

MAILS, via VANCOUVER, for CHINA and JAPAN (specially addressed only) close daily up to May 27th at 6.30 p.m., leaving Vancouver seven (7) days later. For AUSTRALIA (except West Australia), HAWAII and FIJI ISLANDS, close daily to June 9th at 6.30 p.m.

THURSDAY. 23

MAILS for EUROPE, per Steamer NORMANIA, close at Eight (8) a.m. SUPPLEMENTARY MAIL AT G. P. O. TO 9.30 A.M., AND ON DOCK, FIRST ST., HOBOKEN, TO 10.50 A.M.

MAILS for NASSAU, N. P., and SANTIAGO, CUBA, per Steamer NIAGARA, close at One (1) p.m. SUPPLEMENTARY MAIL TO 1.30 P.M.

MAILS for BERMUDA, per Steamer ORINOCO, close at One (1) p.m. SUPPLEMENTARY MAIL TO 1.30 P.M.

MAILS, via TACOMA, for CHINA and JAPAN (specially addressed only), close at the General Post Office daily up to May 28th, at Six-thirty (6.30) p.m.

FRIDAY. 24

MAILS for BOCAS DEL TORA, (via Mobile), close at Three (3) p.m.

CLOSING OF FOREIGN MAILS FOR THE WEEK AT SUB-STATIONS.

	TUESDAY. (Lahn.)	WEDNESDAY. New York.)	WEDNESDAY. (Majestic.)	THURSDAY. (Normania.)	THURSDAY. (———)	SATURDAY La Gascogne.	SATURDAY. (Fulda.)	SATURDAY. (Etruria.)
A	12.20 p.m	6.45 a.m	11.30 a.m	6.45 a.m		A ... 1.30 a.m	A ... 6.45 a.m	A ... 11.30 a.m
B	12.30 p.m	6.55 a.m	11.30 a.m	6.55 a.m	B	B Fri. 10.21 p.m	B ... 6 55 a.m	B ... 11 30 a.m
C	12.15 p.m	6.45 a.m	11.15 a.m	6.45 a.m	C Fri. 10.05 p m	C ... 6.45 a.m	C ... 11.15 a.m
D	12.10 p.m	6.35 a.m	11.10 a.m	6.35 a.m	D	D ... 1.30 a.m	D ... 6 35 a.m	D ... 11 10 a.m
E	12.07 p.m	6 22 a.m	11 07 a.m	6.72 a.m	E	E Fri. 10.20 p.m	E ... 6 22 a.m	E ... 11 07 a.m

MAILS for BRAZIL and LA PLATA COUNTRIES (specially addressed only), per Steamer CATANIA (via Baltimore), close at One (1) a.m.

DIRECT FRENCH MAIL; also Swiss, Italian, Spanish, Portuguese, Turkish and British India closed mails, (via Havre), per Steamer LA GASCOGNE, close at Two (2) a.m. No SUPPLEMENTARY MAIL.

MAILS for BRAZIL and LA PLATA COUNTRIES; also specially addressed for NORTH BRAZIL, per Steamer CUVIER, close at Six-Thirty (6.30) a.m.

MAILS for ST. THOMAS, ST. CROIX, LEEWARD and WINDWARD ISLANDS, MARTINIQUE and BARBADOES; per Steamer FONTABELLE, may close on this date at Nine-Thirty (9.30) a.m. SUPPLEMENTARY MAIL TO 10.00 A.M.

SATURDAY. 25

MAILS for GERMANY; also specially addressed for other European countries, per Steamer FULDA, close at Eight (8) a.m. SUPPLEMENTARY MAIL AT G. P. O. TO 9.30 A.M., AND ON DOCK, SECOND ST., HOBOKEN, TO 10.50 A.M.

MAILS for FORTUNE ISLAND, JAMAICA and SAVANILLA; also specially addressed for other COLOMBIAN PORTS, per Steamer AILSA, close at Ten (10) a.m. SUPPLEMENTARY MAIL TO 10.30 A.M.

MAILS for YUCATAN, CAMPECHE, TABASCO and CHIAPAS, and specially addressed for other Mexican States and Cuba, per Steamer YUMURI, close at Ten-thirty (10.30) a.m. No SUPPLEMENTARY MAIL.

MAILS for VENEZUELA, CURACOA and SAVANILLA, and specially addressed for other COLUMBIAN PORTS, per Steamer PHILADELPHIA, close at Eleven (11) a.m. SUPPLEMENTARY MAIL TO 11.30 A.M.

MAILS for NORWAY, (specially addressed only), per Steamer THINGVALLA, close at Eleven (11) a.m.

MAILS for the NETHERLANDS, (specially addressed only), per Steamer VEENDAM, close at Eleven (11) a.m.

MAILS for EUROPE, per Steamer ETRURIA, close at Twelve (12) m. SUPPLEMENTARY MAIL AT G. P. O. TO 1.30 P.M., AND ON DOCK, CLARKSON ST., N. R., TO 2.50 P.M.

MAILS for PORTO RICO, per Steamer FORT WILLIAM, may close on this date at Twelve (12) m.

DIRECT MAIL for SCOTLAND, (specially addressed), per Steamer CITY OF ROME, close at Two (2) p.m.

(CONTINUED ON PAGE 306.)

Cover and advertisement from The Mackey ABC Guide, May 25, 1895. Rare.

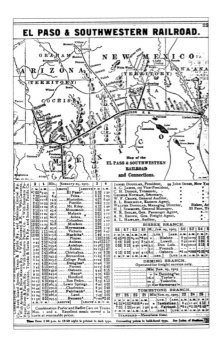

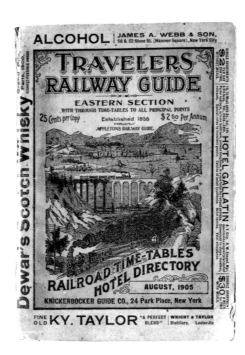

Cover and timetable with map from Travelers Railway Guide, Eastern Section, August, 1905, and Western section, January, 1918. Rare.

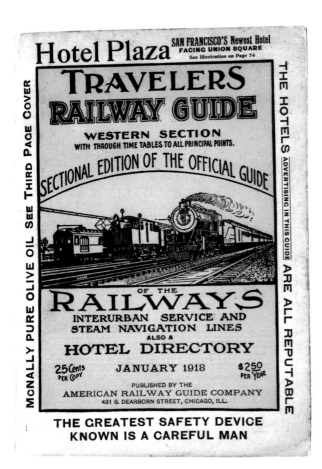

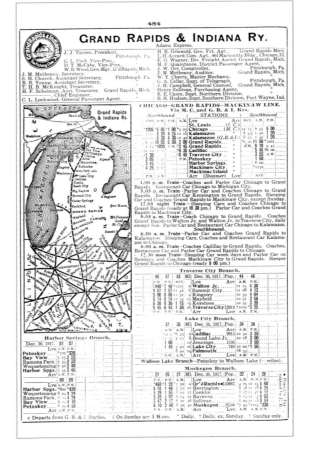

been made by this time from the publication of tourist guides only by independent publishers, the August, 1905, edition included a "List of Summer Resort Books" (brochures) published by the railroads themselves (See Chapter Six).

The Baby Pathfinder Railway Guide

This small, pocket railway guide enjoyed enormous popularity as a complete listing of schedules for railroads in the densely populated northeastern United States. For revenues, it relied on the sales of single copies and subscriptions, with only a few ads in each issue. Begun in 1885, *The Pathfinder* was "issued the fifteenth of each month by the New England Railway Publishing Company" of Boston. This railway guide measured 3 1/4" x 5."

The Railway Hand Book

Close in size and format to *The Pathfinder*, the *Railway Hand Book* was published by The Railway Hand Book Publishing Company of San Francisco on the first of every month. The May, 1891, edition included the complete schedules for "The Transportation Systems of the Pacific Coast." Its pages offer a wonderful look at western history, with ads for legendary railroads like the "Virginia and Truckee," the "Carson and Colorado," the "Nevada County Narrow Gauge," and the "Eureka and Palisade Railway." Also included in its small pages were advertisements for hotels, resorts, land, coffee, breweries, and stage lines along with a "Timetable of Cable and Horse Car Lines" in San Francisco.

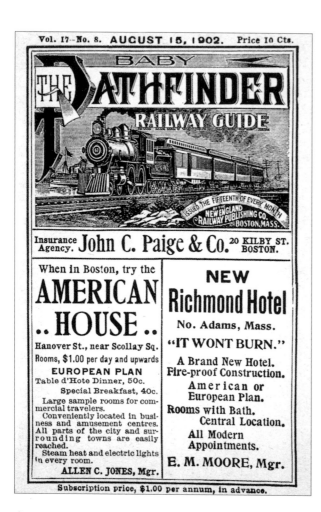

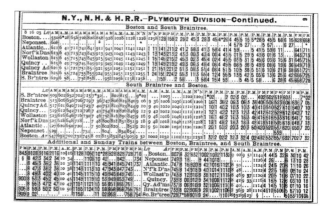

Cover and timetable from
The Baby Pathfinder
Guide, August 15, 1902.
Rare.

Other Regional Guides 1880s - 1940s

The Railroad Gazetteer, Official Organ of Railway, Steamship and Stage Lines of the Pacific Coast, published in San Francisco around the turn of the century.

Russell's Railway Guide and Hotel Directory, Western Section, a midwestern regional guide begun in 1889 by Russell's Railway Guide Company of Cedar Rapids, Iowa and published through the 1930s. It included the schedules of railroads serving Iowa, Illinois, Nebraska, Minnesota, Wisconsin, North and South Dakota, northern Missouri and northern Michigan. The hotel directory included many illustrated ads of hotels found in these states. This popular guide was known as "The Travelers Red Book."

Russell's Railway Guide and Hotel Directory, Southwest Section, a southwestern regional guide, published as above. It included schedules of railroads serving Texas, Louisiana, Arkansas, Missouri, Oklahoma, Kansas and Nebraska.

The Official Utah State Railway Guide, published as "Everybody's City Guide" by The F.W. Gardiner Co. Press, publishers of two Salt Lake City newspapers around the turn of the century.

Kanney's Monthly Steam and Electric Railway Guide, containing complete schedules for trains running between Chicago and surrounding cities in Illinois, Michigan and Indiana. Published by Kanney Advertising System, Publishers, Michigan City, Indiana, around the turn of the century.

The Texas, Oklahoma & Indian Territory Official Railway and Hotel Guide, containing "Complete Time Tables of All Railways in Texas, Oklahoma and Indian Territory, Together with A Reliable Hotel Directory, also A Complete List of Railway Stations, Showing Population, Post Offices, Telegraph and Telephone Station and Express Offices." Endorsed "By All Railway Lines," this guide was published by The Texas Railway Guide Co. of St. Louis around the turn of the century.

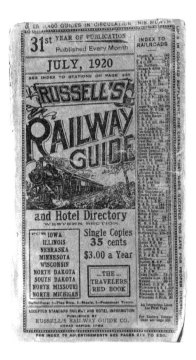

Russell's Railway Guide and Hotel Directory, Western Section, July, 1920. Rare.

The Pathfinder of the Union Pacific, published from the 1880s through the turn of the century, this guide included local and through timetables of the Union Pacific Railroad along with those of connecting railroads, stagecoach, and steamship lines. It was very similar to Union Pacific public timetables from the same period, but was published as a "travel guide" edition.

As the number of different railroads declined, travel guides were less in demand. By the turn of the century, many smaller railroads were absorbed into larger systems. The Depression and the success of automobiles had, by the end of World War II, also greatly reduced the number of passenger trains. As a result, railroads produced and distributed more of their own public timetables, tourist guides and travel brochures. Independently published travel guides would soon become a thing of the past.

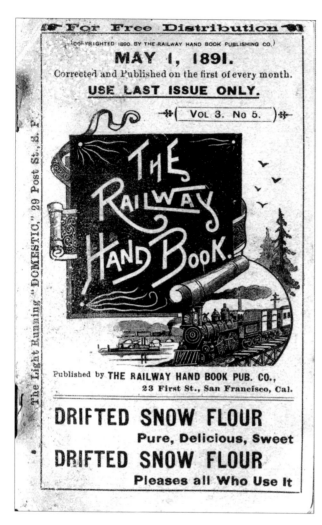

The Railway Hand Book,
May 1, 1891. Rare.

Union Pacific Pathfinder,
September, 1888 (above),
and a later version from
1901. Rare.

Kanney's Monthly Steam and Electric Railway Guide, March, 1910. Rare.

The Official Utah State Railway Guide (center), June, 1915. Rare.

The Texas, Oklahoma & Indian Territory Official Railway and Hotel Guide, February, 1904. Rare.

Peck-Judah, a publicity house noted several times in the text as distributors of timetables, published their own travel guides from the turn of the century to the 1930s. Rare.

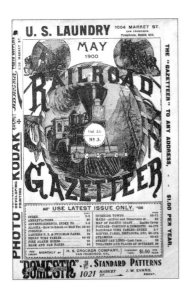

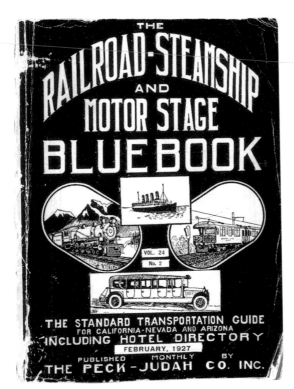

The Railway Gazetteer, May, 1900. Rare.

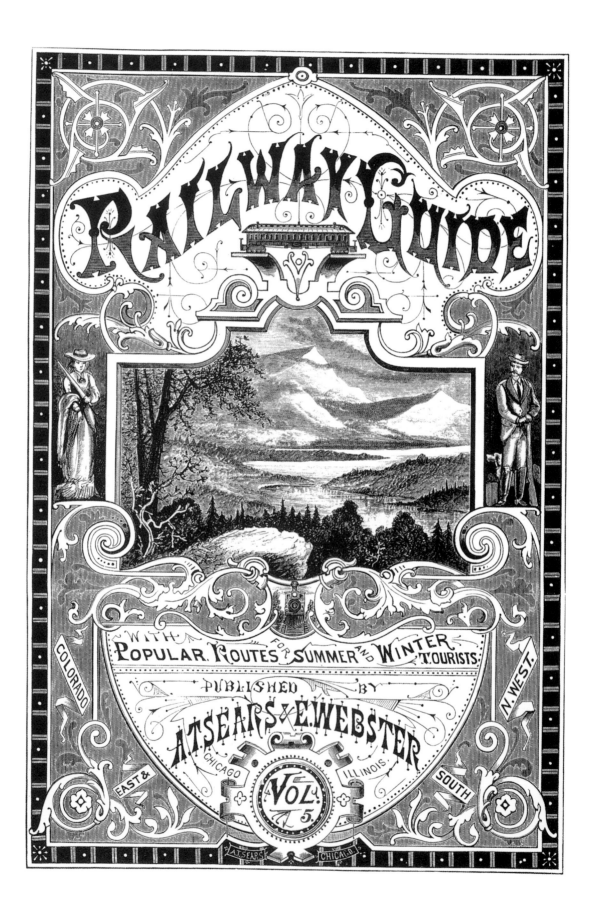

RAILWAY GUIDE

WITH POPULAR ROUTES FOR SUMMER AND WINTER TOURISTS

PUBLISHED BY

A. T. SEARS & E. WEBSTER

CHICAGO ILLINOIS

VOL. 5

COLORADO

N. WEST

EAST &

SOUTH

A. T. SEARS. CHICAGO.

CHAPTER SIX
TOURIST GUIDES AND TRAVEL BROCHURES

RAILROADS emerged in an America rapidly growing beyond its earlier boundaries. Those vast areas of the country still unvisited or unsettled appealed strongly to the imaginations of Americans. They were enthralled by the natural beauty described in the accounts and drawings of early adventurers and explorers who had travelled the seemingly boundless continent.

As railroads reached these areas, railroad-related publications began to provide travel information and advertising about specific regions and their towns and geographical features. Previously such information had appeared mostly in local newspapers and periodicals, and was not available to a broader national audience. These travel publications found a ready response.

With a system of competing railroads now accessing both agricultural land and scenic areas, settlers and travelers could reach these places with relative ease. During these years after midcentury, transporting tourists and settlers became the most lucrative part of railroad business.

Early tour guides, such as this 1882 A.T. Sears & Webster guide shown here (imprinted hard-bound cloth cover) and at left, contained florid narratives written just as much for entertainment as for use in actual travel. Rare.

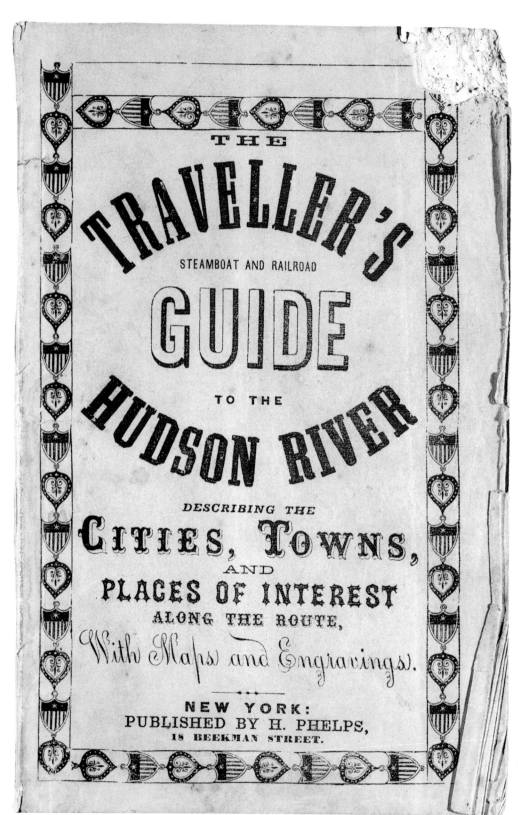

THE

TRAVELLER'S

STEAMBOAT AND RAILROAD

GUIDE

TO THE

HUDSON RIVER

DESCRIBING THE

CITIES, TOWNS,

AND

PLACES OF INTEREST

ALONG THE ROUTE,

With Maps and Engravings.

NEW YORK:
PUBLISHED BY H. PHELPS,
18 BEEKMAN STREET.

This very early travel guide described life along the Hudson River in the 1850s. Very Rare.

Independently Published Tourist Guides

As noted in Chapter Five (Travel Guides), many early travel guides included limited information and advertising related to the regions and locales they covered, but for the most part they were intended solely as compendiums of timetables for planning travel over different railroad lines. However, some independent publishers of early travel guides printed travel information and regional advertising in *tourist guides*. These were designed to be used as companions to travel guides. Only condensed or portions of timetables, if any at all, were included in tourist guides.

Some tourist guides were called travel guides as well. The term was used interchangeably, with one exception: Travel guides (books of timetables) did not usually include "tourist" or "route" in their titles; tourist guides often did so. Generally, the travel guide was more utilitarian since it was focused on timetables, while the tourist guide contained broader additional information.

These independently published tourist guides, supplemented by local periodical advertising and information, were the predecessors of the later railroad-published travel publications. (By the 1880s, railroads were publishing their own tourist guides and travel brochures.) Tourist guides were popular from the 1870s into the 1890s. Many early tourist guides printed as "companions" to travel guides were small booklets. Others were popular-sized (9" x 11") hard bound books. These guides appealed to potential travelers, but were written just as much for entertainment as they were for actual use in travel. The 1882 guide quoted below exemplifies this dual purpose.

Descriptions

Early tourist guides relied heavily on the written word. In many, words painted beautiful pictures, often with verbose style and grandiose terminology. *Railway Guide with Popular Routes for Summer and Winter Tourists*, published by A.T. Sears & E. Webster in 1882, typifies this style in describing the Yellowstone Park's Old Faithful geyser and its environs:

The Geyser Region *is an indescribable passion of nature. Its mysteries awe the most venturesome, and even silence the voice of arbitrary science. In these flinty, elevated ledges of stalagmite, the strata are penetrated by circular wells, which hold beautifully clear, ultramarine water, which one might suppose innocent, spring-fed curiosities. But several times a day, perhaps, this harmless appearing liquid begins to bubble, boil and seethe, while distant phantasmal groans seem issuing from rock crevices. The earth is seized with horror-stricken tremblings, a terrific concussion ensues, clouds of heavy steam rush upward, a gigantic column of water darts heavenward, while jets diverge from its apex in several direction. The very universe seems hushed and awe-stricken while this angry demonstration exhausts itself.*

The Grand Geyser *is the most sublime and mighty type of its kind in the world. The steam clouds rise 500 feet in mid air, while the solid column of water reaches an altitude of 90 feet, surmounted by five water jets from its apex, which attain a height of 350 feet from the ground, surrounded by a celestial halo. The coloring of the rocks in this section is beyond the conception of the most sanguine fancy. Their brilliancy is startling, especially where they are wet most of the time. The rock cavities are filled with little pools, having margins of silica the color of silver. This water being hot, precipitates delicate saffron, coral-like beads, which form into strands and loops and clusters. Other cavities are fringed with meshes of the most delicate lace or fairy frost work. Diminutive columns arise from their depths, crested with small rock tablets. Small white, oval pebbles are gathered in diminutive mounds, as if placed there by human hands. Here and there are stalagmites formed entirely of the most lovely, ingenious and delicate yellow frost work. One of the most remarkable features of this geyser action is the production of rainbows when the water leaps into the golden sunlight.*

Engraved Illustrations

Early travel guides were not completely without images. Some early travel guides used beautifully detailed engravings to supplement their verbal descriptions. Many of the earliest engravings were created by artists from eyewitness accounts of others. Features in these second-hand illustrations were often inaccurate or disproportional. As railroad expansion facilitated travel, adventurous artists were soon able to travel to see their subjects first-hand. They went freelance or under commissions from publishers. Many of these engravings are highly accurate and, where no early photographs exist of the area, of great value to historians today.

One of the most common images was the panoramic view, especially from mountaintops. Almost all engravings and later, photographs, used in railroad travel publications favored this perspective. The popularity of the panoramic image also influenced the writing and graphics of many tourist guides. The *Railway Panoramic Guide* published by the Boston and Albany Railroad in 1878 featured "A Panoramic description of the Cities, Towns and Villages, including Number of Miles, Fare, Bridges, Rivers, Public Buildings, and all Objects of Interest along the Road inviting the Attention of Passengers over the Main Line and its Chief Branches."

Stories

Travel narratives were another important part of early tourist guides. Entertaining storylines followed characters through travel adventures:

Jack Galloway revels in the proud distinction of being the cousin of our family. That accounts for the fact that we are aware that he is the most chivalrous sportsman who ever sallied forth with rod and line. Not that we can positively state what his actual success has been, since none of us ever beheld him capture a leviathan of the deep or a minnow of the shallows. But Jack has a verbal volume of brilliant experience for the entertainment and benefit of his numerous friends, which is remarkably convincing. We admit that he has been unfortunate in the selection of bait and location on many occasions, but we never knew him to give his undivided attention to the amusement, being unattended by companions to distract his purpose, but he returned laden with spoils and triumph.

It may be an "annual epidemic" or a periodical frenzy that attacks Jack as soon as early summer time smiles over the land. We observe the symptoms through the spring and the culmination is reached as soon as circumstances and weather will permit him to take advantage of the summer fishing season and wildwood adventure.

As usual, he was looking over the records of the "clubs"—he is quite the leader of several—during the initiatory progress of his mania. He imparted the conclusion at last, to his immediate family circle that he had decided upon a tournament field. The library table continued to be burdened with maps and charts and tourist's books however, and Jack turned them over and over in an absent sort of way, disturbing his dainty, pretty sister who had been endeavoring to glean the morning news from the "Daily."

"You actually drive me wild," she quoth at last.

"Will you never cease that ghastly rustling? I thought you had decided upon a location, or section, or whatever you term the place of your horrible pleasure! I really expected peace in this house after the stupendous question was settled."

Grace is naturally impatient, and poor Jack's easy-going good nature always exasperated her. His carelessness enraged her.

"Yes—y-e-s"—making a desperate jab at a portrayed lake with his pencil, "but I must get there, Grace! I glance over the different routes, and before I can concentrate my thoughts—"

"Ah!" she exclaimed with a scornful shrug of her round shoulders, "that must be a Herculean task!"

"And select one," he went on penitently, "I forget my object in contemplation of the sport I shall enjoy at Lake Minnetonka, and—"Minnetonka!" cried Grace springing from her chair and running over to him, "are you going there there?"

"Yes, Grace, and—"

"Dear Jack, take me with you, please!"

Such effervescence on Grace's part towards him, was suspicious. He had never heard of such a hereditary horror, but he had heard "they" frequently changed their sentiments in peculiar out breaks. He glanced uneasily towards the door, back again to Grace—but her eyes were filled with a lovely, entreating light; her red lips were

APPROACH TO YELLOWSTONE NATIONAL PARK, SOUTH FORK OF THE MADISON, REACHED VIA THE U.P.RY.

SHEEP ROCK AND POINTS OF OQUIRRH, GREAT SALT LAKE, UTAH, REACHED VIA U.P.RY.

APPROACH TO YELLOWSTONE NATIONAL PARK, HENRYS LAKE AND THE TETONS, REACHED VIA U.P.RY.

THE GEYSERS, YELLOWSTONE NATIONAL PARK, REACHED VIA U.P.RY.

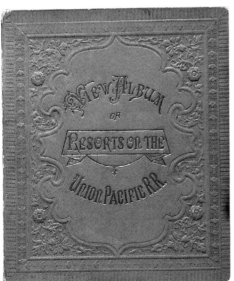
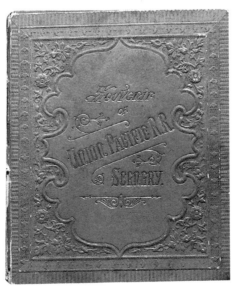

Beginning in the 1870s, railroads published picture albums, often with imprinted covers, as guides and souvenirs. Shown are interior and imprinted covers from three Union Pacific tourist guides. Very Rare.

parted in a sweet, tender smile; and her pretty little hand was resting caressingly on his shoulder.

"Smothered if I don't!" he exclaimed, his warm heart throbbing tumultuously. "Grace, you are awfully nice when you wish to be. Why cannot you always be so?"

"You do get so rough—no—so—com no—

"(So "common" she almost says, which is a harsh insult to a gentleman, especially a sportsman!)

"I'm a grizzly—I know it! never mind—let us seek a way, a path thereto."

"How fortunate!" rippled Grace, running over for her great city daily, "Now just listen to this—"

Thus began the journey for these two 19th-century travelers, as depicted in this 1882 tourist guide. The story line continues to follow their travels, with frequent departures from their amusing banter to describe the scenery they see and experiences they have along the Northern Pacific Railroad's "Albert Lea Route."

These narratives in early tourist guides provide a revealing look into many aspects of American life during the latter part of the 19th century. The tone of their writing set the mood for the adventurous travel spirit characteristic of Americans during this period of rapid expansion.

Souvenir Picture Books

As techniques for printing illustrations improved, other tourist guides appeared in the 1870s that were simply captioned books of pictures. Their titles indicated that they were intended not only as guides for travelers, but also as souvenirs. Early pictorial souvenir guides had ornate, embossed card covers. Their fold-out pages were filled with artists' renderings of important points along the rail line. By the 1910s and 20s, souvenir guides were printed in a photo album format. Colorized photo illustrations with captions were glued on large black pages that were string-tied together in an album. Most common of this style were those published by the Denver and Rio Grande Western

Photo albums such as this 1915 Southern Pacific Shasta Route were printed for travelers in the 1910s and 1920s. Rare.

Railroad with views of Colorado and the Rocky Mountains. This photo album format was also a favorite style for several other large railroads. The cover and title page of a souvenir album published by the Southern Pacific Railroad for "The Shasta Route" in 1915 grandly announces:

A SCENIC GUIDE BOOK, FROM SAN FRANCISCO, CALIFORNIA, TO PORTLAND, OREGON, ON THE ROAD OF A THOUSAND WONDERS—
The color illustrations shown in the following pages are all made expressly for this book from photographs taken by special artists of the most striking objects of interest, which abound to a remarkable extent along the Southern Pacific Railroad between San Francisco and Portland. Great care was taken to select only such views as every traveler actually sees along the line, so that the book truly forms a panorama of scenic wonders which is unrolled every day before the eyes of those who make this trip. Everyone desires to secure souvenirs of the journey, and, knowing this, we have endeavored to make this volume such a record of facts, and such a collection of beautiful, accurate and attractive views, that it will be recognized by all as the most appropriate and interesting souvenir of the journey. For sale only en route on the Shasta Route.

Sold only on the trains, these albums were prized possessions for travelers to share with friends and family.

Souvenir albums produced in the 1940s were collections of colored views in attractive folders. A set produced in 1944 titled "Scenic Grandeur of the West" was a "folio containing sixteen colored views of points of interest along Southern Pacific Lines.—These Attractive Views Are Suitable For Framing."

Picture books were also produced in the 1950s and 60s. These were beautiful color photo albums with postcard views of scenery along the line. As personal photography became more popular, souvenir picture books became much less common, but they can still be found on postcard racks in airports, bus stations, and AMTRAK depots.

Railroad-published Land and Travel Brochures

Railroads had two other profit goals by the late 1860s: land sales and tourist travel. In 1850, approximately 1.4 billion acres of public land in the Midwest and West had become available to settlers. (Native population excluded. Almost all settlers were first generation immigrants of European and African descent.) In order to sell this vast wilderness, the land had to be relatively low-cost. It also had to be made accessible.

Beginning in the 1860s, several laws helped accelerate growth into these large unsettled areas. The Homestead, Soldier's Homestead, Desert Land, and Timber and Stone acts all provided potential farmers, ranchers, and miners with opportunities to acquire government lands for free or at a very low cost. Settlers acquired millions of acres under the provisions of these laws.

It was the Railroad Land Grant Act of 1862, however, that made public land accessibility a reality. Under this law, railroads were granted large tracts of adjoining lands when rail construction was completed into unsettled regions of the Midwest and West. Intended primarily as an incentive for investors to fund a transcontinental railroad, the 1862 act also provided railroads with the motivation to expand into other wilderness areas of the Midwest and West. Investors hoped to profit from the sale of lands acquired. Railroads would eventually acquire four hundred million acres under the provisions of the Land Grant Act.

Railroads and investors knew there could be no profits from these lands without people to create the new markets necessary for freight traffic—primarily agricultural products and manufactured goods—which gave railroads their major support. Railroads needed to sell their newly acquired lands not only to stay in business, but also to pay investors a profit and provide capital for further expansions. Faced with the sudden need to sell so much land and at the same time to compete with free government lands, railroads made an unprecedented sales effort.

By the turn of the century, most independently published tourist guides had become mediums for local advertisers and provided only limited travel information. These covers and ads from the interior of *Whitlock's Guide to California*, 1907, and *The San Francisco and San Joaquin Valley Guide*, August, 1897, are typical examples of those from this era. Rare.

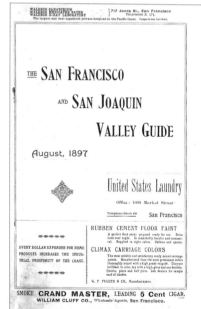

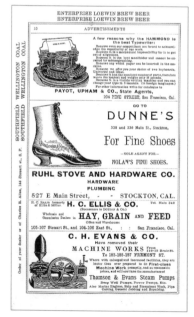

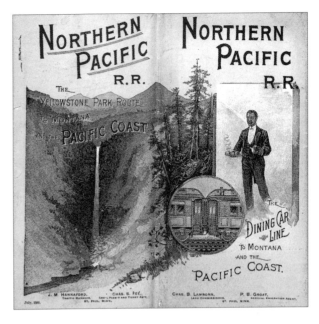

This July, 1889, Northern Pacific Railroad folder exemplifies the information saturation that public timetables had reached at this point in history. They included travel information, timetables, land sales, geographic and demographic information, along with a map, all in one folding brochure. Rare.

The title of this folder of the 1880s describes the nature of bends in the track on the famous Georgetown Loop in Colorado. This early travel brochure carries over the grandiose verbiage of narratives found in tourist guides published during this era. Rare.

This 1882 Oregon Railway and Navigation Company publication is an excellent early travel brochure example. Its panels include information on tourist routes, regions of the Northwest, and train schedules along with a full color map. Rare.

By the late 1860s they had gained enough advertising experience to know their ambitious land sale goals could not possibly be achieved through periodical advertisements alone, so land commissions and sales offices were established for the sole purpose of marketing railroad lands. Commissioners carried out well-organized advertising campaigns that included periodical, travel guide, tourist guide, and timetable advertising. Lands were offered at low cost with payments over time. Fictionalized stories about the successes found by settlers were published regularly to accompany ads in periodicals and tourist guides. Hundreds of thousands of land brochures were printed and distributed in the United States and Europe. Land commission advertising efforts eventually brought thousands of settlers into new areas served by railroads.

By 1890, the swift success of railroad land commissions' efforts had ended the pressing need to sell large amounts of land. (This amazing achievement is considered a landmark in marketing history.) Land commissions were dissolved or became part of railroad land departments. However, the availability of remaining lands for settlers and for industry continued to be advertised in public timetables and travel brochures.

Railroad-published Tourist Guides and Travel Brochures

By the 1870s, the potential for tourist travel was growing as fast as the population. Railroad lines reached well into the nation's beautiful forests, passing scenic lakes and rivers. Realizing the potential for tourism, railroads created an alliance with naturalists to set aside specific scenic areas as "National Parks." Railroads then built lines to these areas.

Beginning with Yellowstone National Park in 1872, others soon followed. By 1916 the National Park Service was created to organize and administer the parks. Eventually, park tourism became the major focus of travel advertising for many western railroads.

By the early 1880s, railroads had fully realized—partly because of their experience with land brochures—the realities and limitations of periodical advertising. It was still important, but it had become increasingly expensive. The large number of periodicals diluted advertising budgets, and the markets and population centers were many. Periodical pages were not focussed on railroads but contained much other advertising as well, including that for local merchants, stage lines, tradesmen, miners, teamsters, medicinal cures and machinery. Most local periodicals served only small areas. This limited marketing potential and the increased advertising costs of local periodicals forced railroads to provide information on their own. Better results could be achieved by marketing railroad travel and lands in their own brochures and travel folders.

Railroad advertising in periodicals continued, but became more general in nature. It appeared in fewer publications, mostly in those with larger circulations, and it now provided addresses for obtaining free travel brochures from the railroads.

Railroads experienced many of the same shortcomings with independently published tourist guides as they did with periodical advertising. In a more complex world, with many more places to go, tourist guide narratives had become too general. More factual information was needed than tourist guide publishers were willing to provide. The guides continued to exist, but in a different role: as a traveler's book of local advertising. Travel information about a particular area was provided as filler for the real focus of presenting local advertisements to travelers and settlers.

Also by the 1880s, travel information had become a large part of many public timetables. More than half a timetable might be travel information and small illustrations. A map might also take up to half. This left little room for train schedules. For all these reasons, railroad land and travel brochures finally ventured out on their own.

Travel Brochure Content and Format

The variety of travel brochure subjects is as diverse as there are places to go in the United States. Starting in the mid 1880s, the race was on to see which railroads could offer the most interesting itineraries and destinations in their travel brochures. The national parks were one theme, and over the years hundreds of different park brochures were printed.

The majority of travel brochures took advantage of the proven public timetable folder format: 4" x 9" folders or stapled booklets. Magazine-sized folders appeared in the 1920s, with full-color illustrations and photos made even more dramatic by their larger-sized pages. These served not only as solicitations, but as souvenirs. Beautiful color cover illustrations by leading artists and illustrators were used to attract attention. The artists included Thomas Moran, Maynard Dixon, Maurice Logan, and W.H. Bull. Inside pages were filled with black and white photographs providing real images of scenery and people. Narratives described scenery, tours, hotels and outdoor activities.

Railroad-published Route Guides and Maps

From the 1880s on, maps with travel information were also printed separately as travel brochures. These were called "route maps" or "route guides." They helped prospective travelers and settlers visualize locations. Information was included on the climate, what crops were being grown where, and with how much success. Points of scenic interest, history, and the best locations for hunting and fishing were also highlighted. Many route guides included sequential lists of towns and cities along the lines with vignettes of information about each: people, industry, population, elevation, climate, etc. A 1927 Southern Pacific Lines brochure titled "Wayside Notes — Sunset Route" states:

"These Wayside Notes have been prepared with the hope that they will add to the pleasure of your journey by pointing out historic landmarks and other places of scenic and romantic interest along the way."

These travel brochure route guides were also intended to help travelers pass the time during a long journey. A 1931 Union Pacific System route guide titled "Along the Union Pacific System" suggests on the cover:

"Take this folder with you on your trip."

Text continued on page 131.

The Adirondack Mountains were featured in this 1893 travel brochure published by the New York Central & Hudson River Railroad. One of the many interesting things in this travel brochure is the transitional mixed use of engravings and photographs. Rare.

COLOR PLATES

Public timetables

Denver and Rio Grande
Railroad, 1895. Rare.

Southern Pacific Railroad
Sunset Route, 1890. Rare.

Southern Pacific Railroad
Sunset Route, 1894. Rare.

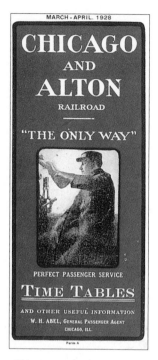

Chicago and Alton
Railroad, 1928. Rare.

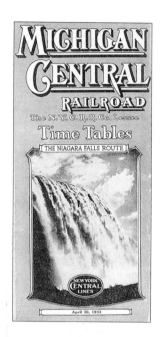

Michigan Central
Railroad, 1933. Rare.

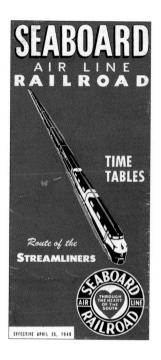

Seaboard Railroad, 1948.
Rare.

Northern Pacific Railroad,
1910. Rare.

Rock Island Railroad,
1917. Rare.

Southern Pacific Railroad,
1893. Rare.

Wabash Railroad, 1952.
Common.

Chicago, Milwaukee,
St.Paul and Pacific
Railway, 1939. Common.

GOLF, DOWN
MAINE

MAINE CENTRAL Railroad

COMPLETE TIME
TABLES

SUMMER SCHEDULE
SHOWING THROUGH PASSENGER CONNECTIONS
MAINE
NEW HAMPSHIRE—VERMONT
AND CANADA
EASTERN STANDARD TIME

TAKE A REST, DOWN
MAINE

MAINE CENTRAL Railroad

1931

COMPLETE
TIME TABLES

SUMMER SCHEDULE
SHOWING THROUGH PASSENGER CONNECTIONS
MAINE
NEW HAMPSHIRE—VERMONT
AND CANADA
EASTERN STANDARD TIME

Maine Central Railroad,
1931. Rare.

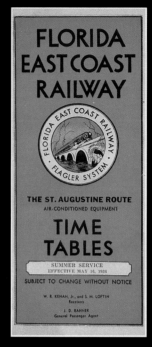

Florida East Coast Railway, 1936. Rare.

Atchison, Topeka & Santa Fe Railway, 1939. Rare.

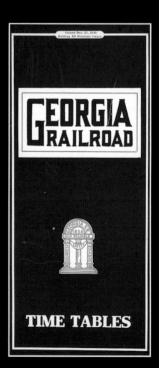

St. Louis-San Francisco Railway Company, 1965. Common

Georgia Railroad, 1934. Rare.

Pennsylvania Railroad, 1951. Common.

Chicago Great Western Railroad, 1917. Rare.

Minneapolis, St.Paul & Sault Ste. Marie Railway (The Soo Line), 1939. Rare.

Illinois Central Railroad, 1951. Common.

San Diego & Arizona Railway timetable/travel brochure, 1928. Rare.

Central Vermont Railway, 1941. Common.

Central of Georgia Railroad, 1938. Rare.

Gulf, Mobile & Ohio Railway, 1964. Common.

Missouri Pacific Lines, 1945. Common.

Kansas City Southern and Louisiana & Arkansas Railways, 1940. Rare.

Rock Island Lines, 1948. Common.

Coast Lines, Atchison, Topeka & Santa Fe Railway, 1915. Rare.

Nickel Plate Road, 1927. Rare.

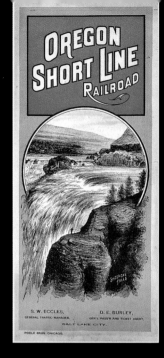

Oregon Short Line Railroad, 1900. Rare.

Western Pacific Railroad, 1900. Rare.

Nashville, Chattanooga and St.Louis Railway, 1941. Rare.

Chicago, Milwaukee and St.Paul Railway centerfold, 1927. Rare.

Kansas City Southern Railroad, 1934. Rare.

Alaska Railroad, 1923. Rare.

Northwestern Pacific Railroad, 1923. Rare.

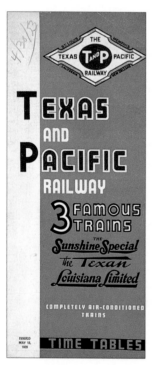

Texas & Pacific Railway, 1939. Rare.

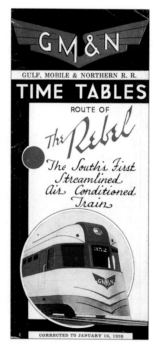

Gulf, Mobile & Northern Railroad, 1938. Rare.

Rail Road from the Atlantic to the Pacific
GRAND OPENING
OF THE

Union Pacific

RAIL ROAD,

PLATTE VALLEY ROUTE.

PASSENGER TRAINS LEAVE

OMAHA

ON THE ARRIVAL OF TRAINS FROM THE EAST.

THROUGH TO SAN FRANCISCO
In less than Four Days, avoiding the Dangers of the Sea!

Travelers for Pleasure, Health or Business
Will find a Trip over The Rocky Mountains Healthy and Pleasant.

LUXURIOUS CARS & EATING HOUSES
ON THE UNION PACIFIC RAIL ROAD.

PULLMAN'S PALACE SLEEPING CARS
RUN WITH ALL THROUGH PASSENGER TRAINS.

GOLD, SILVER AND OTHER MINERS!
Now is the time to seek your Fortunes in Nebraska, Wyoming, Arizona, Washington, Dakotah Colorado, Utah, Oregon, Montana, New Mexico, Idaho, Nevada or California.

CONNECTIONS MADE AT

CHEYENNE for DENVER, CENTRAL CITY & SANTA FE

AT OGDEN AND CORINNE FOR HELENA, BOISE CITY, VIRGINIA CITY, SALT LAKE CITY AND ARIZONA.

THROUGH TICKETS FOR SALE AT ALL PRINCIPAL RAILROAD OFFICES!

Be Sure they Read via Platte Valley or Omaha

Company's Office 72 La Salle St., opposite City Hall and Court House Square, Chicago.
CHARLES E. NICHOLS, Ticket Agent.

G. P. GILMAN,	JOHN P. HART,	J. BUDD,	W. SNYDER,
Southeastern Traveling Agent.	Gen'l Trav. Agt., 72 La Salle St., Chicago.	Gen'l Ticket Agt., Omaha, Neb.	Gen'l Superintendent, Omaha, Neb.

This poster commemorates the May 10, 1869 completion of the first transcontinental railroad. Its bold graphics made it one of the most famous early advertisements in America, widely recognized as such beyond the railroadiana collectors' community. Very Rare.

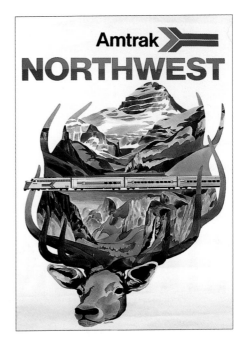

AMTRAK, *American Northwest, 1970s. Rare.*

Southern Pacific Railroad, "Golden State" passenger train of the 1950s. Rare.

Southern Pacific Railroad, Yosemite, 1920s. Rare.

Chicago & Northwestern System/Union Pacific Railroad, "City of Denver," 1948. Common.

New York Central Railroad, "The Mercury," 1940. Rare.

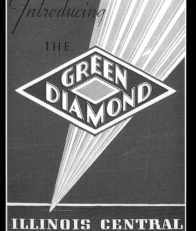

New York Central Railroad, "20th Century Limited," 1940. Rare.

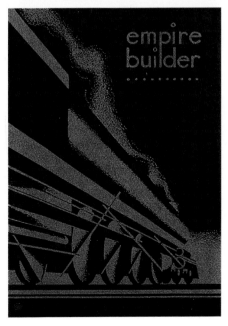

Santa Fe Railroad, "California Limited," 1927. Rare.

Early passenger train brochure for the Great Northern Railway's "Empire Builder." Rare.

Santa Fe Railroad, "The Golden Gate," 1938. Rare.

*Burlington/Rio Grande/Western Pacific Railroads, "The California Zephyr,"
1949. Common.*

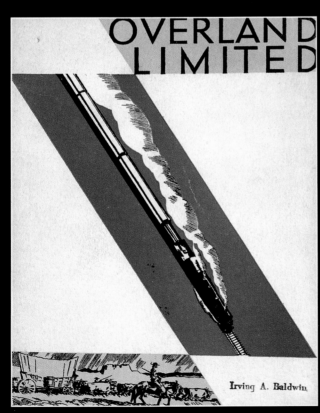

*Southern Pacific Railroad "The Overland Limited,"
1930. Rare.*

*Santa Fe Railroad "El Capitan"
streamliner, 1935. Common.*

The format and colors used in this 1937 Union Pacific Railroad passenger train brochure were part of the train design. Rare.

YOSEMITE VALLEY

SOUTHERN PACIFIC

YOSEMITE VALLEY

THOS. COOK & S
AGENTS
689 MARKET S
SAN FRAN

SOUTHERN PACIFIC

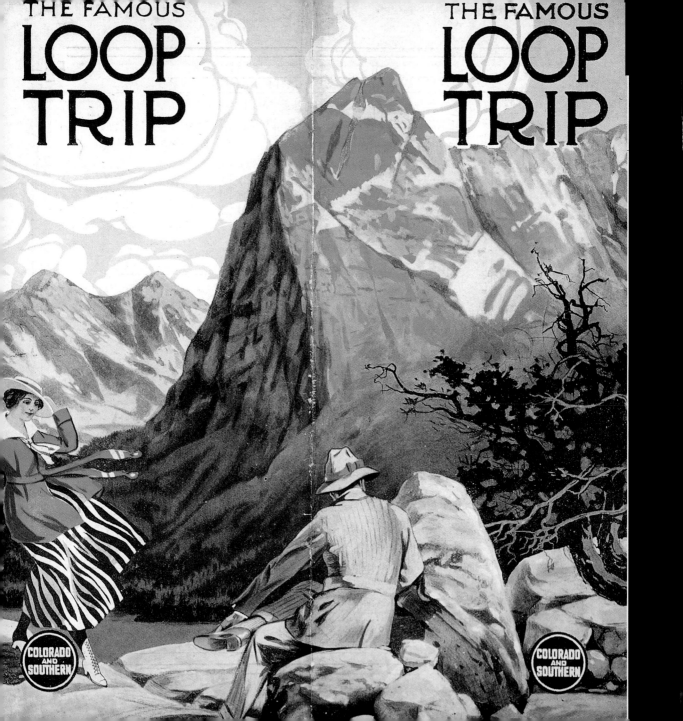

Yosemite Valley, California, Yosemite Valley Railroad Company, 1929. Rare.

Missouri Pacific Lines, c.1939. Rare.

A CENTURY OF PROGRESS EXPOSITION

CHICAGO 1933

TRAVEL BY TRAIN TRAVEL BY TRAIN

The Call of the Mountains

Vacations in
Glacier National Park
Waterton Lakes National Park

Glacier and Waterton Lakes National Parks, Great Northern Railway/Burlington Railroad, 1928. Rare.

Lake Tahoe, with cover art by Maurice Logan, Southern Pacific Lines, 1927. Rare.

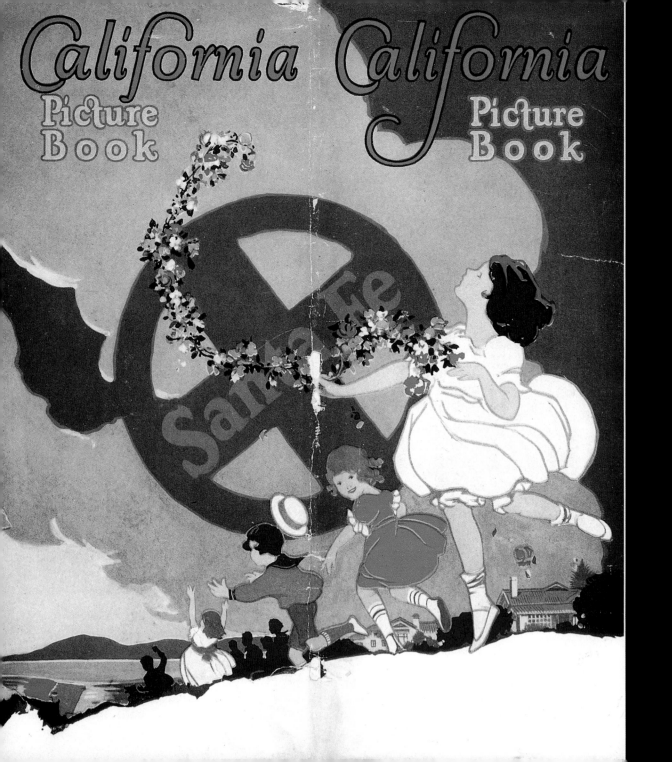

California, Southern Pacific Railroad, 1922. Rare.

The Federal government operated all railroads in the United States during World War I under the entity "United States Railroad Administration." This color brochure is filled with travel information and photographs on travel in the Rockies of Colorado and Utah, 1919. Rare.

VACATIONS
FOR ALL

GLACIER NATIONAL PARK
WATERTON LAKES PARK

NORTHERN
WISCONSIN

CHICAGO
MILWAUKEE
AND ST. PAUL
PACIFIC

M·K·T

SHOULD YOUR BAGGAGE BE MISPLACED
THIS TAG WILL FACILITATE ITS RETURN

SUN VALLEY · IDAHO

AMERICA'S FOREMOST
YEAR'ROUND SPORTS CENTER

CHESAPEAKE AND OHIO RAILWAY

Chessie

· EAST AND WEST ·
VIA WASHINGTON

B&O

N.C.&St.L.

TO AND FROM
Dixieland

c.1912. Rare.

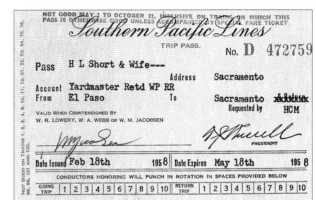

1958. Common.

1906. Rare.

Clockwise from above left: Southern Pacific Railroad Imperial Valley advertising solicitation; Southern Pacific Lines trip pass; International & Great Northern Railroad Company annual pass; and Kansas City, Mexico & Oriente railroad annual pass.

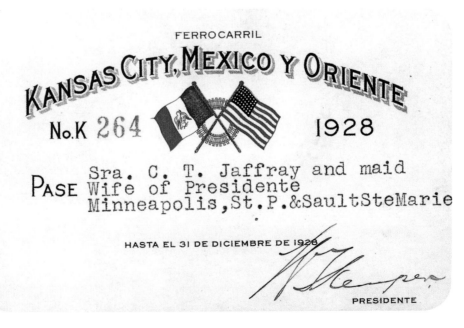

1928. Rare.

Reproduction of Colorado Midland Railway public timetable from 1902.

Text continued from page 98.

Changes to travel brochures

By the turn of the century, railroad public timetables and tourist guides continued to provide some travel and land-sale information, but now advertised their own brochures. These advertisements illustrated the large number of different brochures that were available and the variety of subjects they covered. A 1907 public timetable (illustrated on page 23), listed hundreds of available railroad travel brochures.

Millions of travel brochures were printed from the 1880s up through the 1970s. They could be found everywhere—in the vast number of train stations, passenger terminals and city ticket offices. Publicity houses such as Peck-Judah distributed them to hotels and travel bureaus. They were also available by mail. Their availability, attractiveness, adventurous appeal and price — free or for the cost of postage—made them a tremendously successful advertising tool and a colorful item for today's collectors.

Following is a chronological look at more railroad travel brochures from the 1890s through the 1980s.

THE LIBRARY OBSERVATION CAR

in use on the Great Northern Railway is a modern club house on wheels. It practically has all of the belongings of the ordinary club except the billiard table. It is in charge of a competent attendant, who is an adept in preparing viands usual to club life.

The library contains standard books, illustrated periodicals and daily papers. There are compartments, cozily designed, for card, chess and checker players, and a lounging parlor for smokers. The chairs, elegantly upholstered, are large and easy. The writing desk is supplied with pens, ink, paper and envelopes, and letters are written as conveniently as at home.

The car windows are unusually large and allow extended

LOUNGING ROOM OF LIBRARY CAR.

views of finer scenery than can be had anywhere else on the continent.

Before reaching destination, if the passenger feels the need of a bath, shave, hair-cut, shampoo, etc., the same can be had with all the facilities and comforts of the most complete establishment.

Nominal charge is made for those who do not hold sleeping-car tickets.

PALACE SLEEPERS.

The Great Northern Railway owns and operates its own sleeping cars, built especially to order, containing every feature human ingenuity has been able to devise for the comfort and safety of the traveler. The interiors are designed on a magnificent scale, the

The Great Northern Railway and Northern Steamship Company produced this beautiful folding brochure for the Summer, 1896 travel season. One side of the unfolded brochure has a large map of the northeastern and central part of the United States. Rare.

CALIFORNIA

CLIMATE.

The climate of California is a complete and happy surprise to those who have lived on the same latitudes east of the Sierra Nevada Mountains; there snow, ice, and cold, sweeping winds prevail for half of the year. People and animals require the best of shelter and protection from the intense cold, and field labor is an absolute impossibility during the winter months. Here there is no snow, ice or cold blasts; flowers bloom in yards and gardens the year round. The fields are scenes of the greatest activity in the winter months, plows and harrows are going from early morning till night, from November till May. The whole earth is clothed with a mantle of green, relieved by the brilliant coloring of the varied and luxuriant flora, the woods and groves are vocal with the songs of birds, and the streams swarm with water-fowl that have come here from cold regions.

The cause of this winterless climate is apparent to anyone. Commencing at the extreme western point of the Alaska peninsula, fully 1,500 miles west of our State, there is a continuously high mountain range running southwest into Mexico. This lofty barrier deflects the arctic winds to the east so that they never reach us. In addition to this potent climatic influence, there is a great, warm ocean current which washes the western border of the State. To these two great causes California owes her winterless climate.

A TWENTY-ACRE FARM.

located near a market town or near a railway leading to one, devoted to various products—peaches, apricots, prunes, plums and cherries—say twelve acres; small fruits, strawberries, raspberries, blackberries, currants and gooseberries—five acres; alfalfa, two acres, and one acre for buildings, yard for shade trees and flowers and vegetable garden for family use, will furnish employment for a large family and require the labor of others in the height of the fruit season. Twelve acres in bearing fruit, judiciously planted, well cultivated and pruned, will produce five tons of fruit per year, each acre, or sixty tons on the twelve acres. At the present prices, one and one-half to two cents per pound, will give from $1,800 to $2,400 worth of fruit. Five acres in small fruits will yield an average of $750 per year, and in good years will exceed $1,000.

The alfalfa will keep the horses for farm work, a cow, pigs to make meat, and chickens. The vegetable garden will furnish fresh vegetables for the table the year round.

Such a diversity of products will furnish work for a family the year round, make a beautiful home, support the family in comfort and even luxury, and at the end of the year leave an encouraging balance in the bank. The work will be light, clean and healthy, and the results far more satisfactory than the same labor could accomplish in a winter climate, where the seasons are so short that a single crop is all that is possible.

LANDS.

Califor... ...er borders.
Forty mill... ...nd of profitable cultiv... ...and railway
lands to be...

THE G... ...he most of
which is in... ...of the finest
timber lan... ...ct, for $2.50
per acre,... ...le, and they
will, witho... ...de in them.

RAILW... ...he odd-num-
bered secti... ...onably near
transporta... ...y. It is the
policy of t... ...ment us to
stimulate... ...ave already
made fine... ...lands more.

PRIVA... ...the State in
private ow... ...ost valuable
lands have... ...he develop-
ment of th... ...reasonable
terms as w... ...holder.

GRE... ...CTS.

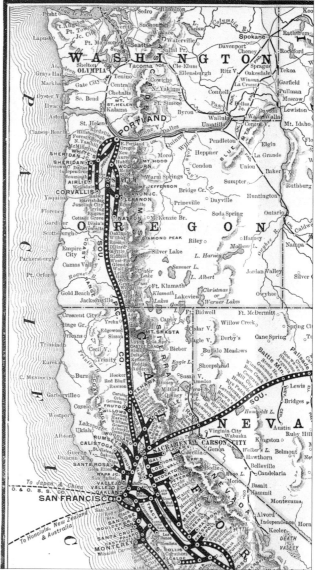

This 1896 "Correct Map of the Railway & Steamship Lines Operated by the Southern Pacific Company" included climate, land, and resort information on California in addition to some timetables. Rare.

THIS FOLDER CORRECTED TO JUNE 1, 1903.

A special Homeseekers' train of twelve cars leaving St. Paul for North Dakota, April 1st, 1903

$25.00 From ST. PAUL to PUGET SOUND, OREGON and BRITISH COLUMBIA points. Proportionately low one = way rates to all western points, effective daily until June 15th, 1903. Stop-overs of 10 days or less at Minot, N. D., and points west. **$25.00**

ONE FARE	Homeseekers' Round=Trip EXCURSIONS	DATES of SALE
Plus $2.00 Minimum Rate $7.00	TO POINTS IN MINNESOTA, NORTH DAKOTA, MONTANA, IDAHO, WASHINGTON, OREGON, THE KOOTENAI AND BRITISH COLUMBIA.	June 2 and 16 July 7 and 21 August 4 and 18 Sept 1 and 15 1903

For information and printed matter on this Great Country, apply to any agent of the Great Northern Railway, or

F. I. WHITNEY,
General Passenger and Ticket Agent,
ST. PAUL, MINN.

MAX BASS,
General Immigration Agent,
220 So. Clark Street, CHICAGO, ILL.

☞Send two cents in stamps for Bulletins on North Dakota, Montana and Washington.

This 1903 Great Northern timetable shows settlers leaving for North Dakota on a Homeseeker's Train. Rare.

133

By the 1910s, railroads were offering railroad/hotel tour packages in special travel brochures such as this 1916 Pennsylvania Rail Road "Eastern Tours." Rare.

Railroad travel brochures (above and on the next two pages) published in the 1910s and 1920s. From the left: Yosemite Valley Railroad, 1925, Rare; Denver and Rio Grande Western, 1928, Rare; Western Pacific Railroad, 1912, Rare.

The MILWAUKEE Railway

from the
ORIENT
to the
OCCIDENT
via
SEATTLE
and the

Chicago, Milwaukee & St. Paul Railway
TO PUGET SOUND—ELECTRIFIED

TRAVELERS from the Orient to the United States desiring the shortest and fastest route should book passage to Seattle, Wash., on Puget Sound. Excellent service is provided by the palatial vessels of the Admiral Line; the Nippon Yusen Kaisha; the Osaka Shosen Kaisha and the Canadian Pacific Ocean Services. The red line map of the Orient, Australasia and the Occident contained in this folder will show the ocean routes used by these steamship lines in cutting down the mileage and time to the United States. With the index finger on the point of embarkation, the traveler will follow these routes to the right and upward. At the end, passing from the Pacific Ocean into the Straits of Juan de Fuca, he will readily distinguish the world ports of Seattle and Tacoma—the western terminals of the great Chicago, Milwaukee and St. Paul Railway system. Seattle and Tacoma combined have a total population of over 500,000, and are modern and typical of American business and social life. Both cities have splendid hotel accommodations. The position of these ports is a dominant one from the standpoint of world trade, the chief industries being lumbering, salmon packing, and flour milling. This is the starting point for the transcontinental journey from the Pacific to the Atlantic seaboard.

First Glimpse of Seattle

Chicago, Milwaukee and St. Paul Railway (above and at left), 1922. Rare.

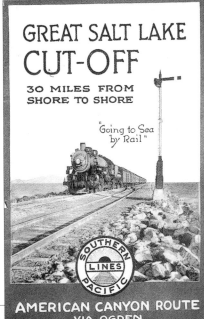

GREAT SALT LAKE
CUT-OFF

30 MILES FROM
SHORE TO SHORE

"Going to Sea by Rail"

SOUTHERN PACIFIC LINES

AMERICAN CANYON ROUTE
VIA OGDEN

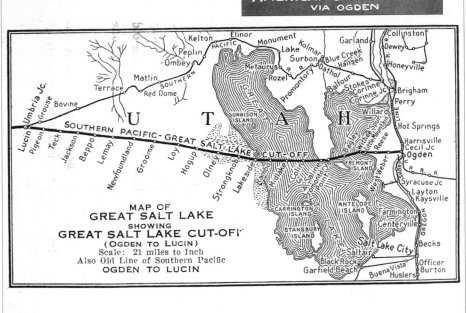

MAP OF
GREAT SALT LAKE
SHOWING
GREAT SALT LAKE CUT-OFF
(OGDEN TO LUCIN)
Scale: 21 miles to Inch
Also Old Line of Southern Pacific
OGDEN TO LUCIN

Southern Pacific Railroad route guide, 1924. Rare.

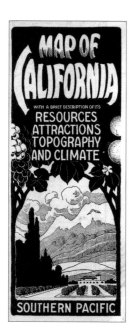

This 1920 Southern Pacific brochure cover shows the usual offerings of land/travel brochures during this period. Rare.

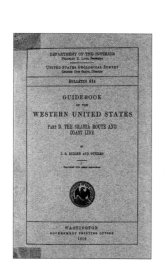

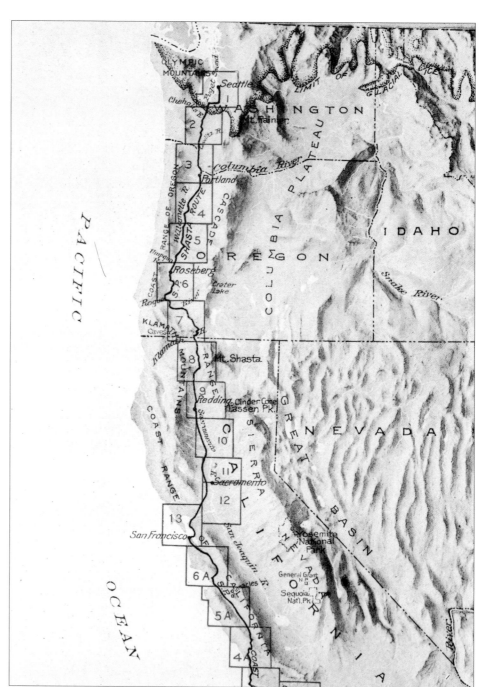

The United States Department of the Interior published a series of comprehensive guidebooks for major railroad routes in the Western United States. Guides were published for "The Northern Pacific Route, with a side trip to Yellowstone National Park," "The Overland Route with a side trip to Yellowstone National Park," "The Santa Fe Route with a side trip to Grand Canyon of the Colorado," and "The Shasta Route and Coast Line," among others. They contained an enormous amount of geographic, geologic, demographic, and natural history information, and are highly sought after by collectors today. (Above and left, map and cover from 1916 Shasta Route.) Rare.

Union Pacific Railroad, 1931. Rare.

This and the next two pages illustrate travel brochures from the 1930s through the 1980s.

Burlington/Northern Pacific/Great Northern Railroads, c. 1940. Rare.

Western Pacific Railroad,
1944. Rare.

AMTRAK travel brochure,
1985. Very common.

Southern Pacific Railroad,
1936. Rare.

Chicago & Northwestern
Railroad, 1942. Rare.

New York Central
Railroad, 1954. Rare.

The Santa Fe "Super Chief" (above and right) was one of many diesel electric-powered streamlined passenger trains introduced in the mid-1930s. Rare.

CHAPTER SEVEN
PASSENGER TRAIN BROCHURES

To THREE YEAR OLD, three foot tall Scotty, the world was a very big place.

And the trains were even bigger.

Scotty's mom was taking him to San Francisco on the "Super Chief " to see his grandparents. This would be his first train ride. She woke him up late at night for the ride to the depot. Still in his pajamas, he was loaded into the back seat of the Ford station wagon. Dad was warming it up for the long drive. He soon fell back to sleep.

As they neared the station, Scotty was awakened by his dad saying "That must be it over there." Looking sleepily out the car window, all Scotty could see was the huge star-filled night sky. It reached way down to the edges of a black sea that was the endless west Texas countryside. The blackness was dotted by the lights of farm houses. As the Ford climbed a highway overpass across the railroad tracks, Scotty had an even better view. He spotted a nearby cluster of lights with one much brighter than the rest. There was the depot, *and the train.*

The local milk train was standing at the station platform in a cloud of steam and smoke. It was 1958, and Santa Fe was still using steam locomotives for some of its trains. Scotty saw two men loading big cans of milk from a truck into the baggage car. He looked toward the hissing steam sound to see the

black, gray, and noise that was the locomotive. It was as big as a mountain. He could barely see the engineer leaning out the window. From way up there, the engineer smiled and waved at Scotty.

But this was not their train. As his dad drove away, Scotty's mom waved good-by and then hurried him inside the depot. The next train to arrive would be theirs.

Inside the small waiting room, Scotty sat on the wooden floor and played with some of the toys that his mom had brought for the trip. His mom talked to the ticket agent behind the tall counter. After a few minutes, he handed her the tickets. She sat down on

the oak bench and, pointing to the clock on the wall, told Scotty the train would be there in fifteen minutes. Scotty looked up at the clock, but did not know what fifteen minutes was.

Soon the ticket agent called out "Super Chief!"

The small group of waiting passengers quickly gathered their belongings and went outside. On the platform, Scotty held his mother's hand and peeked out from behind her coat. He could see the very bright light rushing silently toward them. As the light came closer and grew even bigger, the rails lit up like two bright rays of the sunshine. Now he could hear the train, but this one was different. It was quieter. There was no steam and smoke.

As the locomotive reached the platform, it's bright red nose and yellow logo were visible around the headlight. Way up high and slightly back on the nose were two windows. Scotty could see the silhouettes of two men, backlit by the lights in the cab. The locomotive only rumbled as it went slowly past them.

This was one of the newest diesel electric locomotives pulling passenger trains on the Santa Fe. Its stainless steel sides reflected the dim platform lights and made them dance. Several cars of the train moved past, but the windows were darkened for the sleeping passengers. As the train squeaked to a gentle stop, Scotty's mom tugged him along toward the open vestibule door.

As they climbed the steps onto the vestibule platform, Scotty felt the rush of air from inside the car. It smelled different. They followed the conductor down the aisle, its edges dimly lit from small lights near the floor. He showed them their seats and whispered he would be back for their tickets. This train, and the feeling of being on it, was like nothing Scotty had ever experienced before.

With a waver, the car began to move. The train quickly picked up speed. Scotty looked out the window as the station and platform lights moved swiftly away. The starry sky and black sea of the Texas countryside filled the big picture window.

Scotty's lifetime of travel adventures had just begun.

The stylish simplicity of modern train design is seen in this car interior photo from the 1939 Santa Fe "Scout" passenger train brochure. Common.

Passenger Train Brochures

Most of the major rail travel routes and destinations in the United States were well established by the 1920s. The many smaller railroads of the late 19th and early 20th centuries almost all had become part of bigger systems which offered inexpensive, long-distance passenger train travel that was safe, convenient, and fast. Passenger trains had become the most popular means of travel.

With many railroads now serving the same long-distance destinations, competition for travelers became even tougher. Until this time, railroad advertising had traditionally focused on the scenery along their routes, train accommodations and services. Such information had been part of public timetables, travel guides, tourist guides, and travel brochures since their inception. Only rarely and briefly, however, do any early examples of these publications mention the appearance of the train itself. Now, railroads needed to offer more. Emphasis on the aesthetic beauty of the trains themselves was a new and relatively unexploited avenue for their advertising efforts. Long-distance travel could offer not only the best scenery, but the most beautiful trains. To this end, American artists, designers, illustrators, decorators, and craftsmen collaborated to build some of the most beautiful passenger trains in world history.

Passenger Train Accommodations

In the hopes that passengers would find their trains the most attractive, railroads began publishing special *passenger train brochures*. The first were produced for named passenger trains in the 1910s and 20s. They emphasized the beautiful wood craftsmanship, detailed painting, mohair upholstery, brass fixtures, and cut-glass work that were the heavyweight car builder's "art" during this era. The premise was that the best craftsmanship available provided the most attractive design for all trains built at that time.

Dining-car services on these trains were the finest available. European chefs served fabulous meals on fine china, silver, and crystal. Observation and lounge cars were luxuriously appointed. Sleeping cars included comfortable beds, brass reading light fixtures, and wool blankets. Coaches featured large

This example of an early passenger train brochure is for the Great Northern Railroad's "Empire Builder" of the 1920s. Rare.

143

"THE STREAMLINED TRAIN WITH THE SOUTHERN ACCENT"

Southern Pacific proudly presents
THE NEW **SUNSET LIMITED** NEW ORLEANS-LOS ANGELES

Magazine-style brochures were often produced for the introduction or inauguration of new passenger trains. Southern Pacific's "Sunset Limited," 1950. Common.

brass overhead luggage racks. Cars were air-conditioned with ice in the summer and steam-heated from the locomotive in winter. Services such as nurses, secretaries, and barbers were also offered on these trains. The narratives in these early passenger train brochures clearly emphasize the quality and luxury of the train. Its accommodations, services, and contemporary appearance, both inside and out, were considered part of the design.

Train Design

Train designs soon became more varied by reflecting the simple modern artistry of the *art deco* era during the 1920s and 30s. The works of famous architects and designers directly and indirectly in-

fluenced train designs. For example, Frank Lloyd Wright designed the 1939 20th Century Limited train.

Striking color schemes were developed for many beautiful trains, including the now well-known orange, black and stainless steel of the Southern Pacific's "San Joaquin Daylight" of 1937. These trains were eventually known as "The Most Beautiful Trains in the World." A late 1930s passenger train brochure introducing the new Union Pacific "Portland Rose" illustrates this emphasis on color in passenger train design:

"Today you see for the first time a train into which has been built the "spirit of a city".... a train

named for a city .... a train reflecting the beauty of that city and the region wherein it lies.

The Portland Rose, named for the "City of Roses," was designed to convey to the nation an impression of the scenic charm of Portland, the Pacific Northwest and the beautiful Columbia River along which it travels.

Note how this has been achieved. Note how the design and color of the rose—the decorative motif for the entire train—is in evidence everywhere .... in the rich carpeting, upholstery, lamp shades, stationery, bridge pads, magazine binders and other train accessories.

Step into the exquisite dining room with its rose decorated dinner-ware, menus and soft lights—with its paintings of Pacific Northwest scenery.

Stop as you enter the Pullman cars and glance down the high-vaulted aisles illuminated by the mellow light of parchment shaded lamps. Beauty .... comfort .... rest.

Then the club-observation car known as the "Portland Club"—a bower of roses. Sink into a deep-seated chair. Listen to the radio. Observe the gleaming white fountain from which light refreshments are served.

New Technologies

New materials and technologies developed during the 1930s and through World War II greatly contributed to the designs and construction of modern passenger trains. Lightweight stainless steel and aluminum alloys gave locomotives and cars beauty, strength, and speed. Diesel electric locomotives were cleaner, more powerful, more reliable, and easier to maintain than their steam predecessors. Molded plastics, vinyl upholsteries, and lightweight metals also dramatically modernized the appearance of passenger car interiors. A 1937 brochure for the Santa Fe "Super Chief" illustrates the emphasis on new technology:

In this new streamlined, stainless steel Super Chief, to enter regular passenger service between Chicago and Los Angeles on May 18th, the Santa Fe's guiding purpose has been to create, for this famous train, equipment surpassing all preliminary efforts in the alluring field of modern train design

and construction—in beauty of appointment, in roominess and smooth-riding comfort, in practical operating efficiency.

The Super Chief consists of a 2600 H.P. Diesel locomotive, built by the Electro-Motive Corporation, and nine cars constructed by the Edward G. Budd Manufacturing Company. The entire train is gracefully streamlined, in gleaming stainless steel, and is unique in that it is the first streamliner built exclusively for first-class travel.

And from a 1940 passenger train brochure for the "City of San Francisco:"

The City of San Francisco ... is seventeen cars in length, including three power cars equipped with gigantic Diesel engines that develop 5,400 horsepower. The train is strikingly beautiful ... distinctive in design ... and incorporates many novel features.

Services and accommodations offered on these new trains were an integral part of their overall design. Beautiful dining-car china and silver patterns were developed. Waiters' uniforms, table-

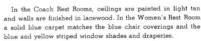

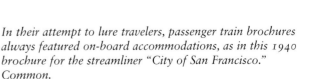

modern appointments for passengers' convenience .... and to allow sufficient space for their comfort.

In the Coach Rest Rooms, ceilings are painted in light tan and walls are finished in lacewood. In the Women's Rest Room a solid blue carpet matches the blue chair coverings and the blue and yellow striped window shades and draperies.

In the Men's Room, red seat coverings form a bright contrast to the blue floor. Window shades and portieres are striped in tan, red and rust. The over-all color treatment is very effective. Wash bowls are a light tan porcelain. There are diffused-lighting fixtures over the mirrors.

Rest rooms are provided with electric outlets for razors and curling irons.

In their attempt to lure travelers, passenger train brochures always featured on-board accommodations, as in this 1940 brochure for the streamliner "City of San Francisco." Common.

cloths, napkins, and menus all complemented the designs. Color-coordinated lounge chairs, dining-car chairs, and passenger seating were more attractive, durable, and comfortable. Cloth headrest covers, towels, paper drinking cups, and packaging for hand soaps were all included in the design. A 1939 brochure for the Santa Fe "Scout" proclaimed:

The modern coaches or chair cars on the Scout are very different from similar cars of the past. They are all new, of lighter weight, and streamlined in gleaming stainless steel. Their seats are deeply cushioned and readily adjustable to several reclining positions. The individual overhead lights may be dimmed, and new type racks provide generous space for baggage. The windows are exceptionally wide, and the seating capacity has been materially reduced in order that the extra space thus obtained can be devoted to a tasteful ladies' lounge and a men's dressing room.

In color effects, fabric designs, and in fixtures, the interiors of these cars have experienced the magic touch of the modern interior decorator, the entire effect being to promote an atmosphere of taste and quiet restfulness. Free drinking cups, pillows, and porter service are also provided.

Diesel electric passenger trains produced from the late 1930s through the 1960s became part of what is now called the "Streamliner Era," the high point to date in American long-distance passenger train history.

Brochure Design and Format

Even passenger train brochures themselves were part of the design for some trains. They were produced in a variety of sizes, but like their advertising predecessors, the most common size was the public timetable-sized stapled booklet or folder. Magazine-sized brochures were also published, usually for the introduction or inauguration of new trains.

Many produced during the "streamliner" era of the 1930s, 1940s and 1950s were the most colorful and are most in demand with collectors today.

Southern Pacific Railroad's "Daylight" passenger train brochure, 1937. Rare.

Passenger train brochures did not end with the nationalization of railroad passenger service under NRPC (National Railroad Passenger Corporation) on May 1, 1971. AMTRAK produces brochures for many of their trains today in their efforts to compete with automobile and airline traffic.

Burlington Railroad, 1933. Rare.

America's First Standard Size Diesel Electri...

CHICAGO -

Illinois Central Railroad, 1936. Rare.

Burlington Railroad, 1942. Rare.

Northwestern/Union Pacific Railroads, 1936. Rare.

Streamlined passenger trains built in the 1930s included specially designed steam locomotives and modern lightweight cars. Accommodations were spectacular! Rare.

1930s Union Pacific Railroad brochure for "The Challenger." Rare.

THE 1934 PULLMAN INNOVATION

IN the new light weight, articulated, streamline trains which Pullman is building for the Union Pacific, the semi-tubular shape of the train has necessitated a re-arrangement of the standard Pullman sections.

Air conditioning permits the use of metal ventilated partitions and sliding doors whereby each section can be transformed into a room, assuring the passenger complete privacy both day and night. And whether he [is] upper or lower, he [controls] the ventilation [he may] desire!

[One of the] novel and use[ful] [innovati]ons is a collap-sible washbowl and illuminated mirror in each berth. A new and improved reading lamp, adjustable to any position, is also found in each berth. When retiring, the occupant of the lower closes and locks a sliding door. The occupant of the upper ascends a folding stairway, undresses in complete privacy and allows the stairway to automatically fold against the panel.

Each section has appliances for the placing of a table. Meals are served to passengers in their own section by a rolling steam table from the buffet coach at the rear of the train.

· 3 ·

In 1934, Union Pacific Railroad published this Pullman seventy-fifth anniversary brochure. Rare.

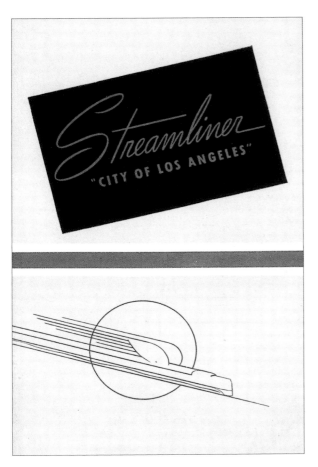

Southern Pacific/Union Pacific/Chicago & Northwestern
Railroads, 1930s. Rare.

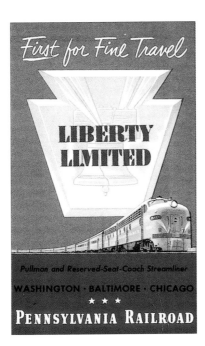

Pennsylvania
Railroad, 1954.
Rare.

Milwaukee Road,
1961. Common.

149

Santa Fe
Railroad,
1963.
Common.

Burlington/Rock Island Railroads, 1941.
Common.

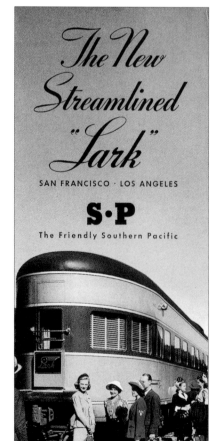

Southern
Pacific
Railroad,
1950s. Rare.

Dixie Route, 1940. Rare.

Southern Railway, 1950s. Common.

Kansas City Southern Louisiana & Arkansas Railways, 1940s. Common.

THE SOUTHERNER
THE LAST WORD IN STREAMLINERS

SERVING the great cities and towns between New Orleans and New York, The Southerner brings to the South the very last word in ultra-modern, Diesel-powered, Stainless-steel Streamliners. Here's the modern way to travel. Luxurious comfort . . . every convenience . . . fast schedules . . . low coach fares.

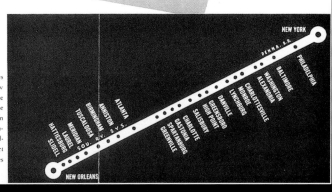

Burlington Railroad, 1957. Common.

Cover and interior of Santa Fe Railroad brochure commemorating Kansas City's centennial, 1950. Common.

*Great Northern
Railway, 1957.
Common.*

*Grand Trunk &
Western Railroad,
1960s. Common.*

White "Economy" Day One-Way Coach Fares:

Detroit-Chicago	$11.00
Lansing-Detroit	$ 3.60
Chicago-Lansing	$ 7.85
South Bend-Battle Creek	$ 3.00
Chicago-Battle Creek	$ 6.45
Pontiac-South Bend	$ 6.95

*Union Pacific,
1959. Common.*

*Great Northern
Railroad, 1950s.
Common.*

*General Motors
Demonstration
Train, 1947.
Common.*

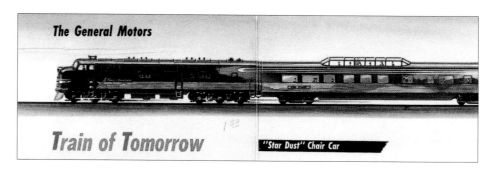

*New York Central's "Explorer," 1950s.
Rare.*

*New trains incorporating unique technical
designs were featured in their own special
brochures.*

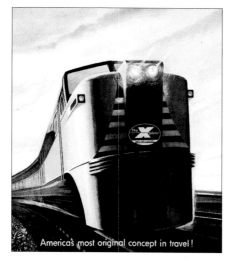

*New York Central
Railroad, 1950s.
Common.*

Pennsylvania Railroad's "Tubular Train," 1956. Common.

By the 1960s, passenger trains had lost the battle with the automobile. This 1960s Santa Fe Railroad brochure romanticizes train travel for children, the great American experience made bittersweet by the fact that the level of patronage no longer supported railroad passenger service. Common.

To compete with car and airline traffic, AMTRAK produces brochures for many of its passenger trains. From left: 1980s, Common; 1970s, Common.

Summer Train Service to YOSEMITE

EFFECTIVE MAY 30th, 1941
and Daily Until September 2nd, 1941

AIR CONDITIONED PULLMAN CARS

Will Be Operated Between

El Portal and San Francisco

On the Following Schedule

Side Trip
Fare . . .

Merced to
YOSEMITE
and Return

$10.25

Including Auto
Stage Between
El Portal and
Yosemite

*2	MAY 30, 1941	*3
	(SOUTHERN PACIFIC)	
11:00 P.M.	Lv................San Francisco................Ar	8:50 A.M.
7:45 P.M.	Lv................Los Angeles................Ar	8:45 A.M.
	(YOSEMITE VALLEY RY.)	
5:30 A.M.	Lv....Merced (So. Pac. Depot)......Ar	10:55 P.M.
5:35 A.M.	Lv....Merced (Y. V. Depot)......Ar	....
9:30 A.M.	Ar.................. El Portal Lv	7:15 P.M.
9:35 A.M.	Lv....El Portal (Motor Stage)......Ar	7:10 P.M.
10:10 A.M.	Ar.................. Yosemite Lv	6:40 P.M.

Trains marked * run daily. Light type A. M. **Dark type P. M.** Standard Pacific
    time.

Train No. 2 carries Standard Pullman cars from San Francisco via Southern Pacific
    Company to El Portal and dining car serving breakfast.

Train No. 3 carries Standard Pullman cars from El Portal to San Francisco and
    dining car serving dinner.

All trains carry observation parlor car between Merced and El Portal.

Yosemite Valley Railway

MERCED, CALIFORNIA

CHAPTER EIGHT
TIMETABLE & TRAVEL POSTERS

THE NEED FOR timetable posters (broadsides) did not end with the increased use of public timetable flyers (handbills). In the 1860s, broadsides could still be found in depots and hotels, on fences and walls, or wherever the opportunity might exist to catch the traveling public's eye.

By this time, the style of timetable posters was changing, becoming less informational and more graphic. Timetable posters no longer included complete train schedules. Instead, only portions of schedules were given for a few important passenger trains. The posters had more illustrations, larger lettering, and color printing to attract attention. Timetable posters also included advertising for tourism and land sales.

The most famous timetable posters in American history were those giving schedules for trains on the newly completed transcontinental railroad. This great historical event revitalized and expanded the printing of timetable posters. The Central and Union Pacific Railroads produced several dramatic examples with beautiful color illustrations. The most famous of these is the "May 10, 1869" poster showing an elk bull superimposed on a prairie panorama with a transcontinental passenger train (see page 110). Other railroads were also quick to seize the opportunity to print new posters showing their train connections with those on the transcontinental line.

Railroad artists created beautiful illustrations for use in timetable posters, using many American scenes. Information was given using many different-sized type styles. With their greater emphasis on the use of illustrations and graphics, timetable posters from this era can be termed the first true railroad travel posters. Those produced from the late 1860s through the turn of the century are considered marvelous examples of early American advertising. Originals are extremely rare.

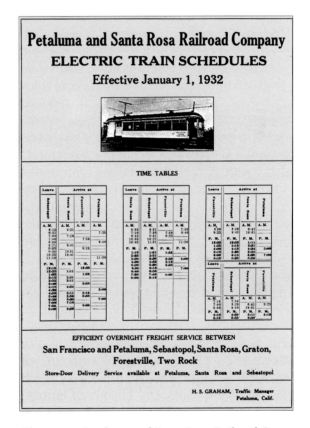

These 1932 Petaluma and Santa Rosa Railroad Company (above) and 1941 Yosemite Valley Railway (left) timetable posters are typical of those found in depots and hotels from the 1920s through the 1960s. Rare.

After the turn of the century, artwork commissioned for public timetable and travel brochure covers was often used to create simple and attractive travel posters. Their content included few if any words. Only the location of the scene illustrated or the name of the train were given. The beautiful images were all that was needed to convey the advertising message.

Timetable posters continued to be used even after other advertising methods were more commonly accepted. A few smaller railroads could still print all their schedules on a single sheet of card stock. Many larger railroads used them to post local schedules in depots. Timetable posters are still used today by metropolitan rail and bus lines to post schedules for the public.

Most travel posters were produced in two sizes, 17" x 23" and 25" x 34" or in these approximate sizes. They could be accommodated by the many locations where they were used, including train stations, city ticket offices, hotels and travel bureaus. Almost all were full-color, although some were produced in two colors or black and white. Travel posters were produced in very small numbers, making originals rare and valuable today.

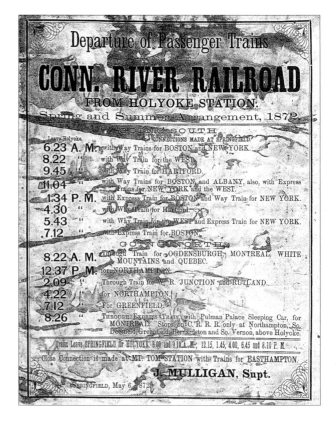

Timetable poster (broadside) from the Connecticut River Railroad, 1872. Very Rare.

In this 1860 timetable poster the South Shore Railroad advertised a change in departure times for their most heavily patronized trains only. Very Rare.

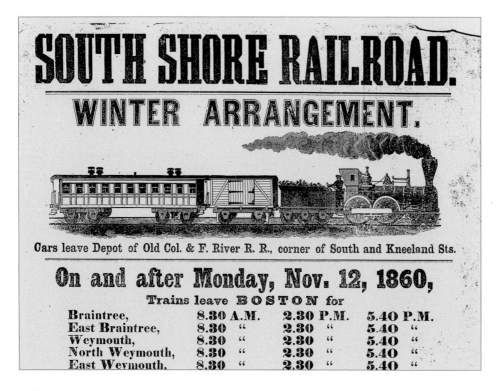

THROUGH [TRAINS]

VIA THE

HOOSAC TUNNEL ROUTE

BETWEEN

BOSTON

AND

SARATOGA.

No. 1, LEAVING BOSTON,

8.30 A.M.

ARRIVING SARATOGA,

3.15 P.M.

THE QUICKEST TIME EVER MADE BETWEEN THESE CITIES

A New Chair Car of the latest pattern, with every modern improvement, runs on this train

THROUGH WITHOUT CHANGE,

WITH NO CHARGE FOR RESERVED SEATS

No. 2 LEAVING BOSTON,

11.15 A.M.

ARRIVING SARATOGA,

7.50 P.M.

WAGNER DRAWING-ROOM CAR RUNS ON THIS TRAIN

THROUGH WITHOUT CHANGE

No. 3, LEAVING BOSTON,

3.00 P.M.

ARRIVING SARATOGA,

10.20 P.M.

CHAIR CAR RUNS ON THIS TRAIN

THROUGH WITHOUT CHANGE

WITH NO CHARGE FOR RESERVED SEATS.

THE ABOVE TRAINS RUN DAILY (Sundays excepted)
Nos. 1 and 3 via the

FITCHBURG, Boston, Hoosac Tunnel and Western R.R. (via Mechanicville) and Delaware & Hudson Canal Co.'s R.R.

No. 2, via the Fitchburg, Troy and Boston R.R. (via Troy) and Delaware & Hudson Canal Co.'s R.Rs.,

All passing through the Finest Scenery between Boston and the Hudson River, including the famous

HOOSAC TUNNEL.

250 Tickets Sold, Seats Reserved in Chair Cars, and Secured in Wagner Drawing-Room Car, at the Hoosac Tunnel Office, **250**

WASHINGTON ST., BOSTON.

This Fitchburg Railroad example is a typical "transitional timetable/travel poster" from the 1870s. With its three-color printing and large letters, its purpose was clearly to catch the eye. Very Rare.

More posters are shown in the color section.

"Follow the Flag"
WABASH

Rio Grande

CHICAGO · MILWAUKEE · TWIN CITIES · SPOKANE · SEATTLE · TACOMA · SPEEDLINER SERVICE
THE MILWAUKEE ROAD
Olympian Hiawatha

Chicagoan

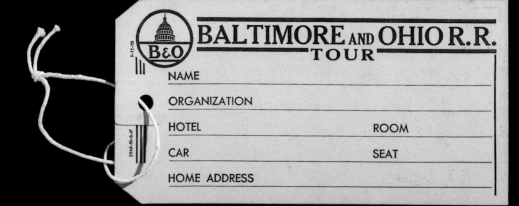

BALTIMORE AND OHIO R.R.
TOUR

NAME

ORGANIZATION

HOTEL   ROOM

CAR   SEAT

HOME ADDRESS

CHAPTER NINE

TICKETS & OTHER SMALL PAPER EPHEMERA

THE KEY TO any travel adventure was your ticket. When you paid your fare, the ticket agent handed you a small piece of paper with the departure and destination stations either handwritten or neatly printed on it. The ticket was a powerful and expensive little piece of paper, and you took care to safeguard it. After travel was complete, it became the smallest symbol of your travel experience. You would tuck it away somewhere safe, maybe in a photo album or a shoe box. Every now and then you would take it out to look at or hold in your hand. It would help to recall memories of the trip and was for your lifetime a ticket to adventure.

Seat checks were small cards placed on clips attached to overhead luggage racks above the seats in passenger cars. They were used as quick reminders to the conductor of the destinations of the seats' occupants. They also helped him keep track of the number of seats available in a car, and to arrange passengers according to their destinations. Common.

Small Paper Ephemera

Collecting tickets, annual passes, trip passes, and other railroad travel paper is a relatively obscure but very popular aspect of the railroad paper hobby. As ordinary as tickets might seem, they are poignant reminders of history, geography, and demography. They are usually the smallest, but perhaps the most nostalgic reminders of actual travel experiences.

Tickets could come in several pieces and sizes. Besides tickets, other kinds of small paper ephemera were useful to the passenger. Following are examples of many types of tickets, ticket envelopes, annual passes, trip passes, baggage tags, and baggage identification tags, all of which are small paper souvenirs for those who ventured on wonderful, long ago travels.

Train Identification Tags were used in terminals with large baggage-handling facilities. These brightly colored tags were used in addition to baggage tags as an easy way for handlers to spot luggage going to one specific train. 1940s and 1950s. Common.

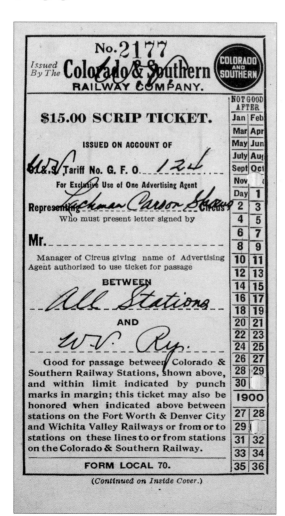

1930.

Scrip tickets were similar to commuter tickets. They were coupons for denominations of fare paid in advance. Scrip tickets were convenient for travelers who went frequently to several different destinations on the same line. Rare.

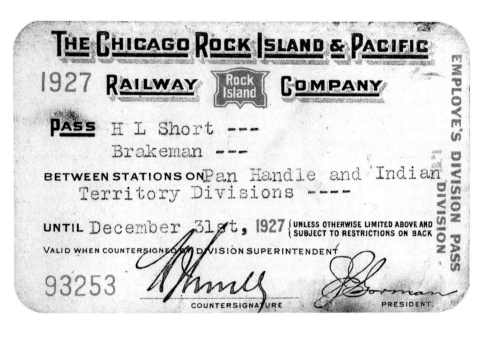

1927.

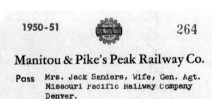

1950-51.

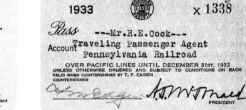

1933.

Annual Passes were issued as a courtesy, either automatically or upon request, to officials and some employees of railroads for travel on each other's lines. They were usually good for a period of one or two years. The number of passes issued between roads was usually equal in number and depended on their financial health. Annual passes were printed on paper card stock or coated linen for durability. Early passes featured beautiful color-lithographed illustrations and railroad logos along with ornate lettering. (Special passes issued by the Rio Grande Southern in the 1890s were made of solid silver!) Each pass had a number that was recorded by the train's conductor so that its use could be tracked by auditors. They are very popular collectibles today. Common.

1925.

Trip Passes were similar to annual passes, but good for only one specific trip on the line. These were much more common than annual passes and usually very plain in appearance. Common.

1926.

Coupon Tickets, or "inter-line coupon tickets" have always been the most common form of tickets used by railroads. This interline system provided a coupon for each train and railroad used by the traveler. The coupons, collected by train conductors, also provided an audit trail for the payment of passenger tariffs between railroads. With some journeys requiring one-way or round-trip travel on many different trains and railroads, several coupon tickets might be required. Some forms with their many coupons reached up to five feet in length! Coupon tickets for common routes to popular destinations were pre-printed with "Going" and "Return" coupons for the trains and railroads ordinarily used. Others were printed with varying numbers of blank coupons for travel on as many different trains and lines as there were coupons. Destinations were either rubber-stamped or handwritten by the ticket agent. Each ticket and all of its coupons were uniquely numbered so that auditors could verify their use when coupons were returned from the carrying to the selling line for payment. Returned coupons insured that only the correct amounts were paid to other railroads for travel on their trains that actually took place. Coupon-style tickets were also used for travel on one or more trains either one-way or round-trip on the same railroad. Common.

Rare.

Common.

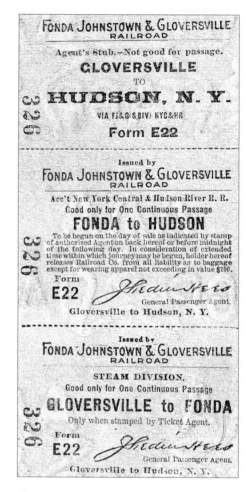

Rare.

Baggage Identification Tags were used to identify baggage with the owner's name and address. They gave additional information to handlers of checked baggage and were a means of identifying ownership of baggage that was carried unchecked in the coaches. They often included railroad logos and advertising slogans of the railroad. Rare (Yellowstone) and Common. See also illustrations on pages 128 and 160.

Baggage Tags (left) were used to identify the destination of each piece of luggage carried in the baggage car. Tags had two parts, each having the same number. The origination and destination stations were either printed, rubber-stamped, or handwritten on both parts. One was placed on the luggage and the other carried by the passenger. This allowed pieces to be tracked during handling, and made them easier to reclaim, or to find if they were lost. Early baggage tags were made of stamped sheet brass and were attached with a leather strap. By the 1920s, most railroads were using tags printed on heavy card stock with string ties. Common.

Book Coupon Tickets first appeared in the 1950s and were a modernized version of the old coupon tickets. Railroads found it easier to bind into one small booklet the many coupons necessary for travel on several trains and railroads. The booklet itself also offered an additional place for railroad advertising. Most book coupon tickets featured full-color covers showing famous, named passenger trains of the line or scenic destinations. Common.

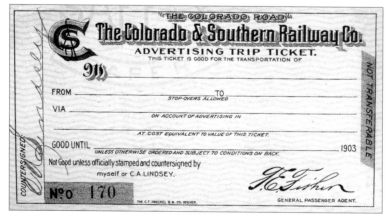

1903.

Advertising Tickets were issued as payment to periodical publishers for railroad company advertisements placed in their publications. This was common practice prior to the turn of the century, when railroads regularly advertised in many different local periodicals and everyone rode the train. Rare.

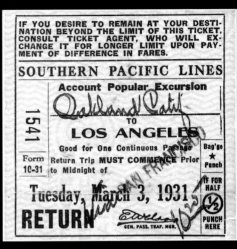

Pittsburgh, Cincinnati & St. Louis Ry. Co.

EXCURSION TICKET—1886.

MIDWAY, PA.
—TO—
BURGETTSTOWN, PA.

62

In consideration of the reduced rate at which this ticket is sold, it will not be accepted unless presented for passage on date stamped on back hereof.

Not good if Detached.

Gen'l Pass. & Tkt. Agt.

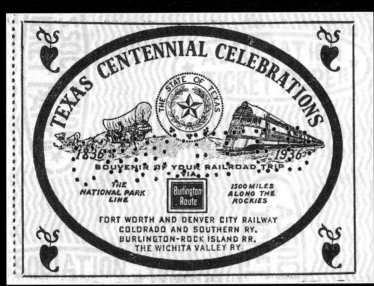

1936

IF YOU DESIRE TO REMAIN AT YOUR DESTI-NATION BEYOND THE LIMIT OF THIS TICKET, CONSULT TICKET AGENT, WHO WILL EX-CHANGE IT FOR LONGER LIMIT UPON PAY-MENT OF DIFFERENCE IN FARES.

SOUTHERN PACIFIC LINES

Account Popular Excursion

Oakland Cal'y
TO
LOS ANGELES

Good for One Continuous Passage

1541

Form
10-31

Return Trip MUST COMMENCE Prior to Midnight of

Bag'ge
★
Punch

Tuesday, March 3, 1931

RETURN

IF FOR HALF

½

PUNCH HERE

GEN. PASS. TRAF. MGR.

1931

Excursion Tickets were printed for trains running on special occasions, weekends, and holidays. The fare was less than what was normally charged. Excursion tickets were used to increase rider-ship, as promotional ventures for land sales and for special trains run to sporting events, fairs, conventions and holi-day outings. Rare.

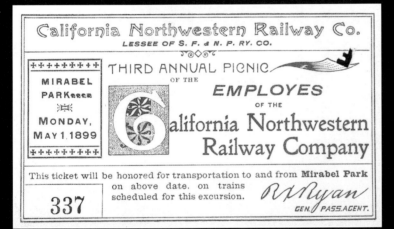

California Northwestern Railway Co.
LESSEE OF S. F. & N. P. RY. CO.

✱✱✱✱✱✱✱✱
MIRABEL
PARK✱✱✱✱
✱✱✱✱✱✱✱✱
MONDAY,
MAY 1, 1899
✱✱✱✱✱✱✱✱

THIRD ANNUAL PICNIC
OF THE
EMPLOYES
OF THE
6 California Northwestern Railway Company

This ticket will be honored for transportation to and from **Mirabel Park** on above date. on trains scheduled for this excursion.

337

R.R. Ryan
GEN. PASS. AGENT.

1899

Conductor's Tickets were sold by the train's conduc-tor to passengers boarding at stops that did not have depots. Normally, the con-ductor sold only intraline tickets for which he had a special ticket book. If the traveler was going to a destination off line, then he was sold a ticket to the next station, where he could obtain an interline coupon ticket from the agent. Rare.

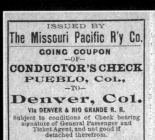

ISSUED BY
The Missouri Pacific R'y Co.

GOING COUPON
—OF—
CONDUCTOR'S CHECK
PUEBLO, Col.,
—TO—
Denver, Col.

Via DENVER & RIO GRANDE R. R.

Subject to conditions of Check bearing signature of General Passenger and Ticket Agent, and not good if detached therefrom.

To be detached by Denver & Rio Grande Railroad Conductor on going trip and sent to Auditor with his Ticket collections.

Book No.	Ticket No.	Form 12.
106	37	

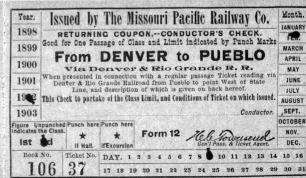

Year.	Issued by The Missouri Pacific Railway Co.	Month.
1898	RETURNING COUPON.—CONDUCTOR'S CHECK.	JANUARY
1899	Good for One Passage of Class and Limit indicated by Punch Marks	FEB.
1900	From DENVER to PUEBLO	MARCH
	Via Denver & Rio Grande R. R.	APRIL
1901	When presented in connection with a regular passage Ticket reading via Denver & Rio Grande Railroad from Pueblo to point West of State Line, and description of which is given on back hereof.	MAY
1902	This Check to partake of the Class Limit, and Conditions of Ticket on which issued.	JUNE
		JULY
1903		AUGUST
		SEPT.
		OCTOBER

Conductor.

Form 12

Gen'l Pass. & Ticket Agent.

Figure Unpunched Indicates the Class.	Punch here	Punch here	NOV.
1st 2d	★	★	DEC.
	II Half.	IfExcursion	

Book No.	Ticket No.	DAY.	1 2 3 4 5 6 7 8 9 10 11 12 13 14 15 16
106	37		17 18 19 20 21 22 23 24 25 26 27 28 29 30 31

1901

Card Tickets were the most common form of tickets used for travel on the same railroad (intraline). Card tickets were pre-printed for popular destinations on the line, resulting in each depot having its own unique supply. Printed on card stock for durability, their small size made them convenient to carry. Like all tickets, each was individually numbered so it could be tracked by auditors. The amounts turned in by ticket agents had to match the totals for the numbers sold in each group.

Clockwise from upper right corner: 1930s, Rare; 1940s, Common; 1959 Rare; 1913, Rare; 1950s, Common; 1910, Rare; 1950s, Common; 1912, Rare; 1969, Common; 1891, Rare; 1920s, Rare; 1908, Rare.

Luggage Stickers were placed on baggage by handlers or the passengers themselves as an additional means of identification and as advertisements for the railroad and its trains. Many luggage stickers featured the same designs used for the train. Most were printed in color on thick, coated paper that was gummed on the back. Owing to their small size and vulnerability to moisture, luggage stickers are relatively rare today. Rare.

CHICAGO & WESTERN INDIANA R.R.

25 RIDE TICKET
— BETWEEN —
CHICAGO
AND
HAMILTON PARK

Good only on C. & W. I. R. R. Suburban Trains. Good only within one year from date of sale.
THE TWENTY-FIFTH RIDE IS REPRESENTED BY THE BODY OF THIS TICKET TO BE TAKEN UP BY CONDUCTOR.

11094   Form T 7 0-8   V. Pres.-Traffic

C. & W. I. R. R.
Accounting Dept. Check
FIRST RIDE
— BETWEEN —
CHICAGO
— AND —
Hamilton Park
NOT GOOD IF DETACHED
25 RIDE TICKET
Form T 7 0-8   11094

C. & W. I. R. R.
AGENT'S STUB
Not good for Passage
25 RIDES
— BETWEEN —
CHICAGO
— AND —
Hamilton Park
Form T 7 0-8   11094

1910s

THIS COVER NOT GOOD FOR PASSAGE BUT TO BE LIFTED WITH LAST TRIP OF MONTH

NON-TRANSFERABLE INDIVIDUAL MONTHLY COMMUTATION TICKET
Good for one round trip daily, without stop-overs, during
MONTH AND YEAR AS INDICATED BY PUNCH MARKS IN MARGIN
BETWEEN

SAN FRANCISCO
AND
VALLEJO

by trains stopping regularly thereat.   No baggage privile

FORM 342G   Subject to conditions printed herein to which p chaser hereby in writing assents.
717E

Sign in Ink—Do not use pencil.   Purcha

MAN ★
Jan | Feb
Mar | Apr
May | June
July | Aug

1937

SOUTHERN PACIFIC GOLDEN GATE FERRIES. Ltd.
SPECIAL RATE 60 TRIP COMMUTATION TICKET
FOR
TRUCK and DRIVER
BETWEEN
San Francisco and Oakland, Alameda, Berkeley or Richmond
Good for 60 days.   This Book expires
Subject to conditions printed herein to which purchaser in writing assents.

Form 107-1
A 1666   PURCHASER (SIGN IN INK)   Vice-President
NOT TRANSFERABLE.   Cover must be presented with Coupons

1939-42

SOUTHERN PACIFIC
WEEKLY COMMUTATION TICKET
For a Male PASSENGER, unless otherwise indicated by stamp or endorsement, thus "W"
BETWEEN
SAN FRANCISCO AND
PALO ALTO
Subject to conditions printed on back hereof, to which purchaser agrees.

Form 301B
91400L

GOOD ONLY FOR WEEK
26
JUNE 29
— TO —
JULY 5
1941

Sign in ink   Purchaser

29 | 30 | 1 | 2 | 3 | 4 | 5

1941

Commuter Tickets were issued for a specific number of trips between two destinations. They were punched for each use until the last trip, when they were taken up by the conductor. By allowing users to purchase multiple trips in advance, commuter tickets made regular travel between two places more convenient. Clockwise: Chicago & Western Indiana Railroad, Rare; Southern Pacific Golden Gate Ferries, Rare; Southern Pacific, Common; San Francisco and Vallejo, Rare.

Ticket Envelopes were helpful for train trips requiring several coupon or card tickets, along with baggage checks, sleeping-car reservations, and passenger itineraries. The passenger needed to keep all of this together. By the 1940s, most large railroads were printing special ticket envelopes for the passenger's convenience. These also served as organizers for tickets prepared in advance by ticket or travel agents. Ticket envelopes were an additional opportunity for railroad advertisement. Most included logos, slogans, showed scenery, or advertised named trains on the line. Clockwise from upper left: 1950s, Common; 1900, Rare; 1920s, Rare.

A NEW TRAIN TO THE
San Francisco World's Fair
"TREASURE ISLAND SPECIAL"
IN SERVICE FROM CHICAGO MAY 22,
AND FROM SAN FRANCISCO MAY 25, 1939
CHICAGO & NORTH WESTERN ★ UNION PACIFIC ★ SOUTHERN PACIFIC

CHAPTER TEN
VARIATIONS

No ATTEMPT to categorize and describe is without its exceptions.

Many different timetable and travel brochure formats and designs were tried by the railroads over the years. The previous chapters presented those that were the most successful in that they became established with the public and railroad employees. However, this success did not mean they were always the very best in their conceptual or artistic approach.

Other ideas on how to reach the public were tried as well. Many were good, some were not. (There was also some overlap between categories, such as small railroads that were always able to include their small public timetable within a multi-page travel brochure.) Presented here are those ideas that were either less common or were unique approaches to the subjects covered in previous chapters. Each variation was a new idea, a fresh approach to being better at providing information or selling train rides. For this, they are worthy of attention by the collector. Examples of these variations are shown in the next pages.

Public Timetable Variations

On occasion, railroads combined the schedules of their best trains under the banner of a separate entity. This created the illusion of a single offering for first-class service. Train travel was made less complicated for those who could afford it. Piedmont Air Line Schedule, 1902; Dixie Line, ca. 1939; San Francisco World's Fair "Treasure Island Special," 1939 (left). Rare.

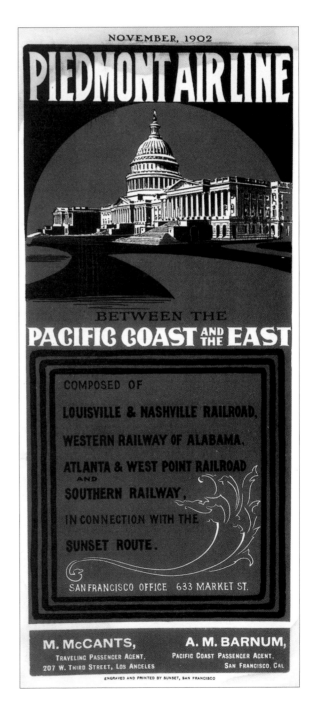

Public Timetable Variations

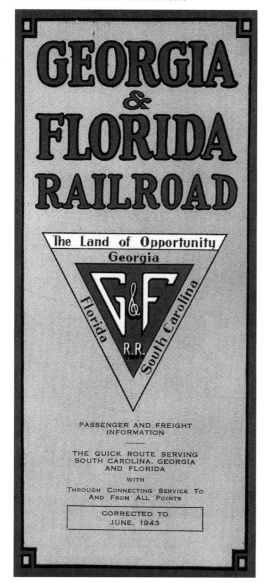

During World War I, the nation's railroads were operated by the federal government under the United States Railroad Administration. USRA-published timetables and travel brochures are rare. Above, Atlantic Coast Line Railroad, 1919. Rare.

When possible, some smaller railroads combined all resources and offerings into one folder. In 1943, the Georgia & Florida Railroad offered this ten-panel folding brochure (above and top center) that included freight schedules and regional information. Rare.

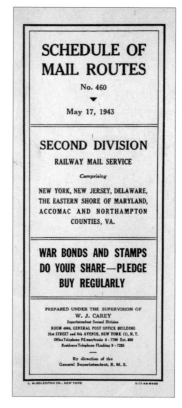

Scheduled mail trains routinely crossed railroad boundaries between their origin and destination. A "Schedule of Mail Routes" was published for each division within the United States Post Office's "Railway Mail Service." At left, "Second Division, 1943. Rare.

Employee Timetable Variations

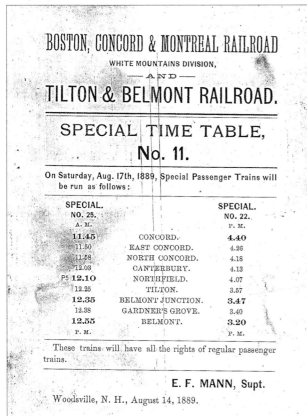

This 1889 "Special Time Table No. 11" of the Boston, Concord & Montreal Railroad, served the same purpose as a general order. Very Rare.

Employees of the Los Angeles Union Passenger Terminal needed to know departure and arrival times for the trains of most railroads sharing the facility, 1939. Common.

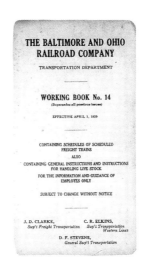

The Baltimore & Ohio (in this 1939 example) and some other railroads printed a combination employee timetable and instruction book giving special information by train number, on the handling and loading of livestock or perishables. Rare.

Southern Pacific Railroad, 1950s. Common.

Union Pacific Railroad, 1950s. Common.

Union Pacific Railroad, 1930s. Common.

Northern Pacific Railway, 1960s. Common.

Train Travel Information Brochures

In their continuing efforts to make train travel as attractive as possible, railroads published informational brochures for travelers. They provided answers to many of the most asked questions, reminders, and travel tips to make the trip more enjoyable.

Train Information Brochures

Once aboard, information brochures provided specific train information to travelers. This included on-board services, accommodations, abbreviated schedules and points of interest along the way.

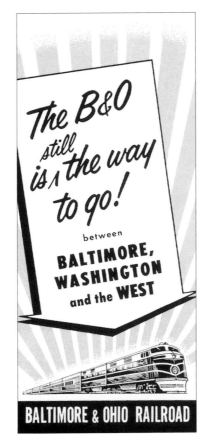

Baltimore & Ohio Railroad, 1950s. Common.

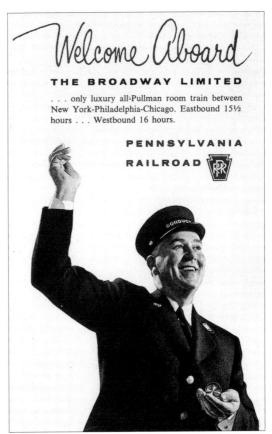

Pennsylvania Railroad, 1960s. Common.

Southern Pacific Railroad, 1950s. Common.

Union Pacific/Milwaukee Road, 1960s. Common.

Northern Pacific Railway, 1950s. Common.

Train Sleeping Car Accommodation Brochures

To help travelers choose sleeping-car accommodations, railroads printed special brochures showing what was available.

Alaska Railroad, 1950s. Common.

Great Northern Railway, 1920s. Common.

Great Northern Railway, 1950s. Common.

Fare Brochures

Special brochures were also printed to advertise regular and special fares on passenger trains.

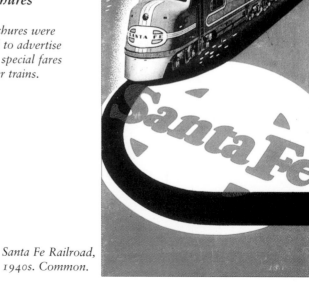

Western Pacific Railroad, 1950s. Common.

Great Northern Railway, 1950s. Common.

Santa Fe Railroad, 1940s. Common.

1953. Rare.

Dining Car Brochures

One of the greatest relationships passenger trains established with the public resulted from their sincere effort to provide the finest dining found anywhere in the country. Nothing was finer than dinner in the diner. Selling this experience to travelers was so important to railroads that entire brochures were dedicated to the effort. Beautiful examples of advertising, such as these Great Northern and Northern Pacific Railroad brochures were printed in limited numbers and are very hard for collectors to find.

The Lewis and Clark

TRAVELLER'S REST

Buffet Lounge Car

A new kind of western hospitality aboard the

Vista-Dome

NORTH COAST LIMITED

1961. Rare.

Reproduction of 1902 Colorado Midland Railroad timetable.
See color section for full-color rendering.

CHAPTER ELEVEN
COLLECTOR'S GUIDE

COLLECTING ANYTHING requires both "categorizing" and "grouping" the material. "Categories" are established by the nature of the different types of materials available. "Groupings" are more variable, depending on a collector's interests and priorities. Categories are more definitive and provide a common language for collectors. Groupings express individualism within one's own collection. There are as many ways to organize collections as there are reasons for saving the paper items.

Major Categories
Timetables, travel guides, tourist guides, travel brochures, posters, tickets and their various subcategories—the categories of railroad paper ephemera discussed in this book—are the most popular and most commonly seen in the hobby. Less common or very specialized categories are: interurban timetables and tickets (for street cars or "trolleys"), train orders, business forms, letterheads, stock certificates, railroad-published postcards, magazine advertisements, wallet calendars, ink blotters, time books, union material, photographs, steam and diesel locomotive technical material, tourist railroad timetable brochures, and framed advertising pictures.

Major Groupings
One of the most popular groupings of all paper ephemera categories is by railroad. Any and all paper from a particular road, no matter what the category, is organized together. This is an easy and practical way for collectors to enjoy looking at paper they have gathered from their favorite railroads.

Also very popular is grouping paper by categories. For example, all public timetables can be grouped together and arranged chronologically in alphabetical order by railroad. Railroad paper collectibles are also grouped by: *regions*, such as Colorado or Western United States railroads; *eras*, such as the 1920s; *name trains*; *personal travel adventures*; or *rarity*.

Collections take on individual themes based on these groupings. Often, personal interests and ways of grouping will change over the years as collectors look through and enjoy their material again.

Keeping the material organized, no matter how you group or organize, is the key to enjoying your railroad paper collecting hobby. This makes it easily accessible, which is very important. Too much unorganized material may be difficult to appreciate. With the wide variety of material available, organizing will also help you make the buying decisions that are most in keeping with your collection themes.

Where To Find It
You are interested, now where do you find it? Generally speaking, so much of this material was produced (after 1890) that it is relatively easy to find. To avoid frustration, some directions will help.

Railroad Collectible Shows
Railroad collectibles shows or "swap meets" occur frequently throughout the nation. Listings for shows can be found in popular railfan magazines, such as *Trains Magazine* (Kalmbach Publishing Company) or *Railfan and Railroad Magazine* (Carstens Publishing Company). Such listings are also found in hobby organization publications such as *The Express* (Railroadiana Collector's Association, Inc.); *Key, Lock, and Lantern* (Key, Lock and Lantern); and *The First Edition* (National Association of Timetable Collectors). These peri-

odicals provide free listings of railroad collectibles shows, along with paid advertisements for same.

Shows are usually independently produced and last for one or two days on weekends. They are held in rented facilities such as fairgrounds buildings and meeting halls. Dealers come from across the country, giving collectors excellent opportunities to purchase a wide variety of material. Expect to pay admissions of from $2 to $6 per person.

Railroad collectibles shows also include many other artifacts, such as hand-signal lanterns, switch keys and locks, dining car china and silver, new and old railroad books, videos, and more. The term "railroadiana" (pronounced like "Indiana") covers all railroad artifacts, including paper ephemera.

Railroadiana shows provide the best opportunities to see and acquire a wide variety of railroad paper collectibles. Dealers who specialize in paper ephemera have a lot to offer, and they love to talk about the history. Looking at the different material and meeting others in the hobby is half the fun and an adventure of its own. It will be easier to focus your collecting interests after you have been to a couple of shows, have seen what is available, and have gained some knowledge of price ranges.

Remember while looking at paper ephemera, especially very old and rare material, that it is paper and therefore fragile. Respect the age and condition of the piece, as well as the dealer offering it, by handling it appropriately. Most dealers will protect their paper items in plastic sleeves, making it easier for the customer, but the burden of careful looking falls on the customer.

Model and Toy Train Shows

Railfan publications also have listings for toy and model train shows. These are separate genres of the railfan hobby that usually do not include railroad collectibles. The major interest of most dealers at these shows will be selling model and toy trains, along with new railroad books, videos, gift items, etc. Model and toy train shows have a broader public appeal, while railroad collectibles shows are more hobby-specific. Occasionally, toy and model train dealers will offer some railroad paper collectibles and artifacts (railroadiana), but

this will not be their main focus. A few railroad collectibles dealers regularly sell at model and toy train shows as well as at the railroadiana shows. Railroad paper collectors will sometimes come across good finds at these shows.

Antique Shows

Antique shows are presented in the same manner as railroad collectibles shows. Generally, it will be much harder to find any railroad collectibles, paper or otherwise, at these types of shows. It is certainly not impossible, though, and sometimes there are great finds. Railroad collectibles dealers can sometimes be found at antiques shows.

Antique shops and malls are also good places to look for railroad paper collectibles. As with antique shows, however, railroad material is scarce there, since it is hard enough to find so that antique dealers usually don't have much in stock, and it is popular enough that it doesn't last long when they do. Antique dealers are nevertheless an important resource for railroad paper collectors, since they are constantly acquiring new items at garage and estate sales. Collectors who visit their favorite antique shops and malls frequently may be rewarded with a find.

If the hunt were always easy, it would not be such fun!

Mail Order

Mail order is another important source of railroad paper collectibles. Dealers regularly place small classified or display advertisements in railfan periodicals. By sending them a self-addressed stamped envelope or a nominal fee, a collector can obtain the dealer's list of railroad paper ephemera. Mail order offers collectors the great advantage of being able to acquire paper from all over the country without incurring the costs of traveling to find it.

The importance of this resource cannot be overemphasized. Many excellent railroad paper collectibles can be obtained this way. Corresponding and receiving items from far away places also adds enjoyment to the hobby.

Want Ads

Want ads placed by collectors also bring new material into the hobby from people who have saved what was handed down to them or acquired through their years of railroad employment. They may want to find a good home for it if they or no one else in their family is interested. Knowing the material is of value, many people prefer to sell the items rather than donate them to museums or historical societies. (Depending on the material, these institutions may not accept it if they already have much similar material in their collections.)

Collector's Groups

Collector's organizations are another important resource for obtaining railroad paper collectibles. Three of the largest groups are the National Association of Timetable Collectors (NAOTC), the Railroadiana Collector's Association, Inc. (RCAI), and Key, Lock and Lantern (KL&L). Meeting others with similar interests is one of the most enjoyable parts of the collecting hobby. These networking organizations can put you in touch with collectors from all across the United States and many foreign countries.

Museums and Historical Societies

The best sources for viewing the rarer railroad paper collectibles are the great collections in museums and historical societies. Through lifetimes of tireless and often unrewarded efforts, many dedicated people have built spectacular collections for posterity.

For those who do not wish to own such material, or for researchers who want only to view many examples, these are the places to go. (Even with generous access to one of the largest private paper collections in the United States, this book could not have been adequately illustrated without examples from the collections of The Railway and Locomotive Historical Society, The California State Railroad Museum Library, The Colorado Railroad Museum, and the Union Pacific Railroad Museum.) One visit will quickly impress upon you the value of such resources. The quantity, variety, and history in these collections is truly profound.

Where is the railroad history kept in your community? How healthy is their funding for such an important endeavor? Take some time to go and see, and get involved!

Scarcity of Collectibles

The most recent railroad paper collectibles were printed *no less than twenty years ago*. Many of the very early items were not printed in large quantities, or were not always saved, or did not survive time and the elements. Timetable handbills from the 1840s and 50s, for example, are extremely rare because, although of good quality paper, few were printed. Because not many were saved, public timetables printed around the turn of the century are scarce, even though many were printed. Because of their large size and poor paper, travel guides from the 1850s through the 1880s are very rare, although they, too, were printed in relatively large numbers. Think of the chances of such a book being kept somewhere undisturbed for so many years.

The initial motivations for keeping such an item and the subsequent circumstances surrounding its storage dictate, for the most part, whether it survives and in what condition. These considerations make it apparent why some items are rarer than others, and their prices higher.

Age is the primary consideration in most cases for determining availability and price. Other factors—the quantity printed, condition, popularity of the region from which they came, and current interest in the specific railroad—affect rarity, demand, and price. Generally speaking, the oldest pieces from railroads having the greatest current popular interest are hardest to find and are worth the most.

Determining Price Factors

Paper ephemera are an investment, so the less you pay for items that are in demand, the more potential they have for appreciation. Although the gray area of pricing may at first appear overwhelming to you, the seven factors discussed below provide a way to evaluate current worth.

First and second, *age* and the *quantity printed*

are the primary factors for determining both the survival and the value of railroad paper collectibles. These factors should be your benchmarks when it comes to pricing.

Other factors then can be considered. In particular the *location* or *train name* and the *railroad*. An 1890s public timetable from the Colorado Midland is a good example. It is from an old Colorado mining railroad, a historical region that is very popular today. The Colorado Midland Railroad lasted only until 1922, and its artifacts are very rare. It printed very few public timetables (one of the most popular collecting categories). Based on its content and appearance, this timetable also gets the highest ratings for *aesthetics*. Public timetables from this era are some of the most colorful ever produced. The Colorado Midland's famous Native American triangle logo (see page 180), which illustrated their public timetable covers, makes them very much in *demand* with collectors today. Finally, a seventh factor is considered: *condition*. If the piece is in like-new condition (mint) or shows a minimum amount of handling, its value is further enhanced. If the item is water-damaged or torn, its value is decreased. Other factors can be affected by the relative weight of condition. The summing up of these factors tells you that this Colorado Midland public timetable in excellent condition will command top dollar.

Taking these seven factors into account will help make pricing railroad paper collectibles more definitive. With age and quantity printed as the benchmark factors for pricing, four rarity-indices are presented in this book. Using this system makes pricing more black and white and less gray for collectors. It must be remembered, however, that the *ultimate factor* determining the value of any collectible is always *the price a collector is willing to pay*. No system for pricing is guaranteed.

Ratings Guide

Very Common – $3 to $8

These are the most recent and most abundant examples found in each category. Particularly, public and employee timetables, travel brochures, and tickets. Their worth relates to a number of factors, including, but not limited to:

age – This is the most recent material, from the 1950s up to and including Amtrak material from the 1980s.

quantity printed – The larger railroads of more recent times printed huge (runs of 50,000-300,000) quantities of timetables and travel brochures.

railroad – For very common material, the railroad it came from matters only to personal interest.

condition – Since this is the newest material, collectors can pick only examples that are in new or very fine condition. Sometimes, scarce ephemera are found in this price range because they are soiled, scuffed, stained or torn.

location or train name – These are the most popular travel locations or are train names for brochures more recently published.

aesthetic appeal – The appearance of these brochures or timetables is ordinary or artistically plain relative to other examples of the same age or older, rarer material.

demand – This material represents the lowest threshold for material that is of any interest to collectors.

Common – $5 to $15

Common railroad paper collectibles are the more popular, appealing and affordable items you will see at shows and on mail order lists. Particularly, public and employee timetables, travel and name-train brochures, tickets, and Official Guides (but not other travel guides).

age – This material is generally from the 1930s, 40s, and 50s.

quantity printed – The largest quantities of colorfully illustrated travel brochures were printed during this time by all roads, both large and small.

railroad – Many railroads from this era later went bankrupt or merged into larger systems.

condition – Common material is often found in very good to new (mint) condition. Collectors can discriminate to find the best examples for their collections. Sometimes older and rarer ephemera are found in this price range because items are soiled, scuffed, stained, or torn.

location or train name – Travel brochure subjects include popular regions of the country and national parks. Named passenger train brochures from the 1950s and 60s are also common.

aesthetic appeal – Travel brochures and timetables are aesthetically appealing with colorful logos, illustrations, and photography. Appeal of this material is greater than what is very common and is slightly less than material found in the rare category.

demand – This material is most in demand because of variety, availability, and price.

Rare - $12 to $75
Rare paper collectibles are the uncommon items you will find at shows or only occasionally on mail order lists. Includes: public and employee timetables, travel and name-train brochures, travel guides, tourist guides, travel and timetable posters, and tickets.

age – Rare ephemera include material produced from the 1890s through the 1940s. The odds of survival for material from this era are considerably less than for more common railroad paper collectibles.

quantity printed – Generally, rare ephemera are those originally printed in smaller quantities (runs of 5,000, 10,000, 20,000 to 50,000 in increments of 10,000) by a fairly large number of railroads. Still, enough were printed so that collectors can find them with reasonable effort.

railroad – Most rare ephemera come from the many different railroads of pre-1950s vintage. The popularity of these first- and second-generation roads greatly influences the availability and price of surviving ephemera.

condition – Rare material reflects its age more clearly, although it is not uncommon to find examples that are in very good to new (mint) condition.

location or train name – These are the more rare, early examples of travel guides, brochures, and other paper collectibles. Passenger train brochures from the first streamliners are included.

aesthetic appeal – Because of the age group, rare material has the most popular appeal of all paper collectibles. Generally, the most colorful artwork and most interesting content appear in publications from this era.

demand – This material is more in demand with advanced collectors who are willing to pay the higher prices.

Very Rare - $40 to $250
Only the rarest and oldest material is considered here. Very rare ephemera will generally be hard to find, no matter where you look. Demand for rare material exceeds supply. This is reflected in the prices. Includes: broadsides, public timetable flyers, early employee timetables, travel and tourist guides, timetable posters, and land brochures.

age – This is the earliest material produced, from the beginning of the 1840s through the 1880s. The chances of material from this era having survived in good condition is small.

quantity printed – This material is from the era when the largest number of small railroads existed. Items were printed in very small (runs of 200, 500, 1,000, 2,000, 3,000) quantities. Also, fewer different kinds of publications were produced. For example, travel brochures were not printed until the late 1880s.

railroad – The greater number of smaller railroads in existence during the early years further increases the rarity and desirability among collectors for their ephemera. Small early lines later became part of larger roads that were also very popular.

condition – Since this material tends to be the oldest, collectors can expect most examples to be worn. Very rare ephemera can occasionally show up in very good or new (mint) condition, partly because of the higher rag-content of papers used during the mid 1800s.

location or train name – These are the earliest examples of all categories, including public timetables with travel and land information, travel and tourist guides, timetable posters, travel posters, and employee timetables that included operating rules.

aesthetic appeal – The appearance of early guides and timetables reflects the unique but enticing limitations of illustrations and printing methods from this time. Because of their age, the content of material produced in this era is extremely interesting.

demand – The availability of very rare material is met with a consistent demand from collectors and institutions, making it difficult to find. Prices reflect this.

Dating Material

With relatively few exceptions, railroad paper collectibles can be easily dated. Most collectibles include the month, day and year—a necessary part of frequently revised publications. This applies to the earliest broadsides, public timetable handbills, public timetables, employee timetables, rule books, timetable posters, and travel guides. The information in later publications—land, travel and passenger train brochures—was less time-sensitive. They were designed and printed with a larger, more flexible life-span in mind. Obvious dates for these publications were often intentionally omitted from the cover or the text. Coded dates were usually included in small print on the last page or panel of the publication. Dates were shown in numerical month, day, and year form, often in parentheses, such as (03/12/12), meaning the release or issue date was March 12, 1912. Later, dates showed only the month and year. For example, (04/18) meant a release or publication date for this folder of April, 1918.

Quantities Printed and Printer

Often, very early souvenir guides and travel brochures (Chapter Six) did not include a date as part of their content, even in coded form. This leaves only the content as a means of dating these publications. Studying the detail in illustrations can provide valuable clues: the location, buildings, types of locomotives, and route names. Or, you sometimes need to research the history of the line to place the time of publication. In most cases, using the content to determine the age of a piece can ultimately be almost as accurate as a date code, it just takes a little more effort. This makes a rare acquisition that much more fun.

Two additional bits of information of interest to collectors were also included with dates in travel publications: the quantity published (shown along with the date) and, sometimes, the name of the printer, usually in parentheses. For example, a travel brochure from the Great Northern Railway from 1908 would show the following in small print on the last page or panel of the folder: "(05/08 20M) Rand McNally and Co., Chicago." Translated, this small amount of fine print yields valuable information to collectors: 20,000 of these brochures were printed for the Great Northern Railway, with a publication date of May, 1908 for release to all railroad passenger agents and ticket agents, city ticket office agents, publicity bureaus, and the public, printed by Rand McNally, and Company, Chicago, Illinois, U.S.A. Not bad for one inch of small print!

A variety of publishers established themselves early on in the business of printing railroad maps, travel guides, tourist guides, and posters. The names of these companies were often included with the date and quantity-printed codes on timetables, travel brochures and timetable posters from the 1890s on. Two names commonly found are Poole Brothers and Rand McNally.

Familiarity with dates, quantity printed and publisher names can provide collectors with a sense of who published the most accurate or most aesthetically appealing travel brochures, and how rare they are.

Archival Storage and Protection

This entire book is dedicated to railroad historical paper and our enjoyment of it. This material has often survived because care was taken in its storage. With a few simple precautions, collectors can easily protect their investments and ensure that the material will be around for later generations to enjoy.

The survival of all paper is dependent on several environmental variables. Excessive moisture, temperature extremes, acid migration and micro-organisms (molds and fungi) are the most important. Storage conditions can mean the difference between your collection surviving indefinitely or being quickly destroyed.

Moisture is the most obvious enemy of paper. Water can damage paper very quickly when applied in large amounts, or more slowly if the paper is semi-protected from its effects. For example, paper items will slowly absorb, or wick, moisture if stored unprotected in a cardboard box on a damp basement floor. Make sure items are stored where they will be safe from exposure to moisture.

Temperature extremes can also affect the survivability of paper. Freezing and heating, endured as a result of storing in a garage or rental-storage unit, can have long-term detrimental effects.

Museums and libraries housing large paper collections maintain stringent temperature and humidity conditions with sophisticated heating and air conditioning systems. Most modern homes can provide almost the same level of protection.

Direct sunlight and incandescent lighting can accelerate decomposition of many inks and papers, causing them to fade and yellow. This is primarily a concern where items are displayed, but must also be considered for safe storage. Make sure framed items hang where direct sunlight will not hit them. Avoid direct lighting from incandescent or track lights. Use non-glare glass in frames to help minimize lighting-caused deterioration. Store items where they will not be exposed to light.

Paper items stored next to one another are susceptible to acid migration, the effects of acid from higher-content papers being absorbed by those that are more neutral or "balanced." In this slow process, the more acidic materials are trying to become more chemically stable. Unfortunately, the results are unsightly yellow or brown stains on the affected papers. Most railroad paper collectibles were printed on better-quality papers having a well-balanced mix of more acidic cellulose fibers from trees and more neutral "rag" fibers from plants. More modern coated papers are also less susceptible. Still, the effects of acid migration can most often occur at such a slow rate that you will not notice any damage until it is too late. Depending on the quality of paper and storage conditions, acid migration can cause significant damage.

Another concern is the growth of molds and fungi. This damage is most commonly associated with paper that has become very wet at one time or is being stored where it is damp. Warmth will provide the perfect conditions for the growth of molds and fungi. They will cause very unsightly stains on paper items, cause pages to stick together, and in many cases completely ruin them.

Under normal ambient temperature and humidity conditions, all paper items can be safely protected from the environmental factors discussed above by using some basic archival materials that are inexpensive and easily obtained. The most popular protection for paper today are polypropylene "sleeves" or "protectors" available in a wide variety of sizes. These are also available in a more expensive material called "mylar." Both materials are "inert," which means they are chemically stable and will not react with materials stored in or next to them. Poly sleeves cost only pennies each, which is a small price to pay for protecting valuable paper collectibles. Mylar sleeves cost more, but provide more durable protection. These are more often used by museums and libraries.

Acid-free paper envelopes, mounting boards, and storage boxes are also available for the safe storage of paper collectibles. The papers used in these archival storage materials are "buffered" to help them maintain a neutral "ph" and prevent acid migration. Mounting boards are especially valuable for use in the safe framing of prints or posters. Backing boards are also available for use with poly or mylar sleeves. Poly or mylar sleeves with acid-free backing boards are an excellent and inexpensive archival storage system for most railroad paper collectibles.

Archival storage materials are available from a variety of sources, including office and art supply stores, framing shops, and mail-order firms (see resources). Poly sleeves are available at packaging (shipping supply) stores. Collectors will be glad they took the time to properly protect their valuable paper items.

Resources

Collectors' Organizations

National Association of Timetable Collectors
(NAOTC)
Norbert Shackletter, Membership Director
125 American Inn Road
Villa Ridge, MO 63089

This organization has provided a forum for collectors all over the world since 1962. Members' interests include timetables from all forms of transportation; railroad, bus, airline, and marine. Memberships available are: $13 junior (under 18), $20 regular, $25 contributing, and $25 for outside USA per year. Included is a monthly newsletter titled "The First Edition" and the quarterly magazine "Timetable Collector."

Railroadiana Collector's Association, Incorporated
(RCAI)
Joe Mazanek, Secretary
795 Aspen
Buffalo Grove, IL 60089

As a non-profit educational corporation since 1971, RCAI has brought hundreds of railroadiana collectors together through the annual publication of its "Directory" and quarterly magazine *The Railroadiana Express*. Members' interests cover all categories of railroad collectibles including railroad timetables and travel brochures. Memberships are $20 Regular and $40 Contributing per year. Add $3 each for family members in either category.

Key, Lock and Lantern
(KL&L)
Sandra Shaw Van Hoorebeke, Treasurer
3 Berkeley Heights Park
Bloomfield, NJ 07003

Although emphasizing railroad hardware collectible categories, many KL&L members collect paper as well. Membership is $21 per year for the U.S. and Canada, $26 elsewhere. Add $4 each for family members. Membership includes the quarterly magazine by the same name—*Key, Lock and Lantern*.

Archival Supplies
Quality archival storage products and conservation materials can be obtained from a number of companies, including the following:

Conservation Materials Ltd.
P.O. Box 2884
Sparks, NV 89432
(800) 733-5283

Light Impressions
P.O. Box 940
Rochester, NY 14603-0940
(800) 828-6216

University Products, Inc.
P.O. Box 101
Holyoke, MA 01041-0101
(800) 762-1165

Gaylord Brothers
P.O. Box 4901
Syracuse, NY 13221-4901
(800) 634-6307

RAILROAD AND RAILWAY COMPANIES

INDEX

PICTURE CREDITS

Golden Hill Press would like to thank the following for their help and the permission to use material from their collections.

Author's Collection: frontispiece, pages 16, 21 *(below left)*, 24 *(below left/center)*, 27 *(below center, right)*, 28, 30 *(right)*, 31, 32, 33, 34, 36 *(below)*, 37, 38, 39, 51, 53 *(above left/right)*, 54, 57, 59, 61, 65, 66 *(above left/right, below center/right)*, 67, 68, 69, 84 *(above left/right)*, 85 *(below right)*, 86, 87, 91, 92, 100 *(above center right, below right)*, 102 *(left above/below)*, 103 *(below left, right)*, 104 *(left above/below, below right)*, 109,111, 112, 113, 114, 115, 116, 117, 119, 120, 121, 122, 123, 124, 125, 128, 129, 132, 134 *(below left)*, 135 *(above right, below)*, 136, 137, 138, 139, 140, 141, 142, 143, 144, 145, 146, 147, 148, 149, 150, 151, 152, 153, 154, 155, 156, 157, 160, 161, 162, 163, 164, 165, 166, 167, 168, 169, 170, 171, 172, 173 (left), 174 *(left, center above/below)*, 175 *(above right)*, 176, 177, 178, 179.

William J. Neill: pages vi, viii, xiv, 3, 13, 16, 17, 18, 19, 20, 21 *(above, below right)*, 22, 23, 24 *(above)*, 25, 26, 27 *(left, above center)*, 29, 30 *(left above/below, center)*, 35, 36 *(above left/right)*, 40, 41, 47, 53 *(below)*, 56, 58, 66 *(below left)*, 70, 71, 72, 75, 76, 78, 80, 81, 82, 83, 84 *(below)*, 85 *(above, below left)*, 88, 94, 95, 96, 98, 99, 100 *(above left/center left/right, below left/center left/right)*, 101, 102 *(right, above/below)*, 103 *(above left)*, 104 *(above center left/center right/right, below center left/right)*, 105, 106, 107, 108, 118, 126, 127, 131, 133, 134 *(left, above, below center/right)*, 135 *(above left)*, 173 *(right)*, 174 *(right)*, 175 *(below left/right)*.

California State Railroad Museum: page 12.

Central of Georgia Magazine: page 7 *(left)*.

Colorado Railroad Museum: pages 130, 180.

Fawcett Publications: pages 5, 6.

Railway and Locomotive Historical Society Collection, California State Railroad Museum: pages 4, 7 *(right)*, 8, 9, 10, 11, 42, 43, 44, 46, 49, 62, 63, 158, 159, 175 *(above left)*.

Union Pacific Museum Collection: page 110.

Dust jacket illustrations: are from the author's collection except front, left, Courtesy W.J. Neill.

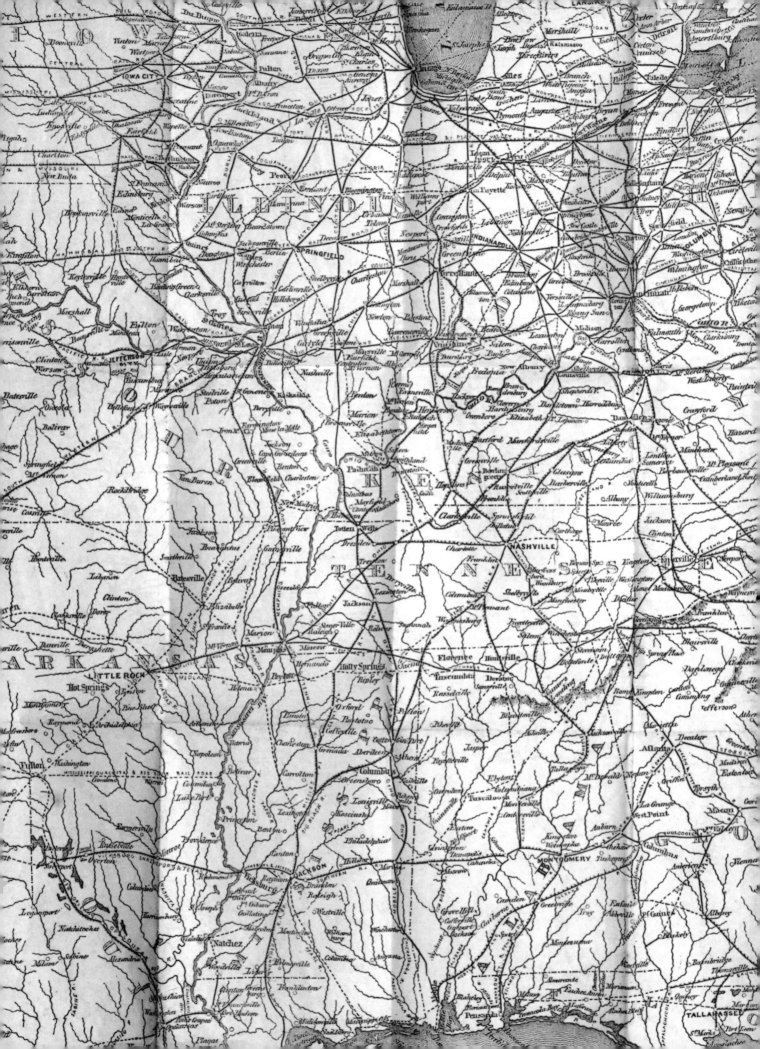